# ONE GOD
# CLAPPING

*The Spiritual Path of a Zen Rabbi*

## ALAN LEW
with Sherril Jaffe

*For People of All Faiths, All Backgrounds*
**JEWISH LIGHTS Publishing**
Woodstock, Vermont

*One God Clapping*
*The Spiritual Path of a Zen Rabbi*

2001 First Jewish Lights Quality Paperback Edition

**Library of Congress Cataloging-in-Publication Data**

Lew, Alan, 1943–
One God clapping : the spiritual path of a Zen rabbi / Alan Lew with Sherril Jaffe.
    p. cm.
Originally published: New York : Kodansha International, 1999.
ISBN 1-58023-115-2 (pbk.)
1. Lew, Alan, 1943– 2. Rabbis—United States—Biography. 3. Judaism—Relations—
Buddhism. 4. Buddhism—Relations—Judaism. 5. Zen Buddhism. I. Jaffe, Sherril,
1945– II. Title.

BM755.L485 A3 2001
296'.092—cd21
[B]

00-054451

10  9  8  7  6  5  4  3  2  1
Manufactured in the United States of America

Book design: Michelle McMillian

*For People of All Faiths, All Backgrounds*
Published by Jewish Lights Publishing
A Division of LongHill Partners, Inc.
Sunset Farm Offices, Route 4, P.O. Box 237
Woodstock, VT 05091
Tel: (802) 457-4000     Fax: (802) 457-4004
www.jewishlights.com

for Isaiah Lew
*zicharon livrachah*

# Contents

# CONTENTS

# PART I

*To Leave*

*Everything*

*That Is*

*Familiar*

## Prologue THE WAY THINGS ARE

When does the spiritual life begin?

I can remember watching my mother sitting up in her bed, nursing my baby sister, Carol. I could not have been older than three. I was sitting opposite them in the big chaise lounge. The doorbell rang. "It's time to go to bed, now, Alan," my mother said. My father was answering the door. Some people had come over to visit. There were a lot of people. It must have been a party.

I got up and started walking toward the room I shared with my sister, and my mother followed with Carol in her arms. I got into my bed carefully so none of the stuffed animals would be disturbed. My mother put Carol into her crib and strapped big metal braces onto her legs. As she did so, Carol began to cry. "She has to wear these. It's for her own good," my mother said to me. "They will make her legs straight." Then she tucked me in, kissed me, and turned out the light.

I could hear people laughing through the walls.

Carol continued to cry. Her cries got louder and louder. She started to scream. She was in an agony of pain, and I knew what it was—the braces were hurting her!

Finally, I got up out of bed and ran into the living room. Finding my mother, I pulled her desperately by the hand. She looked down at me. "They hurt her!" I said.

My mother took me by the hand and led me back to my bed. "Carol has to wear the braces," she told me, tucking me in again. I watched her dark silhouette leaving the room.

Carol continued to scream; she screamed and she screamed.

Could it be that there was nothing my parents could do to make it stop? Carol's screams were filling up the world, and now even my dresser and my shelf of toys were filled with them, and they became the very stuff the world was made of.

Another evening, when I was about five, I was lying in my bed with my eyes wide open, when the night began to cascade down around me like a blue velvet curtain. Outside, a deep royal blue was filling up every corner of the universe. It was filling the world, and now it was coming into our house, and, finally, even my little room was awash in blue. My bed lifted and began to float inside of it, and blue velvet filled every cell of my being.

In the very center of the infinite blue was a small orange orb that the whole universe was funneling out of. I floated in my bed watching it vibrate, watching the vibrations going out from it in concentric circles, radiating out forever.

The head of my bed faced an open door. Across the hall, in the kitchen, my father was sitting alone at the Formica table, smoking in the dark. The glowing orange orb was the burning end of his cigarette.

Why was he sitting alone? Why was he sitting in the dark? Was he, too, transfixed by the cascading blue curtain? He stood up, then, stubbing out his cigarette. I could hear the scrape of his chair against the linoleum, and I could just make him out as he walked toward me through the inky darkness. For a moment, when he reached me, he stood absolutely still. Then he sat down on the side of my bed. "Are you all right, son?" he asked.

"Yes," I said, inside a blue-black dream. He pulled the covers up around my chin and stroked my hair, looking into my eyes, and a great love passed between us.

# 1   A VIVID DREAM

The world I had become part of was completely Jewish. This was Brooklyn in the forties and everyone spoke Yiddish; there were pickle barrels out on the streets and candy stores full of penny candy on every corner. My father's father, Zayde Isaac, came to our house one day to see me. He was a rabbi, like I am now, and though he may have been no older than I am now, he was a little old man. He had thin white hair and a round white face. He was carrying a satchel.

My mother retreated down the long hall with baby Carol on her hip, leaving Zayde Isaac and me in the dining room, alone with each other. He put his satchel down on the table. It looked like a doctor's bag, and I came closer to see what was in it. "These are Hebrew letters," he said, opening the bag just a little. I peered inside. They were large and beautiful, and they seemed to be moving in rows. I stood back as he took them out.

Zayde Isaac put some raisins in my hand. The letters seemed to be dancing. "Yes, they are alive," he said.

This was how I was introduced to the *aleph bes*, the Hebrew alphabet.

I did not know Zayde Isaac very well; I did not see him very often. He came only one other time to show me the contents of his wonderful satchel. Only years later did I realize—this was not education; it was initiation.

I did not know Zayde Isaac as well as my maternal grandfather, Zayde Sam. When I think of Zayde Sam I picture him standing on the balcony of his apartment, bending over the rail to talk with people down in the park below. I have crawled out the window to join him. Zayde Sam would be arguing with "Uncle" Zaretsky, who was called "The Red" because he was a tall thin man with red hair and because he was a Communist. Old Mrs. Greenberg would stand nearby, but she never opened her mouth. No one had ever heard her speak. Sitting on a bench next to her would be Mr. and Mrs. Moran, who lived inside the Cyclone roller coaster in Coney Island. I had been in their house when the Cyclone was going. Everyone just stopped talking and everything shook. But everything in their house was nailed down, and nothing ever broke.

Molly Moran alternated as president of the local chapter of Hadassah with Bubbe Ida, my grandmother. Bubbe Ida was always very busy raising money for Israel. One day my cousin Arnie and I were playing hide-and-seek in our grandparents' apartment and I ran into their bedroom to hide under the bed. But I couldn't fit because there were too many guns under there—rifles, machine guns, and pistols. A whole arsenal was under my grandparents' bed, even the Samurai sword Uncle Eli brought back from the war in the Pacific! Bubbe was collecting weapons to send to Israel for the War of Independence, some-one whispered to me later. But I must never tell. Now it was al-most Pesach, and Bubbe Ida was turning the whole apartment upside down. There had already been days and days of chop-ping and cooking.

At the seder I sat by Zayde's side and asked the four ques-tions. Later, I crawled under the long table that stretched the length of the apartment and looked at all the feet. Laughter shook the table above me. Zayde read on and never missed one single word of the *Haggadah*.

Zayde Sam loved words. He would sit in his chair in the evening reading the dictionary. He loved music. He led the choirs in the neighboring synagogues. When he sang or lis-tened to music, his eyes would gloss over and begin to close. He was also in love with America. Songs began in his throat as synagogue melodies, but when he opened his mouth, "Cherry Pink and Apple Blossom White" came out.

One day on Yom Kippur when he stood with the choir on the altar, the *bimah,* of Beth El, the great synagogue in Borough Park, my aunt signaled to him from the congregation. She didn't have the fare to take the subway home. He signaled back for me to come up to him. When I got up to the bimah, he blessed me and slipped a five dollar bill into my hand. I was too young to understand that, according to Jewish law, you aren't supposed to handle money on Yom Kippur, and moreover, that you aren't supposed to take the subway home from synagogue. But I knew the blessing he gave me wasn't real. My aunt laughed devilishly as we were leaving.

On Simchat Torah Zayde always took me to a little shul in Coney Island where old men danced ecstatically, some of them holding Torah scrolls and others waving Jewish flags with candy apples stuck on the ends. They snaked around the synagogue in a long, delirious line, their faces flush with passion.

In the summer we would go to a farm in upstate New York with several other families. My most vivid memory of this farm was the day they slaughtered the pig. The farmhands performed the slaughter in ritual fashion. The pig hung from a hook high above a platform in front of the barn. The families from the city watched with dropped jaws and a mixture of awe and horror. Life was being taken before our eyes. Blood covered the wooden platform.

I loved all the animals, but especially the cows. Every morning I went with the farm boy to milk them. I loved the sweet smell of the barn and the comfortable sounds the cows made. I would stroke their heads and they would gaze at me with their large shiny eyes. I knew they liked me. Then we would lead them out to pasture. In the afternoon I would go out to the fields to help lead them back.

One day I was walking out to the fields to lead the cows in when I saw a large cloud of dust coming toward me. The ground beneath me began to shake. There was a thundering sound—the cows were stampeding! Just then I tripped. I was now lying right in the path of hundreds of stampeding animals, each weighing more than a ton, and there was no time for me to stand up. I could see my parents and the other grown-ups through the cloud of dust, their hands extended toward me, helpless. The cows were coming closer and closer, their hooves and my heart pounding, when all of a sudden they parted like the Red Sea, and went around me.

Why did they spare me? Was it because they liked me? Was it because God liked me? Was it because that's just how cows behaved? Or was it because life, at bottom, is good?

One day my father and mother bought property in West-chester County, and there they built their dream house. I was seven when we moved there from Brooklyn. I didn't want to go, and I told my girlfriend Michelle that I would come back for her on the horse I was sure to get when I moved to the country. But we moved, and the Jewish world of Brooklyn sank beneath the surface of my world, and when it emerged again it was a vivid dream.

## 2 | JEWISH KARMA

On weekends Bubbe Ida and Zayde Sam would come from Coney Island to visit, and we would watch TV. When the news came on, Zayde would explain to me that the elections were fixed, like baseball. He said my favorite quiz show, "The Magic Horseshoe," was fixed, but I didn't believe him. On Friday nights we watched the fights together. I loved the fights more than anything. I didn't care if they *were* fixed.

I had a little set of boxing gloves of my own. My father was very proud of the way I could box. I wanted a real set of boxing gloves, however, the kind that was a prize on "The Magic Horseshoe."

A kid could be a contestant on this show if he or she had a sponsor, a second kid who wrote a letter to the show about a heroic act the first kid had performed. The hero was given questions in certain categories, and if the questions were answered correctly, the kid could have whatever he wanted. It would all come out of the magic horseshoe—ponies, bicycles—whatever he had asked for. Then, at the end of the show, all the heroes would compete for the jackpot, which was an endless stream of prizes pouring out of the magic horseshoe: trips, clothes, and best of all, an Everlast Boxing Set, which included satiny Everlast boxing shorts with the word "Everlast" written on the buckle, real professional Everlast boxing gloves, a little punching bag to punch fast, and a big punching bag that was like punching a body. There were springs to pull to expand your chest and grips to squeeze to make your fists and your arms stronger. When I saw this set, I said, "I must have that." I never wanted anything so much in my entire life. So to get this boxing set, for the first and only time in my life, I devised a devious scheme.

Our house was out in the woods in a cooperative community called Usonia, Frank Lloyd Wright's experiment in building houses for ordinary people. Most of the people in Usonia were young Jewish professionals, and we were surrounded on all sides by Revolutionary-era towns full of WASPs. We were at least four miles from any of them. The people in these towns thought of us as the Commie Jews on the hill, and not one of them would agree to give us fire protection. They wouldn't come even when there was a fire. So the Usonians started their own volunteer fire brigade, and whenever a fire was spotted, someone would race around alerting everyone, and everyone would come with shovels and hoses and buckets and put the fire out.

There was a kid named Jonathan Gable who lived down the hill from me. He was the smartest kid I knew, especially in science. Science was one of the categories you could choose to be quizzed about on "The Magic Horseshoe."

I went down to the baseball field just south of Jonathan's house. There were often brush fires there in the summer, and I lit one now. Then I ran up the hill. Jonathan was standing outside his house. "Jonathan," I yelled, "there's a fire! You'd better go warn everyone." He hopped on his bike and rode off. In a few minutes, some men came running down the hill and they stomped the fire out. It had only been a little fire. I went home and sat down at my desk and wrote a letter to "The Magic Horseshoe" explaining how my friend Jonathan had saved an entire community from being burned to the ground. In a few days we got a call from the people at the show. I was on!

My mother went out and got me a powder-blue jumper because at that time everyone knew that powder blue looked best on black-and-white TV. On the big day my mother and sister and several of my relatives were in the audience. The whole town of Pleasantville was watching at home. A picture of me had been on the front page of the local newspaper.

Just before the show, Jonathan and I were taken backstage. "I just want to warm you up so you won't be nervous," the man said to Jonathan. He then asked him several very easy questions about science. Finally, he said, "Now, Jonathan, when half of the moon is lit up we call it a half moon. What do we call it when the moon is all the way lit up?"

Jonathan was confused. It seemed too easy. He thought this must be a trick question. He just sat there thinking, and then the man said, "Now look, Jonathan, if a bathtub is half full of water we say it's half full. When it's all full of water, we say it's full. Now, let's go back to the moon."

"It's a full moon," Jonathan said.

We were the first contestants to go on. I looked great in my powder-blue jumper, and I told the story of Jonathan's great heroism with many flourishes. Then they started asking Jonathan the questions. They began with a few ridiculously easy science questions. Then they got to the final question. If he answered this right, everything he wanted would come pouring out of the magic horseshoe. "Now, Jonathan," the man began, "when we can see half the light of the moon we say it's a half moon. What do we call it when the moon is all the way lit up?"

Now Jonathan was really stumped. How could they be asking him the same question again? Now he was sure it must be a trick question. The man started in again with the bathtub analogy—"Suppose a bathtub is half full of water—" Suddenly Jonathan got it: He knew the answer to the question. The answer to the question was that the world was fixed. He said in a very small voice, "A full moon." Bells started ringing and lights started going on and off, and out of the magic horseshoe came a beautiful girl holding the thing that Jonathan Gable had asked for: a Gilbert Chemistry set worth two dollars and fifty cents.

They led Jonathan off in a daze, but brought him out at the end of the show to compete against the other two heroes who were pretty nearly complete idiots. They showed the heroes an aerial photograph of about a hundred soldiers marching in formation. "How many soldiers are marching?" the man asked. "Six," the first idiot said. "One thousand," the second idiot said. "Ninety-eight," Jonathan Gable said, and prizes and gifts started pouring out of the magic horseshoe. I had made a deal with Jonathan before the show that he could have it all. All I wanted was the Everlast Boxing Set.

The next day my father made a shed down in the yard for my Everlast Boxing Set. It was a miniature gym. The little punching bag that you hit fast was hung from the ceiling next to the big punching bag that you punched like a body. There was a hook for my chest expander and a shelf for my hand grips, and nails to hang my silky Everlast boxing shorts and my professional boxing gloves from. I never went down to the shed once. In short order, some dogs bit a hole in the big punching bag, and little by little everything else was stolen.

To console me, my father bought me a rabbit. We kept it in the house for a few days, long enough for me to come to love it, then put it in the shed and the neighborhood beagle broke in and ate it.

Although I was only nine, I understood the implications of all this immediately. My grandfather was right; the world was fixed, and God was the fixer. Later, when I was a Buddhist, I would recognize this story as a manifestation of the doctrine of karma, and later still, as a Jew, I would recognize it in a passage from the Talmud, *Pirke Avot:* "Rabbi Akiba used to say everything is given on pledge and a net is spread for all the living. The store is open and the storekeeper allows credit. The ledger is open and the hand writes. Whoever wishes to borrow may come and borrow but the collectors go around every day and exact payment from us whether we realize it or not."

## 3 PLEASE THROW ME A ROPE

One night, when I was almost thirteen, I was lying in my bed and I heard the maid in her room next to mine singing Jamaican spirituals along with the radio. She was taking care of me and my brother, Jason, who was only six. My sister was in the hospital on the east side of Manhattan, having an operation on her legs. My father was in the hospital on the west side of Manhattan, dying from an intestinal disorder. My mother had rented a hotel room in the middle of Manhattan so that she could run back and forth between them.

Tears burst from my eyes. I did not know then that my sister was going to heal so perfectly that one day she would be a cheerleader, nor did I know my father would survive his operation, and many more, for the next thirty years. Each time he went under the knife I was terrified, and I prayed to God to spare him.

I prayed all the time as a child, and I always felt there was some response to my prayers, even when I didn't get exactly what I prayed for. When it was raining, I would pray that someone would pick me up when I was walking into town, and someone usually did, even though sometimes people would pass me by screaming "Jewboy!" out the windows of their cars. When we went to temple I prayed for girlfriends. These prayers, however, were never answered.

But it was in nature that I always had my strongest spiritual feelings. I felt God's presence in the woods and the swamp. I made a circle of stones in the swamp, and I went there often, alone, to feel the beauty of the universe.

My mother never asked me what I did when I was out in the woods or sitting in the swamp. She was too busy raising money for Israel to pay attention to me. I was familiar with God, but I had no clue what Judaism was about. Outside of Hanukkah parties and Pesach seders, there was no Jewish observance in our house. My mother never once lit candles for Shabbat. Jewish ritual was scorned, especially by my father. It was discounted as irrational superstition. Nonetheless, when my father got really sick, rabbis appeared in his hospital room. They came to change his name so that if the Angel of Death came asking for Isaiah, it could be truthfully said that there was no one named Isaiah there, only Alter-Isaiah.

The morning of my bar mitzvah, while everyone was dressing to go to the service, I sat alone in my room playing "Somebody Up There Likes Me" and "I Believe" on my record player. My father had been extremely sick for most of the year, but now he was better. My rabbi had helped me write my bar mitzvah speech about this. The speech said something about a mountain and a lot about the fact that my father had almost died. I

17

felt like a phony later when I read it in front of the congregation. There wasn't a dry eye in the house.

I delivered this speech after reading a portion from the Torah, as custom demanded. I had practiced my Torah portion over and over with my father during the summer up at Cape Cod. My father told me reading Torah was a skill I had to master. He did not tell me that the Torah was divine because it wasn't, in his opinion.

One day up on the Cape my father took me out in a little sailboat. He had never learned how to sail, but how hard could it be? The wind died and the current began to carry us away. My father pulled on the ropes and moved the boom back and forth. We were drifting out to sea. We were never going to see my mother, my brother, my sister, or our dog, Falla, again. The shore disappeared and the sky grew dark. My father tried different things with the ropes. I turned toward the last bit of light in the west and asked God to save us.

A little fishing boat appeared on the horizon.

## 4 HOW I LEARNED TO LOOK BENEATH THE SURFACE

When my father wasn't in the hospital, he was commuting down to his dental office in Manhattan, where he had a thriving practice. He was also the inventor of dental implants and went all over the world to lecture about it. This supported our comfortable life in this beautiful place, this place where I walked with God in the swamp every evening and experienced countless episodes of anti-Semitism every day. The nearest town, Pleasantville, was where I went to school, but it was a place where people belonged to country clubs I couldn't enter. It was a place where it was considered rude to say what you really meant.

There was one other Jewish boy in my class at school. He was about half a foot shorter than me. He had sandy hair in contrast to my black hair. Everyone was always getting us mixed up.

And yet, not all of the anti-Semitism I experienced was negative. Once when I went to a wake for my friend's father, his mother leapt up and put her arms around me. "You see this!" she said. "This is Alan Lew! He's so smart! He gets such good grades!" This was weird because I was practically flunking out of school, and the only thing that was stopping me was that I was copying her son's lab notes.

At all times of the year, kids passing me in the hall at school would greet me with "Happy Hanukkah!" Being Jewish was my caricature identity. People would sing "Lew Alan, Lew Alan—sounds more American." All these things made me feel painfully self-conscious about my Jewishness. I was never allowed to forget that I was different from everybody else.

The family that made me feel that the most was my friend Blair's. His parents drank all the time, listened to Glenn Miller, and played golf. They belonged to the restricted country club and lived in a big colonial house. When there were parties at their house, all the adults would get drunk, but when they were eating dinner, they were all quiet, prim, and proper. That was when I always seemed to be talking too much. And it didn't help that I was always breaking things in their house.

Blair died of leukemia when we were sixteen, and his father died of another form of cancer within a month. One day just before he died, when I was walking through town to his house to visit him one last time, I saw the outlines of the buildings stand out sharply from their surroundings. Everything was suddenly in super-focus, so much so that it hurt my eyes. It was death I was looking at.

When I arrived at Blair's house, I heard his father screaming from the next room, "Forget about me! Take care of him!" It shocked me to hear this coming from the lips of this repressed gentile. Blair had bruised patches of blood all over his face. He was in kind of a bad mood. I was sitting next to his bed on a little chair. I broke the chair.

That was the last time I saw Blair. Recently, I was a guest in another house. Although I had never been there before, there was something familiar about it. Then I realized what it was— like my father's dream house, it was the house of a dentist. But it wasn't just the refrigerator magnets in the shape of teeth and other dental knickknacks that gave it away. There was something naked about it. It was a house where the rough edges weren't covered over, where the cracks were showing.

My father had this same naked quality to his consciousness. He knew that the mouth is a secret portal into people. We dress it up with lipstick or moustaches, but the dentist sees the bone and the blood and the fluid, not the veneer.

I remember the smell of my father's hands. It was an organic smell, a rank sort of smell, a mortuary smell. His hands were inside of people's mouths all day long. And because of this, I think my father saw how things really were—devoid of illusions and facade. He was always trying to teach me how to fix things, but I was too clumsy; he couldn't teach me carpentry or mechanics. But, inadvertently, he taught me something else, something much more important: he taught me to look beneath the romantic surface to see the truth about the world.

FREEDOM IS A SPIRITUAL STATE

The University of Pennsylvania accepted me even though my grades weren't very good because I was a football star in high school. But I never played football after I got there. Penn and Columbia were the only two Ivy League schools that didn't have quotas. Consequently, Penn was half Jewish, and Columbia was even more than that. This was 1961. Actual quotas restricting Jewish admission had been outlawed, of course; these were virtual quotas, geographical quotas.

I joined a Jewish fraternity. The fraternity brothers would make comments if you didn't dress in the right preppy garb. A sophisticated freshman clued me in on where to go to buy these clothes—at a shop right on campus. The owner of the shop was Jewish; he reminded me of one of my uncles, except that he was impeccably dressed. There were a few people in my high school who had dressed in this preppy way, but I hadn't understood why back then. These clothing stores at Penn were places of transformation. You would walk in dressed like a Jew and you would walk out looking like a WASP.

In those days, a family might make sacrifices to send a son to an Ivy League school, but they usually wouldn't do it for a daughter. Consequently, most of the women at Penn came from extremely wealthy families. In my sophomore year, I fell in love with a girl named Randi Usher who lived in a penthouse on Park Avenue. Once when I went to pick her up for a date, I rang the doorbell of the apartment next to hers by mistake, and the actor Don Ameche, in a silk smoking jacket, opened the door. He looked at me like he knew I knew who he was. "Mr. Usher?" I said.

Randi always liked to have two or three nice boys like me in her entourage. She was mean and careless, and she would string us along, but what she really liked were big guys who weren't so nice. Once when we were out on a date, she said she had a headache, so I took her home. I later found out that she went right out again with one of those big mean guys.

She had an uncle who was a sophisticated restaurateur. All the glittery New Yorkers ate at his restaurant. One day she took me there to lunch with him. While we were talking, I suddenly felt a clammy feeling on my throat. I looked down and saw that my tie was in the soup, and it was siphoning it up. That was our last date.

It was now the summer between my sophomore and junior years. I had decided to go to the March on Washington. When I was small, Zayde Sam's partner in his floor-scraping business had been a black man named Jack who had been like part of the family. Jack used to take me fishing. One day my grandfather got a contract to scrape floors in Virginia, but when he went down there, they wouldn't let Jack share his room in the hotel. So my grandfather went to the black section of town to sleep at a black hotel with Jack.

There had always been a tradition in our family of being for civil rights. This was true for the other families in our community, Usonia, as well. When Jackie Robinson was told that he couldn't buy a house in a town in Westchester that had a restrictive covenant, I wrote to him and suggested that he move to Usonia. "We have people from many different places here," I wrote. "Holland, Germany." "Thank you for the invitation, Alan," Jackie Robinson wrote back. "But my wife and I have decided to move to Stamford, Connecticut."

I thought that if blacks were finally treated with respect then Jews might have a chance to be treated that way, too. So as soon as I heard about the March on Washington I wanted to go. When I was all set to drive down, at the last minute, the friend who had planned to come with me backed out, and so I went alone.

On my way down, I stopped off at my apartment in Philadelphia. On impulse, I called up one of Randi's friends, Linda Shur, who lived in Cherry Hill, a suburb of Philadelphia, because she was the only person I knew who was around. She invited me to dinner. She told me her parents really wanted to meet me, but I told her I was on my way down to Washington. "Then come tomorrow night, on your way back," she said, and I told her I would.

When I got to Washington I checked into a motel and called up several people I knew who lived there. They all told me I was an idiot to be joining the march, that the KKK was going to be there, and that it would be a bloodbath. All hell was going to break loose. There was going to be a huge race riot and I was sure to get killed.

The next morning, early, I went downtown. Washington was like a ghost town. Many buildings were closed. I went to the Washington Monument where the march was to begin. People were just arriving. As more people gathered, the entertainment began. Joan Baez; Bob Dylan; Peter, Paul, and Mary; Lena Horne; and Harry Belafonte sang. It was turning out to be a very joyous day. The crowd got bigger and bigger, and I saw every single black guy who went to Penn walk by. When they saw me, they said, "What are you doing here? Why did you come?" I was not with any group. I was alone. They couldn't figure me out.

Just then, a white guy who had been standing next to me struck up a conversation. He, too, had been moved to come, and like me, he had come alone. He was an art student from Pratt. He was very friendly and attached himself to me.

Finally, we started to march. The whole mall between the Washington Monument and the Lincoln Memorial was full of people. The art student and I were close to the head of the line. When we got to the Lincoln Memorial, Mahalia Jackson and Marian Anderson were there singing gospel songs.

The day had taken much longer than I had anticipated. I had assumed that a march down the mall wouldn't take very long, but now it was so late that it was clear I would never make it back to Cherry Hill in time for dinner at the Shurs' house. And there was no way that I could get to a phone to call them. I was also starting to get nervous about the art student. He was becoming very clingy, and it made me uncomfortable. So I said to him, "Well, good-bye. I have to leave now."

25

"What?" he said. "How can you leave now? The Reverend Martin Luther King is just about to make his speech!" I could see Dr. King walking toward the podium. "I just have to go," I said.

As soon as I got to my car I turned on the radio, and as I drove through Washington, desperately looking for a phone booth so I could call Linda Shur and tell her that I couldn't make it for dinner, I heard Martin Luther King make his "I Have a Dream" speech. The words poured over me and mesmerized me. I had never heard a public figure speak like this before. When I heard the ringing refrain, "Free at last! Free at last! Thank God Almighty, we are free at last!" I felt in my bones a great longing to be free myself—free from my fear of art students, free from my guilt for letting the Shurs down, free from my desire for glamorous rich women, and free from the need to dress a certain way. King was speaking about my own secret heart, imprisoned and yearning to breathe. But what could help me? How would I ever find my way to freedom? As I drove into a gas station and around to the back where the phone booth was, I heard the answer, just for a second, imbedded in King's words: "Thank God Almighty," he said, "we are free at last!"

# 6 SUBLIMATING SPIRITUALITY

One day, late in November of my junior year, I was in my frat house when I heard a horrible scream coming from the street. Just then the girlfriend of one of my fraternity brothers burst in the door. She had always seemed like a placid girl, but now she was hysterical. "The president's been shot! The president's been shot!" she screamed. "Are you sure?" I asked. "Let's go down and turn on the TV and see. If the president's been shot, it'll be on TV." We ran down to the basement where the TV was. The basement was where we held our parties and it reeked of beer. No one ever watched TV there except for Frank Kern, "The Eye," an inert guy from Miami. He was sitting now in a big ratty chair watching a soap opera. "Frank!" I said. "Turn the channel! We have to see if the president was shot!" He did, but there were soap operas on every channel. Then suddenly a news announcer cut in and said that Kennedy had been shot, and then he said he was dead.

At that moment, I was supposed to be over at the women's dorm to pick up a girl I had been seeing named Betty, another friend of Randi's. Linda Shur had fixed us up. Now, in shock, I went to my car and drove there. Betty got in the car, and we started to drive around Philadelphia, aimlessly. As we drove through the black neighborhood that was next to the college we saw people staggering in the streets, publicly weeping. One man was weeping so hard he walked right into a mailbox. There was a feeling of total suspension of order in the universe.

I was an English major at Penn, and I had, coincidentally, just been studying *King Lear*, where the medieval idea, the biblical idea, that there are spheres of order in the universe, is expressed. When something is wrong in one sphere, the disorder radiates outward and inward at the same time. When Lear becomes spiritually sick, his family starts to fall apart, the kingdom starts to fall apart, and nature itself dissolves into a stormy chaos. I was now experiencing the spiritual reality that *Lear* portrayed. Betty and I drove aimlessly through the senseless streets, the wind lifting old newspapers and candy wrappers up from the gutters and swirling them into the air all around us. When we got back to the fraternity house a crowd had gathered around the TV. Lyndon Johnson was being sworn in, Jackie Kennedy standing next to him with blood all over her. The interregnum was over.

When I was an undergraduate, I did not engage in any formal spiritual activity, but besides the Kennedy assassination, three other very powerful experiences took me by surprise and reminded me of the spiritual dimension of reality, which I had been familiar with as a child and which I would come to think

28

of as being harbingers of my later spiritual life. The first happened when I took a class in James Joyce. I had to write a paper on Molly Bloom's soliloquy at the end of *Ulysses*. I read it to myself over and over, for several weeks, until one day my own mind started to work like a Joycian stream of consciousness. I was enjoying it, but then it got to the point where I was not really able to control it. I walked around in this altered state for several days. It was as if a dam holding back language had broken. I could no longer think the way I used to think.

Studying Beethoven led to something similar. I had a great passion for music, and I decided to study it while I was at Penn. I signed up for an evening course in symphonic music. One night I was walking along on my way to this class and I realized my perceptions had heightened. All my senses were acutely sensitive. This was before drugs, so there was no chemical explanation. I stopped and looked at a red light. The intensity of the red against the black of the night nearly broke my heart. When I got to class, the professor started to play Beethoven's Ninth Symphony. As the last movement began—the chorale—I felt my soul leaving my body and soaring through a pool of stars. Afterward we read the text. That's exactly what it's about: flying through the stars. Art, like religion, can give you an experience of transcendence. But art and religion are not the same thing. Religion makes the experience repeatable. Art brings us the news. It tells us there is something out there we had never before imagined.

The third experience occurred on a snowy night. Although Betty and I had been seeing more and more of each other, our relationship had been troubled right from the start, and our fights were getting progressively worse. One evening we had a really bad time, and I dropped her off at the door to the women's dorm believing that it was over. Then I walked away, down the bridge and over the moat for several hundred yards. It was snowing very hard. There was no wind. The whole world was silent. The walkway was suspended high in the air. I walked down to the street, past the pharmacy on the corner, when suddenly I felt something powerful preventing me from continuing home. I stopped and turned around. Betty was still standing in the doorway. A long time had passed, but she hadn't moved. So I started walking back toward her. Against my will, I was being pulled back into this relationship. I knew somehow that despite logic or even my own desire, this was the fate I was going to have to live out. Only by doing so could the rest of my life unfold.

In Judaism there is this sense of destiny, the force you feel compelling your life forward and giving it its meaning. The patriarchs discover their destiny in their encounters with God. "I will make of you a great nation," God tells them. Your destiny is not always positive, however, and this moment with Betty in the snow certainly wasn't. I was being pulled back into a troubled, entangling relationship that was going to take us years to extricate ourselves from. Encounters with God are not always pleasant; they are not always aesthetic, and they often leave you with an injury you bear for the rest of your life.

# 7    *LECH LECHA*

My parents wanted me to become a doctor because my father had wanted to be a doctor. He had ended up at Penn Dental School instead because my mother wouldn't leave her family to follow him to medical school in Arkansas. But I couldn't go to medical school because I had no aptitude for science. In college I had accidentally dropped a very delicate and expensive instrument in my chemistry lab and they had asked me not to continue. So my parents said they would settle on my becoming a lawyer. I had no interest in being a lawyer, but I applied to law school. I had to be in school anyway so that I wouldn't be drafted and sent to Vietnam, and it never occurred to me to challenge my parents' idea of what I should do with my life. Part of me actually thought law school might be a good idea— the speech-making part—and I did well enough the first semester because I found the courses in constitutional and criminal law interesting.

I married Betty that winter. We had a huge formal Jewish wedding in Atlanta, where she was from. We then moved into our new home, a garden apartment in a middle-class neighborhood in Maryland, which our parents paid for and furnished with middle-class furniture. Then law school started up again and it was all procedures, torts, and contracts. I had difficulty concentrating and barely made it through. The next year it was the universal commercial code. Now, no matter how hard I tried, I couldn't concentrate and I couldn't focus on it. I was heading for disaster.

Then Betty got pregnant. We were twenty-two, not really old enough to be parents, but since we were about to be, I realized that if I were to drop out of law school now, I wouldn't be drafted. My unborn child, who turned out to be Steve, had come to protect me. My parents were thrilled that they were going to be grandparents, but they would be less than thrilled to be the parents of a dropout. It scared me to think of how they were going to react. I called them and told them my decision. They were horrified.

Up to this moment, I had never considered it possible for me to do anything other than what my parents wanted, and they hadn't either. "How could you do this to us?" they wanted to know. They were profoundly disappointed in me. After I hung up the phone, I lay down on the couch, trembling. The door to my parents' safe, predictable world was shutting behind me. My heart was beating so loudly that I was afraid it would wake Betty, asleep in the other room. A great weight was pressing on my chest, making it difficult for me to breathe. I couldn't move my arms and legs. I was bathed in sweat. I lay pressed into the couch the rest of the night, unable to call out, waiting to die.

But I didn't die. We moved back to New York, and I got a job with a newspaper in Yonkers.

At first I did only obituaries and the weather, but then I was assigned a series called, "Narcotics, the Seventh Hell." I received a lot of favorable attention for my writing from the owners of the newspaper chain, and in the course of all this, I learned to write very fast. It was the Summer of Love, and we went to a Be-In at Fillmore East, where Timothy Leary sat in a half-lotus position on a stage with psychedelic slides projected behind him, chanting "Tune in, turn on, drop out."

Betty was now very pregnant. She was unhappy about having had to give up her job teaching elementary school in Maryland, unhappy about moving to New York, where she never felt comfortable, unhappy about sitting alone all day in our apartment in Riverdale. The '67 war had just broken out, and I stood in the newspaper office all day by the ticker. It suddenly seemed as if Israel was going to be wiped off the map: all the Arab countries were declaring war. Israel didn't seem to have a chance in the world. I felt that I really should go and fight, like my cousin Robbie. But how could I endanger my life when I had a wife who was about to give birth?

The U.N. held meetings where many lies were told about Israel. The whole world was against Israel except for Adlai Stevenson. Even the left was turning against the beleaguered country. The blacks started identifying with the Arabs. But by the end of the miraculous Six-Day War, everything was different. The Israelis were suddenly heroes in the eyes of Americans, the kind they most respected—military heroes. A right-wing senator stood up in Congress and said, "We oughta get that Moshe Dayan and send him to Vietnam! He'd take care of things!" Then the Yiddishization of American culture began. Everyone started eating bagels, saying "shmooz" and "shtick," and suddenly every acclaimed author was Jewish. Jews, who had been despised, were now revered.

Jews became incredibly sentimental about the liberation of the Western Wall, the Kotel. My parents were now listening to albums of Israeli war songs that had been released overnight. "Don't you realize thousands of Arabs died?" I asked my parents, horrified, as they sang along with this music.

Betty went into labor on July 1, 1967, and, as it happened, it was exactly nine months from the day there had been a city-wide blackout in New York. All the maternity wards in Manhattan were jam-packed, there was total confusion, and Steve was misplaced as soon as he was born. When he was finally found, they brought me to see him. He was in a glass case. "Congratulations! This is your son!" they said. I looked at him. He had breasts. His face was swollen and funny looking. I felt like I was having a hallucination. They took him upstairs to Betty's room so that he would be there when she woke up, and I walked out into Central Park. "I'm a father!" I said to the trees, amazed.

Bubbe Ida came and posted herself outside the window of the nursery, and whenever anyone came by and said, "Look at that cute Chinese baby!" she would scream, "That's not a Chinese baby! That's a Jewish baby!" In a few days, the swelling went down and Steve turned into an adorable kid.

During this time my former roommate, Jeff Linzer, had been taking jobs at the graduate schools at Rutgers and Princeton as a subject for psychological experiments. For months, he was hypnotized every day. Some days he would be hypnotized to believe that everything he saw was yellow, others he would be told that he would see everything without depth perception. Like Leary and Alpert at Harvard, these Princeton psychology professors were dipping into hypnotism, psychedelic drugs, and Eastern religions. Then they started giving Jeff massive amounts of LSD. One of the psychologists introduced him to a group called the Institute of Ability. Here people would sit across from each other asking "Who are you?" for twenty-four hours at a stretch. They would begin by saying, "Well, I'm John," and then, when asked again, "I'm a teacher," and then, "I'm Jewish," and then, "I'm fat," and so on. The idea was that when people got down to the bottom of the list, they would discover their suchness, their essential selves, and then they would go to the leader of the group and he would confirm it. Jeff very quickly became a leader at the Institute, as he did in all the subsequent spiritual groups he became involved with.

Meanwhile, it was becoming clearer and clearer to me that all I had ever wanted to do was write. But not for a newspaper. I wanted to do serious writing, literature. Some relatives of Betty's had a summer house on an island in the Tennessee River in northern Alabama and offered it to us rent-free for the winter. We could live there on my bar mitzvah money and the monthly checks Betty got from her wealthy family. I had decided to apply to the Iowa Writers' Workshop. I would use this time in Alabama to write some stories to send with my application.

Our house on Pine Island was like a dream. There was no one else on the island. We had no television; we had a little boat. We read, took care of Steve, and I wrote. One day we were sitting on our porch watching the sunset turn the water in the river into brush strokes when a huge Titan missile came down the river on a barge. It looked like a malevolent twenty-story building lying on its side. It was coming from Huntsville, where Werner Von Braun had made it, and it was on its way to Florida.

It made me feel weak. We were living on the largesse of Betty's family. They had no idea why I didn't have a job. They had no idea what it was to go off and write.

One night, we were watching television at Betty's parents' house in Atlanta when Martin Luther King came on the screen. He was in Memphis, speaking before the striking garbage workers there. He spoke like a man possessed, someone out of his body altogether. His face was flushed and radiant. The words came tumbling out as if he were channeling them from another world. He spoke of his own death.

"I'm not fearing any man!" he said. Longevity has its place, he said, but it wasn't a very important one for him. I was stunned. He seemed to be predicting his own death, and he was absolutely persuasive. Moreover, he seemed to be speaking from the other side of that great unconscious fear that enslaves us. He was free at last. I was not in the least surprised when he was killed a few hours later.

There were pictures on the TV of Jesse Jackson slumped over his body on the motel balcony, his shirt soaked with King's blood. It was strange to see what was so clearly a monumental religious event on television. It was like Elijah rising in a pillar of cloud on live TV. That sense I'd had in Washington was now confirmed. His voice was the voice of the ancient Hebrew prophets, a clear clarion call to social justice. The vision that launched him on his crusade for civil rights was Ezekiel's vision. King was a prophet, a pure religious voice mistaken by almost everyone for a political one. Like all the great Hebrew prophets, he was completely misunderstood.

Dignitaries from all over the world began to pour into Atlanta for the funeral. The Kennedys came, the Johnsons came, Hubert Humphrey came, and they all crowded into the Ebenezer Baptist Church. The radio stations in Atlanta said people should turn on their headlights to honor King. I turned on my headlights. No one else had their headlights on. A pick-up truck forced me off the road.

One of the stories I wrote that year was about a guy who runs away from his life. He goes to Miami and spends a few feckless days at the dog races. Then he drives home through a hurricane with the news of the Kennedy assassination coming in through the radio. It was supposed to be an evocation of the spiritual drift of the country. To research it, I drove down to Miami myself and got a room at the seediest hotel on the strip. The hotel was small and extremely run-down. As I was standing in the hallway trying to get the door to my room open, one of my old fraternity brothers stepped out of the elevator with his new wife. He was there because he had won an all-expenses-paid vacation at this hotel for selling a certain amount of furniture in his family's furniture business. Most of my fraternity brothers had gone into their fathers' businesses. He couldn't figure out what I was doing there.

I drove back through a hurricane like the guy in my story. I was planning to have him crash and die in this storm. I tried to write as I drove along. The rain was so heavy it made big circles on the pavement as it fell. In Jacksonville the water was coming out of the St. Johns River in huge waves.

Leave-taking is a universal religious theme. Jesus goes out into the wilderness, Buddha leaves his parents' palace, and in the Jewish tradition, God says to Abraham, *Lech lecha,* "You absolutely must leave." Abraham must leave his father's house, he must leave the place where he is from, and he must go to the land that God promises to show him. But Abraham does not know where that land is, and he can't know, or be there, until everything that was once familiar is far behind him.

## 8 THE WAR BETWEEN THE TWO SIDES OF THE BRAIN

One day soon after I arrived at Iowa, a package arrived in the mail from my kid brother, Jason, now an undergraduate at Tufts. In it was a pair of overalls (I wore those overalls every day for five years). In one of the pockets was a railroad watch, and in another there was some LSD.

When the drug started to come on, I looked over at the sheet of paper sticking up out of my typewriter, and at the words I had just written. A glow appeared around it. Its neon rainbow shadow was now visible. I knew then that I was right to have come to Iowa. What I had decided to devote my life to was good. Narrative was a divine implement; it had the power to heal.

But the power of stories wasn't all that LSD showed me. It showed me and all of my friends the dazzling pure beauty of the universe. It showed me that I was made out of pure energy. It showed me how everything connects, that there is a oneness to the world.

According to some brain specialists, most of us are usually incapable of anything more than a very weak experience of spiritual reality, because the part of the brain where these perceptions are formed is almost completely unused. American education and American culture rely on the other side of the brain, the dualistic side, the rational side, and so we live in tremendous imbalance. Psychedelic drugs temporarily correct the imbalance by weakening this side, the left side, of the brain. When the left side blocks the right side, the right side seems stronger, but this is just an illusion.

While I was experimenting with drugs, there was a war going on against the war in Vietnam. Thousands of college kids were marching and rioting. One day we woke up to find one of the classroom buildings on campus had been blown up. There were armed soldiers on the streets. That was the spring the students were shot at Kent State. The whole world was coming apart at the seams, and it seemed that a revolution was about to erupt.

I had become friendly with Norman Fischer, a brilliant student in the workshop whose writing was as wild as his wiry hair. Norman was a few years younger than me, unmarried and childless, and so still vulnerable to the draft. He received a very low number in the draft lottery and was called to Des Moines for his induction physical. There was no way he would ever serve in the army. If need be, he would go to jail, but meanwhile, his other friends and I decided it would be easier if he simply failed his physical. We kept him up the night before so he would be physically depleted, and we gave him LSD so he would appear crazy. The next day when he went to Des Moines, it turned out that the sympathetic doctor from the university who had given Norman a physical had written a letter saying that he had an ulcer, and he was immediately exempted from the draft.

We were out marching every night, and every morning I had to go down to the jail to bail out one of my friends. One night Norman was out very late marching with some blacks. The police started clubbing the blacks, and Norman reached out to protect them, so the cops started clubbing him and arrested him. I went to the jail to try to bail him out, but they wouldn't let him go. He was a political prisoner. So I bought him Mao's *Little Red Book*.

Meanwhile, Betty got pregnant again—with twins. I had assumed I would have a teaching job after leaving Iowa, but the teaching jobs had suddenly dried up because so many people had gone to graduate school to avoid the draft, and people with graduate degrees were now a dime a dozen. How was I going to support a wife and three kids? I walked to my classes through a cloud of tear gas and gray anxiety. What was I going to do? Every night when I lay down in my bed now I shook with terror, and every morning when I woke up the terror was still there. This, of course, is the problem with suppressing the left side of the brain. When you start to walk around with your rationality and defense systems chemically altered, the result can be weakness, paranoia, and madness, and this is what I was experiencing.

Then Betty started to bleed. We rushed to the hospital, but she miscarried the twins. School let out for the summer, and all the undergraduates went home for vacation. Apparently, it had only been a pretend revolution.

Norman and I now discovered that we had a common interest besides writing: Buddhism. Years before, I had gone to an

Eric Hawkins dance concert back in New York. There was a blue backdrop on the stage. "What do you see?" Hawkins asked the audience. "I see the ocean!" someone said. "I see the sky!" another chimed in. "Doesn't anyone just see blue?" Hawkins asked. This blew me away. Later it was explained to me that Eric Hawkins was a Zen Buddhist.

After that, I read everything I could find on Zen, all the books of D. T. Suzuki. But I knew nothing about Zen meditation practice or that it was the basis of the whole thing, because it is never mentioned in these books. Then Norman and I met Julian Hartzel, who had studied at the San Francisco Zen Center, and Julian showed us how to sit *zazen*, Zen sitting meditation.

I was very stiff and tight at first, and I found it almost impossible to get into a half-lotus position. Julian kept piling pillows under me until I was practically standing up on my knees. Nonetheless, I was soon hooked.

When I began meditating, I stopped taking drugs. In contrast to drugs, spiritual activity such as yoga, meditation, and prayer does not suppress any part of the brain. Instead, it works to stimulate the mostly unused but potentially powerful part. It allows the left brain to relax naturally, instead of being burned up as if by a forest fire. I began to calm down, and I stopped having terrors.

## 9 DEATH RECYCLES INTO LIFE

One day a guy came into the graduate students' office looking for someone to caretake a house on the north coast of California, in Gualala. I had completed my degree but had failed to find a job and had no idea what I was going to do. Here was the answer. Besides, I had always dreamed of going to California. As we approached the California border, I got very excited, but then I suddenly became afraid. It was summer and the bare hills were weirdly yellow. I felt as if I had arrived on another planet. Betty was terrified. She wanted to turn back. But there was no turning back.

We spent our first night in California on the Calistoga Road, on the land of an acquaintance of ours from Penn. He had dropped out of college to join the army, and when he was discharged, he came to San Francisco for the Summer of Love. Now everyone was leaving the Haight Ashbury for the country, and he was living in a primitive cabin. We set up our tent on his land. We could hear rattlesnakes shaking their rattles all around us in the grass. We were afraid to close our eyes all night.

I felt I was undergoing some sort of initiation. Later when I read in the Torah about how Jacob, fleeing from the wrath of his brother Esau, has a dream of a ladder, and he says, "How fearful this place is!" I thought of the land on the Calistoga Road. All the biblical places of transformation are fearful places. In the Zen tradition, anxiety, confusion, and disorientation are characteristic of the moments preceding enlightenment.

Gualala is the farthest point west on the American mainland. It's on the part of the coast called the Banana Belt, between Point Arena and Stewart's Point, which hold the fog at bay. It is at the very end of the San Andreas Fault. There are warnings on all the nautical maps of the area that there is something strange about the magnetic field here so that compass readings will always be a little off.

When we first arrived at the address we had been given, we didn't see a house, only a gray fence on the ocean side of the Coast Highway. We rang the bell and a gate opened, disclosing a gray-haired woman with a watering can in her hands. She was framed by roses, as if in a tableau, and behind her, taking up the entire background, was the huge blue ocean. "You're here," she said. "This is the right place."

The house itself was nondescript and middle class; it was not funky or handcrafted like the houses of the people we would soon become friendly with, and this would be the source of some embarrassment to us. But we barely registered that at the time because the entire back wall of the house was one large

44

window divided into panes, and each pane framed a view of the dazzling remorseless ocean.

"I have to go now," she said. "Here is the key."

The gate closed behind her. We turned and looked at the ocean. The wind blew our hair back and carried our words away. A chorus of sound rising and falling from the waves poured into our ears. This was not like the Atlantic, the ocean I had grown up swimming in. You couldn't swim in this ocean; it was too cold. This was not an ocean you played in. This was an ocean you watched.

For the next two and a half years, I would spend some part of every day watching this ocean. In that time, there weren't two days that it looked the same. Some days it was made of silver shards; others, sapphires. I hadn't known that there are infinite permutations of gray, blue, green, and brown. The angle of the light affected it, and the wind, and the clouds.

It filled the world outside and it filled the house. It was not pretty or nice; it was strong, and it was very, very grave. It ebbed and flowed; it rose up and it receded. It had no substance. It was all gray and dark, turgid and brown; it was a delicate Mediterranean blue. One minute it was turbulent, the next it was coming into shore on long gentle rolls. It was all chaos with a thousand disparate movements. I couldn't grasp it. I couldn't wrap my mind around it. It was bigger than the field of my vision. I felt I was looking at death.

Almost as soon as we got to Gualala, Betty went into an almost total collapse. My nights of lying on the couch shaking in terror in Iowa, my failure to find a job, the radical breakdown of the world around her, and the horror and terrible sadness of the miscarriage were now all taking their toll. I said, "It's a good thing that all your defenses are breaking down. You're going to be reborn. I'll get you through this." So I cared for her and Steve twenty-four hours a day.

Out in the yard, I made a little garden. Years later, at a party, I overheard friends from that time say to each other, "Remember Alan's garden?" and burst out laughing, so perhaps, objectively speaking, it wasn't such a great garden, but I loved it. I would put my eye down low to the ground to see the sprouts poke miraculously out of the dirt. Eventually Betty began to believe what I was telling her—that she was going through a transition, a process leading to spiritual rebirth—and she started to get better.

When she was well enough to be left alone with Steve, I started looking for work. The first job I got was digging ditches at Sea Ranch, a new sprawling clifftop community of aesthetically perfect second houses built to blend in with the environment. But I hated digging ditches and was glad when they offered me a job as a lifeguard at the pool there. These were the first of a series of jobs I took that required only my physical attention and left the rest of me free.

I began to notice that there were many shell-shocked people living in the woods all around. Vietnam veterans were pouring into Mendocino County to heal. One of them was Don Shanley, who became a friend. One day, while he was studying at Berkeley, Don had walked off the street and into a marine recruiting station where he signed up for the war in Vietnam. He had a few weeks of training at Officers' Candidate School and was then rushed to the front. Riding in a helicopter over Quang Tri Province into Khe Sanh, he saw the most beautiful countryside he'd ever seen: a lush, dense, green jungle full of wild elephants and monkeys.

Unbeknownst to him, he was flying into the Tet Offensive,

the engagement that turned the Vietnam War in favor of the Vietcong. Don arrived at Khe Sanh as a captain in command of a troop full of distrustful enlisted men who would shoot an officer in the back if they suspected he didn't know what he was doing, and Don, whose entire military experience consisted of two weeks in O.C.S., had no idea what he was doing. Then the Tet Offensive began. Waves and waves of Vietcong came up the mountains in black pajamas, multiplying far faster than Don and his soldiers could kill them. When the smoke had cleared, 80 percent of Don's men were dead, and Don was hysterical.

He was flown off the mountain for a little R and R, and when it was time for him to return, he refused. He just couldn't go back. But an older officer who had taken a liking to him convinced him he had to return to Khe Sanh. He told Don he would get over his fear, that he would never be able to live with himself if he didn't go back, so Don took another helicopter back to Khe Sanh, this time over a desolate, burned-out wasteland. The lush jungle, the monkeys, and the elephants were all gone. The helicopter touched down on the side of the mountain and Don jumped out. As soon as his feet hit the ground, a Vietcong sniper's bullet entered his helmet and whirled around his skull. By the time it came to rest, Don had had it. He refused to stay on the mountain; he demanded to be taken away. They took him to the loony bin, the officers' mental hospital at Phoo Bai, and after he got out of there, he started smoking tremendous quantities of dope, and he became very active in the burgeoning antiwar movement within the military, until finally he made such a nuisance of himself that he was discharged, and that's when he came to Stewart's Point.

We worked together as lifeguards at Sea Ranch. The Sea

Ranch pool was sunk at the bottom of a natural bowl surrounded by ridges covered with golden California grass. No one
ever swam there. Don told me all his stories as we sat alone by
the pool, the ridges looming over us in the inky night. He told
me these stories until we were both shaking with fright, and the
Vietcong in their black pajamas were almost visible over the
hilltops, swarming out of the black sky.

Like Don, Betty and I had come to Mendocino to heal, and
gradually I began to feel the landscape softening and opening
me. Sometimes I would take off all my clothes and walk naked
in the forest. When I sat alone on the soft loam beneath the
redwoods, it was impossible not to be aware of a divine intelligence acting on everything. The loam was what fed the trees. It
was made up of trees that had died. Death recycled into life.
Everything was moving up to the light, and then falling back
down. The seeds I saw sprouting in the loam were made of pure
intelligence. They took what they needed from the loam and
reorganized it to reach for the light. Where did this intelligence
come from? It was obvious to me that it was from God.

## 10 THE QUESTION IS NOT WHETHER A TEACHER HAS REAL SPIRITUAL POWER, BUT HOW THAT POWER IS USED

When I reached California, I found I was in the midst of a perpetual demographic earthquake. No one else had been here much longer than I had. In California everyone is floating, no one is holding on. There is a constant letting go toward the new and the innovative. But there is no grounding. The East Coast is *all* grounding. It faces the whited sepulchers of Western civilization, Europe. The West Coast is buffeted by a fresh breeze blowing in from Japan. But faults run through the land; it's unstable. Each coast distrusts the other and each lacks what the other has.

In all the major religions today, there are battles being fought between the dogmatists, who are old, tired, and dull, encased in their forms, and those advocating renewal and seeking to enliven the tradition at all costs, even to the point of embracing the latest spiritualist fads and leaving tradition in the dust altogether. Both sides lack what the other has. Those who reject tradition suffer because they have no standard outside themselves, and those who see God's word as frozen end up worshiping a dead God.

My friend Norman and his girlfriend had followed Betty and me out to California. They got a place in Berkeley, but Norman also got a little place up in Gualala where he would stay half the time. One day Norman and I saw an advertisement for yoga lessons on a bulletin board in the health food store. A disciple of B. K. S. Iyengar's had a farmhouse in Manchester, the next town up from Point Arena. It was a beautiful ride through farmland. There was an entire small yoga commune living in the farmhouse, and out in the barn lived a guy named Michael. He lived without plumbing or electricity, like a yogic ascetic, and he took Norman and me on as his students.

Michael was an excellent but gentle teacher. He had long, long hair and a long, long beard. All he ever did was yoga. Like many people I met experimenting with Eastern spiritual practices, he was Jewish. He told me one day he had had a nightmare that his little room in the barn was a cattle car on the way to a concentration camp.

My posture had always been very bad. One day I was sitting in my house looking out at the terrible ocean and I spontaneously began to pray. "Please God," I prayed, "allow my posture to improve." When my prayer was finished, I continued to sit very still on the couch. Then suddenly I heard laughter, the loudest laughter I had ever heard. It was as if the whole universe was laughing, even though it was completely silent.

So I did yoga twice a day, and my posture improved enormously. Even my mother noticed when she came to visit. Yoga got Norman and me very high. We always ended yoga by doing "the dead man." After the stretches we would lie flat, and going from the crown of our skulls to the tip of our toes, we could feel our awareness inhabit each muscle until we felt our souls hovering above our bodies, and sometimes we could feel our souls flying all around the room. When we walked out of Michael's barn, the world would be shimmering and radiant. Sometimes Norman and I would walk in the woods then, just experiencing the trees.

Meanwhile, my old college roommate, Jeff Linzer, had become a leader in the Institute of Ability. When everyone at the Institute had peeled off their masks, they realized that basically, underneath everything, they were just men and women, and they started hopping into bed with each other. Jeff invited my brother, Jason, to go to one of the Institute's retreats, and there Jason met a woman named Nancy, who later took Jason to see a guru named Rudrananda, or, as he was known, Rudi.

Rudi's real name was Albert Rudolf. He was a Jewish guy who grew up in Brooklyn. The story was that a man from India came to Rudi's house when he was a kid to get him because Rudi was supposed to be a swami in India. No one ever explained, however, how it was that Rudi's mother let him go.

Rudi's teacher was Nityananda, who also taught Muktananda—one of the most popular and successful swamis who came over during the seventies. All of the Institute of Ability people ended up with either Rudi, Muktananda, or Trungpa. Jeff eventually followed Muktananda; Jason went to live in Rudi's ashram.

The next summer when I took Steve back to New York to visit my parents, Jason took me to see Rudi. I found myself in a long narrow room full of people sitting on cushions. An old woman gave a very strange talk, which I couldn't follow. Then

51

Rudi spoke. He was very fat and had a shaven head. He gave a general talk about the spiritual journey, and I could tell immediately that he was fairly sharp.

Several months before, back in Gualala, I had begun giving Ouija board readings. Although I did yoga and shopped at the health food store, I wasn't really an orthodox hippie; however, the houseful of people who lived across the way were, and we became good friends. The house was rented by a young Jewish couple from the San Fernando Valley. Lynn, the wife, started the whole Ouija board thing when she came to me to talk about her marital difficulties. Some people who had been passing through had left a Ouija board in our house. I had been playing with it, and now I took it out to consult it on her behalf. What it told her really helped her, and she developed a fervent belief in it. The news spread, and gradually, other people began coming for consultations, until they were lined up outside my door. This is how my career as "the Guru of Wood" began.

In the middle of Rudi's talk, I found myself wanting to ask him about the Ouija board. I was concerned about it. I didn't understand it. I was transmitting information of a depth and specificity that I didn't ordinarily have access to. I would say things that I didn't know consciously about people, general spiritual advice that I had no way of knowing would have special significance in their lives. People were coming from all over the coast to consult with me. They were showing up by the dozens. I wouldn't take any money, but people were so grateful they were coming back later and leaving gifts on my doorstep. They would ask me questions and the Ouija board would speak.

People came every day. It was worrying and, moreover, it was exhausting me. I was beginning to feel bone weary all the time, empty and drained. One day some people brought me their mother, an ordinary middle-aged housewife. The Ouija board started telling her not to take acid anymore, and I said to myself, They're going to come and arrest me! I can't be saying this to this woman! But it turned out that she *was* taking acid, and this was a problem.

When I would give readings, people would always say, "How did you know that! That's exactly what I needed to hear!" When they said this to me I wondered if they were just gullible or if what I was doing was real. After a while, it occurred to me that it wasn't the Ouija board that was the instrument of divination, it just helped focus something in me that knew more than I did, so I stopped using it. Sometimes when Lynn came over we would just be talking in my living room and I would go into "that place." There was a subtle but real difference between my own thoughts and the thoughts that came from this source.

One day Lynn's husband, Richard, came over with a bunch of people from the city. They wanted a psychic reading. They were all giggling, and it was clear they thought it was a big joke. I gave them a vindictive reading inspired by spite rather than the mystical source. This was the first time I had abused this gift.

As I sat there listening to Rudi now, a question formed inside my head. I desperately wanted to ask him about all of this, but I was afraid to. All of a sudden Rudi stopped in the middle of his talk and said, "Go ahead, ask the question."

No one said anything.

He said, "Go ahead. I feel someone needs to ask a question."

I didn't say anything. I was too afraid.

He said, "We're not going to go on until you ask the question. So ask the goddamn question."

I knew then that he was talking to me, so finally I said in the most general terms, "There's this thing I've been doing and people have been coming to me and I've been answering their questions and—"

"If you continue what you're doing you'll be dead in a year," he said.

I immediately saw the truth in what he was saying. I had been becoming more and more exhausted and depleted. I was putting out energy that I didn't know how to replace. It was like losing blood.

In the Torah there is the story of Nadav and Abihu, sons of Aaron, the high priest, who make an offering of "strange fire" to the Lord and are instantly and literally zapped—burned to a crisp, completely consumed. Some say it was because their worship was not of the prescribed method and that was why they perished. Others say it was because they had drawn near to God at an unauthorized time, so that they weren't protected, and that was why they became completely depleted, exhausted, and used up. As I was leaving Rudi's talk, he came up to me and said, "That was very good that you asked me that question. Come to my store tomorrow to talk about it."

It was a large store in the middle of a commercial block in Manhattan east of Union Square, a mixed neighborhood, not Bohemian and not uptown. Upstairs was a loft where all of Rudi's students lived. The store was filled with tonkas, Tibetan tapestries, and priceless Buddhas. Some of them were very large, over six feet tall, and all of them were exquisite. Rudi had stood at the Indian border when the Tibetans were fleeing the Chinese, buying all their priceless Buddhas and art treasures.

Now he was an art dealer, selling his treasures to museums and extremely wealthy people. I had to wait a long time while he obsequiously waited on museum representatives and millionaires, periodically going to the back of the store where one or two of his students were meditating on him. He would put his hand on their heads and somehow transmit energy to them, and they would go into convulsions. Other students were coming to him for consultations. It was as if Rudi was giving off electricity. The more advanced the students were, the more electrified they would become until they were trembling, all in the midst of high-powered transactions over statuary. The millionaires who came to buy art objects seemed totally oblivious to everything that was going on and never got jolted.

It was in the midst of all this that Rudi told me I should drop everything and come study with him, that he would make me rich, and that I would get laid all the time. "You should have seen the knockers on the woman I was just with in Boston," he said.

He told me to come to a beginners' class. It was upstairs, in the loft where students were living in every corner. The class was in the living room. Rudi sat at one end, and before him sat all his students, facing him. They were meditating on him in half lotus and going into convulsions. Behind them was a big TV screen. Rudi was addicted to TV, and he was watching *I Love Lucy*.

Ironically, Rudi was the one who was dead within the year. He died in a small plane crash. He was the only one who died, and the others on board said that he had protected them with his death.

When I got back to Gualala I put the word out that I wasn't going to do readings anymore. And I never did, except for one time, a few months later. One day Lynn came to me and said, "I know you don't do your thing anymore, but you have to discover where this guy is. This friend of ours has just disappeared. They found some of his stuff along the beach. We're afraid he's committed suicide. The police and the coast guard can't find him. Would you please come out of retirement just for this?"

I had a vision of a hill and a tree and a number. (I often had visions, and I still do.) There were mile markers all along the highway. She took me to the parking lot by the beach where all the hippies were gathered. We went to where the mile marker I had seen in my vision was. We looked all day, from hill to hill and tree to tree. But we never found him. It was a great humiliation for me. There were a hundred trees and a hundred hills that looked just like what I saw in my vision.

# 11 CENTERING

Betty had lost a lot of weight because of her depression, but gradually she started to get better, to put on weight, and to go out more and more. When she was finally cured, she emerged with an entirely different personality. Before, she had been passive and so painfully shy that she would never speak at all in a group. Now she was assertive; she dominated conversations. But as she started to get better, I fell into a depression. Both of us were completely different people than we had been at Penn. She couldn't stand my depression, and it soon became apparent that we needed to get away from each other.

Since she was now able to take care of Steve, I moved out, and for a month I lived in a tent deep in the woods. I fasted and read Thoreau's *Walden;* Jung's spiritual autobiography, *Memories, Dreams and Reflections;* Martin Buber's *I and Thou;* and *Autobiography of a Yogi* by Yogananda. Then I came back and we tried to live together again, but it didn't work and I moved into a trailer that was owned by friends.

While I was living in the trailer, the people who owned the house we were caretaking demanded it back. "You were only supposed to be there for two months," they said, "and you've been there two and a half years." There was no place for Betty to move to in Gualala. People spent years trying to get a place to live there. So I decided to leave, too, because although Betty and I weren't exactly together, we weren't yet ready to be apart either, for Steve's sake if for no other reason. We decided to try to find some place where we could both settle. Gualala was a place that had a strange capacity to take people in, almost magically. It had come all the way out to Iowa to get us. But when it was done with us, it spit us out.

We didn't know where to go, so we just set out, figuring we'd settle in the first place that felt right. The first place we got to was Los Angeles. Betty and I couldn't see ourselves there, so we decided to press on, but before we left I went to find Yogananda's headquarters. Yogananda was dead, but when I had read his book in my tent in the woods, I had been very inspired by his story. In the book he had talked about the Self-Realization Fellowship, which he had started and which had its headquarters in Hollywood. When we got there it was all locked up. There were plaster models of the Taj Mahal and pink flamingos. It looked like a miniature golf course.

The next place we went to was Tucson, where we stayed with my cousin Leah, whose twins Steve played with while we were there. She took us hiking in the mountains and showed us trees and plants I had never seen before and have never seen since. They were beautiful, but I couldn't relate to them or the whole alien landscape. So we decided to go to Mazatlan in

Mexico, where we could live cheaply and where the culture was rich and vibrant.

Mazatlan was a beautiful town with whitewashed churches where European Catholicism married Indian idolatry. We got a hotel room on the waterfront. The beach was full of international drifters. On the beach Betty and I met two single women, drifters from Australia trying to meet Mexican men. They told us they were leaving and asked if we wanted to take over the house they had been renting.

It was pleasant, whitewashed, and tiled. One day the plumbing got stopped up and we didn't know how to fix it. So we left.

We slowly made our way back to Gualala, where another place had magically become available, but we realized that we didn't want to be in Gualala after all. So we headed north to Eugene, and then Seattle, neither of which felt right either.

Meanwhile, Norman had moved to Berkeley full time. I myself had thought of going to Berkeley, and now Betty and I decided that Berkeley was as good a place as any to settle. We had friends there; I could get a job and pursue my spiritual interests.

I still felt mystically drawn to Yogananda. I would look at his picture on the cover of *Autobiography of a Yogi* with love. I figured he was my guru; however, he was dead. Then I happened to read an article about Dennis Weaver, the actor who played Chester on *Gunsmoke*, which said he was a student of Yogananda's, and I realized I, too, could study and practice what Yogananda had to teach if I sent away to the Self-Realization Fellowship for the mail-order course. I wanted to get an ordinary job in a store selling things so that I could devote all my psychic energy to doing Yogananda. I thought I could do yoga on my lunch break. While I looked for a job I tried to do the Yogananda program, which had begun to come in the mail, but

I was having a hard time with it. I would pick it up and drop it. I couldn't get into the visualizations, and it was too cluttered with Hindu dogma for me. There was also a sappy devotional side to it that I couldn't stomach. I yearned to have a spiritual practice, but this wasn't it.

One night I dreamed that I went to the *Oakland Tribune* and got a job there, so I went to the offices the next day to apply. I had never been there before, yet everything looked exactly as it had in my dream: the bar on the corner across the street, the tower, the entrance to the building. Only there were armed guards at the door, and they wouldn't let me in. I told them I wanted to speak to someone about a job, and they handed me an application. But I didn't fill out the application. I wanted to speak to someone. Clearly I had had a predictive dream, but it hadn't predicted what I thought it did.

Finally, I looked up bus companies in the yellow pages. I had driven the school bus in Gualala, and that experience was enough to land me a job with a small company called Gateway.

During this whole period Norman had been sitting zazen and practicing Buddhism. One day he invited me to come with him to the San Francisco Zen Center to hear a famous Japanese Zen master talk. At least half the people at the Zen Center were Jewish, but the Japanese Zen master, thinking that since he was in America everyone was Christian, based his lecture on a text from the Gospel: "Unless ye be as little children you will never enter the kingdom of heaven." He gestured emphatically saying, "I mean little, little children, just born; one week old is already too late." The Zen consciousness he was describing was that of a newborn; after a week, you already had too much cognitive consciousness. This was the path to cosmic consciousness, the experience of reality. You had to go back beyond all your old ideas, preconceptions, and assumptions before you could see what was really there. I looked around the simple, beautiful Buddha hall, at the single flower in a vase, at everyone sitting in black robes on black cushions, balanced between relaxation and tension. Everything was clean, clear, and uncluttered. After having considered a dozen other paths, I had finally found the spiritual discipline that I would follow. A few nights later, I was walking home and saw a mass of people standing in the street, looking up into the sky, their faces filled with innocent wonder. A plastics factory was on fire, and it was filling the sky with gorgeous multicolored flames.

At that moment it really did seem to me that this was where I was supposed to be. I had just gone south, then north, and then south again, until I had come to rest in the geographical center of my journey. I had been circling, zeroing in on the place where I would feel centered, grounded, where I might find myself.

# 12 MEDITATION

Whenever Betty and I were together it was very depressing. As soon as I got my first paycheck from Gateway, I moved out of the house on Hillegas and rented a room a few blocks away over the Claremont Delicatessen. The room was filled with huge pieces of furniture, and I told the Greek delicatessen owner I would only rent it if he would take all the furniture out, which he did. I set it up as a perfect little Zen space. I tacked a straw mat to a door, which I used as a sitting mat, and I slept right on the floor in a sleeping bag. I had a folding table for the Royal portable typewriter I had gotten for my Bar Mitzvah on top of it, and a folding chair I had gotten at a thrift shop. That was all I had in the way of furniture.

Norman picked me up every morning at five. In those days, the Berkeley Zendo was in the attic of a Victorian house on Dwight Way near Grant. The staircase came up into the center of the room. There was a polished wood floor and redwood rafters. About fifteen tatami mats were set up symmetrically all around the periphery, each with two round black pillows, *zafus*, set up on two rectangular black pillows, *zabutans*. As soon as you entered the zendo, every movement became highly ritualized and conscious. The first thing you would do when you emerged was bow to the Buddha facing you. Flowers and incense were arranged in front of it. On the altar was a picture of Suzuki Roshi, the founder of the San Francisco Zen Center and author of *Zen Mind, Beginner's Mind*, and also a picture of Dogen Zenji, a fresh, unconventional, original thinker who brought Buddhism to Japan. Zen prided itself on being anti-establishment, and Dogen was famous for challenging even every assumption of Zen and standing it on its head. You would bow to these pictures, in *gasho* position, hands together in front of your chest. Then you would fold your right hand over your left and walk very carefully and consciously to your place, never crossing over in front of the altar. When you reached your place, you would bow to it and carefully turn 180 degrees and bow to the room. Then you would sit down, turn to the wall, and assume a half- or full-lotus position. Mel Weitsman, the Zen priest, would already be seated.

There was not a huge crowd at 5:00 A.M. We would sit for forty minutes, followed by ten minutes of walking meditation. The second sitting was at 5:50. There were usually only about four to six people present at any session. Sometimes we would joke about how there weren't enough for a minyan, realizing most of us were Jews—Mel, his wife, Liz Horowitz, Norman, another man named Ron Nester, and me. After you got to your seat you would take a minute or two to settle in, leaning to the left and right, stretching, centering. Then someone would ring the bell, a teacup-sized temple gong struck with a stick, signaling the beginning of the period of meditation. It was not polite to come in after the bell rang. The acoustics in the zendo were perfect and the bell would make a vivid sound.

The idea of sitting was that you were supposed to be conscious of your breath, watching and counting it and making sure that your mouth was closed, your teeth were open, and your tongue was resting on the bottom of your mouth; conscious of your posture, continually checking and adjusting it so that your chin was tucked in, your arms were held alertly but loosely at your side as if there were eggs in your armpits that you were holding up, and your torso was cocked forward at the base of your spine as if an imaginary rod ran from the base of your spine to the pit of your belly and was the fulcrum on which you were sitting.

All the tension and weight of your body would then be in your legs; your upper body and your belly would be relaxed, which was important, because that was what controlled your breathing. You had to let your shoulders drop and relax the muscles of your upper body, but leave your sternum slightly lifted. You were to imagine a skyhook pulling you up by the crown, so that it wasn't only the muscles of your body but energy that was holding you up.

Your eyes were to be neither open nor closed. You were facing the wall, not really looking at anything, neither seeing nor not seeing the wall. You had to relax your cheek muscles; your hands were to form a *mudra*, a mystical hand position forming a perfect oval, thumbs touching, relaxed but alert. Every part of your body was to be at the balance point between being tense and relaxed.

When you are concentrating on sitting correctly and watching your breath coming in and going out, you are focusing on the present moment. This is the object of Zen meditation. But during the course of forty minutes, you inevitably drift off into random thoughts, and every time you become aware that this has happened you take note of it and allow the thoughts to fall away, and then you bring your awareness back to your posture and your breathing. You become aware of how much you daydream and you become aware of your daydreams, and your unconscious material becomes more conscious. I became aware that there were constant arguments going on inside my head, with other writers, my in-laws and parents, and even my closest friends.

Because you are more highly attuned to your breathing when you are sitting zazen, you become more highly attuned to everything. Between 5:00 and 5:40 A.M. the world is just waking up. When I sat on my zafu in the zendo, I heard people talking on the street, cars going past on the road, radios going on, and birds beginning to sing. As the meditation period went on I would start to relate to all these things differently. They became more vivid. If I heard the sound of a car, I would not think "car" but would just experience it as sound, very beautiful sound. I would start to go through this process with everything, experiencing things exactly as they were. The sunlight came across the floor, and I didn't say to myself, "Oh, the sun is coming up." I would experience an incredible eruption of light.

The other present-moment reality you experience when you sit zazen is physical pain. It can really hurt to sit absolutely still in half-lotus for extended periods of time, and in the beginning it was very painful. At first I would be holding on for dear life not to succumb to the pain for almost the entire forty-minute period. My tolerance for pain was very low when I began. I was afraid of it. But as time went on, I got better at tolerating it and it seemed to lessen. Still, it accounted for a large part of my experience when I was sitting, although as I was to find out later, the period before I learned how to get through the pain was actually the easiest time in my practice. The pain riveted my attention and kept me tremendously focused and right in the present moment, not daydreaming for a moment. Later, when pain was no longer the consistent focus of my meditation, my mental state became much more diffuse, and concentration, more difficult. This happened after I learned to let the pain go through the same transformation as the sights and sounds of the zendo had. The pain became a primary occurrence. I didn't name it any longer or think to myself that it was a terrible thing because it hurt. The pain just became a wave of sensation; the idea of pain disappeared and the pain itself disappeared shortly thereafter.

At the end of the first period of zazen, the bell would ring again, and we would get up (bowing first in the sitting position to the wall), stretching left and right and forward and back, then unfolding and swiveling around on all fours, fluffing up our zafus. We would stand, bow to our cushions and bow to the room, and walk around in ritual fashion maintaining our posture and breathing, taking halting steps not to break the spell. After ten minutes the bell would sound again, we would return to our seats and the whole thing would be repeated.

After pain, the next problem one encounters trying to sit zazen is sleep. The signals your body gets from meditation are the same as the ones that tell it to sleep. The compulsion to sleep is very powerful and bothersome, but sleeping through meditation is a waste of time, so each period one person was given the job of hitting people with a stick if they started to fall asleep. It was one of the first signs of rank to be given this re-sponsibility, like being asked to lead chanting or ring the bell. The stick would be laid out by your place. Then you would get up, take the stick, bow to the Buddha, and in walking medita-tion form, make your way around the zendo until you came upon those who were fighting sleep who would request the stick by putting their hands together in the bowing position. You would then tap them or whack them on the soft part between the neck and the shoulder bone. They would lean over side-ways to give you more of a target. Afterward, you would bow and they would bow. It wouldn't really hurt; it was like a slap to get the blood circulating, not a hostile act. The stick was al-ways voluntary at the Berkeley Zendo. You had to ask for it.

At the end of the second period, we would put our hands together and recite the four great vows in unison: "Beings are numberless—I vow to save them. Delusions are inex-haustible—I vow to end them. Dharma gates are boundless—I vow to enter them. Buddha's way is unsurpassable—I vow to at-tain it." All the Buddhist dogma made wonderful sense to me, but dogma was almost incidental to the practice, which was mainly based on the direct experience of sitting. Zen distin-guishes itself from other forms of Buddhism as the direct expe-rience of the *dharma,* the path beyond scripture and dogma. After the vows, we would straighten our pillows, stand up, and do a series of full prostrations to the ringing of the bell. We would finish by sitting on our haunches to chant the *Heart Sutra* to the beat of a drum. "Form is emptiness, emptiness is form," we would chant, and after that, a *dharani,* a Japanese transliteration of a Chinese nonsense chant, all in singsong ro-botic fashion. The kind of consciousness we came to just sit-ting, watching our breath, and focusing on our posture, we now tried to bring to the act of chanting, doing prostrations, standing, and walking. The purpose of the service was to carry the meditation experience into other parts of our lives. The service was a bridge between sitting and being in the world.

The teacher would leave first, then the two lines would step forward, bow together to the Buddha two at a time, and step down into the stairwell. Everyone would move up and continue in this same fashion until everyone had left the zendo. Downstairs they would serve coffee in the living room of the house. There were no sofas, only a few chairs. On the wall was a wall-hanging of Bodidharma, the teacher who brought Buddhism from India to China. He was burly, black-haired, and had a moustache, which added to the fierce and scary expression on his face.

I didn't drink coffee in those days, but I would hang around for a while, anyway, just to be with everyone. Then I would leave and go about my day with a very deep consciousness. The world would have a dimension of depth it hadn't had before. The sky, the flowers—everything—had become heartbreakingly beautiful.

## 13 THE GATEWAY

From zazen I would take the bus down to the Gateway Bus Company in West Oakland, stunned by the beauty of my fellow passengers. At times I would get off the bus and there would be fresh pools of blood on the sidewalk. Gateway was in a very dangerous, decrepit black neighborhood that was rapidly being eaten alive by the largest post office in the Pacific Northwest. It was under the freeway overpass and next to the army yards, and there were several wonderful restaurants where I would go for lunch. In the restaurants they would be playing soulful rhythm-and-blues music on a jukebox. There would be a lot of kidding and constant banter going on between the customers and the waitresses. I would be the only white person there, but they would take me in right away, calling me honey. I'd go to a restaurant for lunch one day, and the next day it and most of the block would be gone, and there would be an adjunct building of the post office under construction or already erected on the site.

Sometimes the job entailed long trips, and one day I was given a load of tourists to take to Yosemite. After I dropped them off in the valley, I was free to do whatever I pleased until the next day, when I would drive them back. I set off alone to hike, starting out on the loop trail around Mirror Lake. After I had been hiking for a while, the trail began to skirt a rapid river. Suddenly I caught a glimpse of the headwaters up on the mountain. They were incredibly beautiful and powerful; they seemed to beckon me. I left the path and set off along the edge of the river to climb up to them.

A chill wind blew from the churning water, but the headwaters seemed closer, and I marched on until I came to a place where the water forked and I could go no farther without crossing the river. I took off my shoes and put one foot in the water to see if it was possible. But as soon as I did, the water pulled me in, and then I was being swept downstream in the powerful current. The water was ice-cold—fresh snowmelt—and the current was so fierce and so rapid that there was nothing I could do to fight it. I was being hurled against the rocks, heading straight for the falls, sure to be tossed over and smashed to smithereens on the rocks below.

Then suddenly I saw a branch hanging over the river ahead of me, and just at that moment I remembered that I had dreamed this—the granite cliff walls all around, the roar of the water in my ears, the swiftness of the water carrying me along, the branch appearing overhead—and I remembered that in my dream I had reached up, grabbed the branch, and pulled myself out of the water.

As soon as I remembered this dream, everything stopped.

The churning noise silenced. The headlong current paused. Time stopped. I now had all the time in the world to carefully lift my arm out of the water and to reach up and grab hold of the branch. And that is what I did.

As soon as my fingers encircled the branch, the current started up again; the rushing was back in my ears and the water was churning past me, pulling my legs forward in the direction of the falls. But I held on to the branch for dear life and pulled myself out of the river.

I was battered and numb and sure I was going to die. Idly, I wondered which I was going to die from, the cold or the shock of the battering I had just taken on the rocks. Then I felt a force rising from my belly, an animal force, a force other than me. It compelled me to stand up, though I was sodden and shaking. Carried by this force, I began to tramp barefoot back through the cold woods. I, the part of me that was my personality, observed in amazement. After I had gone about a mile, I was led to a patch of bright sunlight. Then, painfully and desperately, I stripped off all my clothes and lay down on a rock in the sun.

The sun began to warm my naked body, and I heard a woman's voice say, "Look! It's our bus driver!" And then my whole busload of tourists came traipsing by.

When I thought about this experience later, it was clear to me that I was saved because there was something inside me, inside my body, that knew more than I did, something that had been looking out for me. That fall when I turned thirty, I had evidence that this same force existed in the world outside of me as well.

On my thirtieth birthday, I took myself out during lunch break at Gateway to one of the homey little restaurants gradually being devoured by the post office. When I finished my lunch, I had exactly $1.80 in change. This was all the money I had left before the next payday. I would use it for my dinner, and then on the next day I would commence to starve. When I came out of the restaurant an old black man approached me. "Could you spare me $1.80 so I can get me a hamburger, french fries, and a large coke?" he asked me. I laughed and gave it to him.

Now I had absolutely nothing, only my bus transfer. At the end of the day, I got on the bus to go home. The older women sitting across from me in garish clothes were perfectly beautiful, like paintings. When I got home Jeff Linzer was waiting outside my empty room over the delicatessen with a woman I didn't recognize. He had broken up with Charlotte, his wife. "This is Susan," he said. They had driven across the country to surprise me on my birthday. "We're flat broke," Jeff said. "Can you feed us?"

I didn't know whether to laugh or cry. I had just given away my last dime. "This is a fine kettle of fish," I said. We sat around in my empty room for the rest of the evening worrying and trying to think of what we could do. Then suddenly the doorbell rang. It was a special delivery letter from my Bubbe Ida. When I ripped it open, a birthday check for thirty dollars floated out.

## 14 FORM IS EMPTINESS

One day I was riding home from Gateway on the bus, enjoying looking at the other passengers who were as vivid as characters in a Fellini movie, when I noticed a gorgeous Filipino girl sitting in the front of the bus. To my surprise, she came over and began talking to me. I couldn't believe it—she was inviting me to come to dinner.

Dinner was discolored spaghetti in a huge mansion up on the north side of campus. There were about a hundred people there. Half of us were bewildered, and the other half were Moonies, trying to recruit us. Moses Durst, the Reverend Moon's right-hand man, came out and started to give a lecture with charts and graphs. The Filipino girl had also brought along her high school teacher from Alameda. The woman was in shock; the girl had been her star student until dropping out of school altogether. After the lecture three or four people gathered around us to try to convince us to join. One was a Cornell graduate who seemed reasonably intelligent. It was exactly like a fraternity rush. They were trying to overwhelm us with good feeling and camaraderie, but I could see we were like pelts to them. They wouldn't let us go. They were trying to get us to go up to their country place in Boonville where they practiced a form of classical brainwashing. They wanted to make us slaves of Reverend Moon.

The next week, Margie Johanson, another of the drivers at Gateway, asked me back to her house, and we went out a few times after that. Margie was a Berkeley graduate who was working at Gateway because she didn't believe in being part of the middle class; she was involved with the leftist underground. One day she asked me to go with her to return a car she had borrowed from a friend of hers named Emily Harris. Emily greeted us from the top of a tall staircase. She had big hairy legs. Apparently, she needed the car back because the following week she and her Symbionese Liberation Army friends were going to kidnap Patty Hearst.

When Norman would pick me up in the mornings, it would be in his Dodge Dart. This was the same car he had had in Iowa, and even then it was old. The door to the driver's side was broken, and Norman had to slide in and out of the passenger's side. After Patty Hearst was kidnapped, dozens of cops started coming out every morning to look for her, and Norman and I were often stopped and frisked.

"Get out of the car," the cops would say, leaning into Norman's lowered window, but because he couldn't open the door on the driver's side, I would have to get out of the car so Norman could slide out the passenger side. This invariably made the policemen very tense. While they frisked us they would ask where we were going, and we would spend the next fifteen minutes trying to explain to them what zazen was. Some of them seemed really interested. One cop asked for instruction in sitting and got right down on the curb to try it out.

After I stopped seeing Margie, I developed a crush on a woman named Suki at the Zen Center. But I was painfully shy and afraid to ask her out. I sat in my room and said to myself, "You're an idiot." I knew that she lived near me. I knew the block, but I didn't know her address. "You're going to go out there right now," I told myself, "and you're going to go up and down her block and knock on every door and ask for her, and when you find her, you're going to ask her out," and then I got up and marched out the door. I knocked on twenty different doors, but I didn't find her.

In the course of my search, however, I had had twenty different glimpses into twenty different lives. I forgot all about finding Suki and ran back to my room and began to write about all the things I had just seen. I realized that to write with honesty and depth, I didn't have to make things up or write poetic reminiscences from my childhood. I didn't have to chase after the strange or exotic in order to find the truth. I had only to look at the reality right in front of my eyes and just write in the present moment. I was suddenly very happy.

The impulse to avoid living the reality one has been given, to have things somehow be otherwise, is the greatest impediment to happiness. Buddhism says that, in fact, all suffering is caused by *tana*, the selfish desire for something other than what is. Looking for Suki that night I got a glimpse at all those ordinary lives instead, and I realized that my sitting was helping me see things as they really were, without embellishment, without reification, without fantasy, even without meaning. Groups like the Moonies and the S.L.A. put a romantic overlay over life. The members of the S.L.A. were middle-class kids who saw themselves as an exotic revolutionary band and history as a fairy tale. The Moonies with their charts and graphs covered over reality with a thicket of romantic illusion, such as the idea that Reverend Moon was a savior. But the Moonies had captivated thousands and the S.L.A. had seized the attention of the world. They were playing on the most ancient of all human impulses, the desire to cover over the yawning emptiness of our real experience with something else, anything else, a fairy tale, a savior.

From that night forward, when I was waiting in my bus outside a school or even when I came to a stop sign, I would take notes about what I was seeing right in front of my face, then later, sitting at my collapsible desk, I would render this material into poems and stories. I loved this desk because at the end of each writing session I could just fold it up and put it away. Then, once again I would be in a totally empty room.

I was willing to go through all this inconvenience and discomfort for the sake of this final clarity. The emptiness of my room at the end of the day reflected my passionate embrace of a Zen aesthetic. Moreover, it comforted me after the confusion and messiness of my marriage. Our marriage house had been exactly as messy and disordered as it had been unhappy.

But, to be fair, I had been feeling oppressed by the objects in my environment ever since I was a child. I remember once lying feverish in my little bed in Brooklyn looking across the room at all my toys. They were piled to overflowing in a big basket and they filled every shelf. Half of them were broken, half I had never even played with once. I could feel the weight of all these toys pressing down on my chest. As I lay helpless in my bed, I yearned to clear all these things away so that I could breathe. Now at last I was fulfilling that yearning. My room was completely empty. There was nothing in it I didn't need, and nothing in it that I did.

## 15 SPIRITUAL PYROTECHNICS

When I first came to California and was actively exploring various spiritual paths, a guru from India called the Mahara-ji had a brief but strong run in the American spotlight. We used to call him "the little fat boy" because he was quite plump and extremely young, a child, really. I knew dozens of people who had gone to see him, and they all claimed that they saw a radiant white light when they were in his presence. Many of them were so impressed with this that, at his suggestion, they sold everything they owned and went off to follow him. Their friends and families were properly horrified. They tried to talk them out of what they had seen. "You just imagined you saw a white light," they would say. "It's simply mass hysteria."

For my part, I had no doubt that he had made them see a white light. They were all reasonable and relatively honest people, and they said they had seen a white light. Why shouldn't I believe them? What I had trouble with was the part about selling everything they owned and going off to follow him. I didn't see what one had to do with the other, and the fact is, all of them came to feel the same way. The little fat boy's popularity swelled for a while. He filled the Houston Astrodome with his followers at about the six-month mark, but shortly after that, people began to say, "So, I saw a white light. So what." And they began to say to themselves, "Why did I sell all my belongings? Why did I give up my life?"

The experience of seeing a white light had become both empty and mundane. There was nothing behind it, there was nothing beyond it. It was just a white light. In their spiritual naiveté, the Mahara-ji's American followers had come to resemble those African tribesmen who worshipped the pilots of airplanes, or villagers in the Asian hinterlands who were dazzled to the point of religious awe by a man who could produce light by pushing a button on a flashlight. Americans are very naive about spirituality and are constantly being duped by charlatans. Their own experience of spirituality being so limited, they have no sense of the complexity of the spiritual endeavor. If a person shows any sign of spiritual power whatsoever, they immediately fall to worshipping him. The idea that someone could be spiritually powerful but also evil or venal, or simply crazy, is beyond their ken. I have always known that people could have spiritual aptitudes in the same way they might have an aptitude for music, but because spiritual power is somewhat rare in the West, when most Americans encounter it for the first time, they are utterly defenseless and unable to distinguish between its abuse and its legitimate exercise.

When Jeff and his girlfriend, Susan, came to Berkeley it was actually because they were following Muktananda, a teacher of yogic-style meditation with a large following who was staying temporarily in a mansion up in the hills. Jeff offered to take me to see him, and I drove us up there in Mel's VW bug, which I sometimes borrowed to drive Steve places.

Muktananda held court all day, and people came to him for audiences bearing gifts. "You have to bring him a gift," Jeff said, as we were getting out of the car. I had forgotten, so I looked in the back seat to see if there was anything I could take. All I found was one of Steve's little plastic animals, a smiling lion.

We were ushered into a large room where we sat meditating in preparation for Muktananda's appearance. We sat for quite a while, a half hour or so, with our eyes closed. Suddenly I saw something I had never seen in meditation before—a radiant white light as vivid as a lightning bolt. The light had an elegant natural shape. It was beautiful, luminous and powerful. When I opened my eyes, I saw that Muktananda had come into the room.

He was twinkly-eyed and yet he had a powerful presence. People came forward one at a time to give him gifts of flowers, books, or fruit. They would bow before bestowing the gift and he would bow back, and sometimes he would bless them. When it was my turn to come forward, I bowed and handed him the toy lion. He took it and his whole body began to shake with laughter. Then he leaned back and began to roar. Finally, he handed it back to me. It had been smiling with its mouth closed when I handed it to him, but now it had its mouth wide open in full roar. My own jaw dropped.

My name, Lew, was actually pronounced "Lev" in Poland, where my Zayde Isaac was born. The Polish letter that sounds like V looks like an English W, however, and when Isaac came through Ellis Island, they changed his name to "Lew." In Hebrew, *lev* means "heart," but in Yiddish, *lev* means "lion."

To this day, I have no idea if Muktananda was a genuine teacher or not. I have no idea if he ended up sleeping with his students or appropriating their money dishonestly. I didn't care about these things because he wasn't my teacher. All I knew was that he was far more subtle and far more charming than the little fat boy had been, and he seemed to be the bearer of an important message for me.

Was it a trick Muktananda had done with Steve's toy lion, or was my own mind playing tricks on me? I couldn't be sure. But finally, it was irrelevant, because in our brief encounter, Muktananda had managed to raise the central question of my life: How can I realize my strength? How can I make my lion roar?

# 16　DOKUSAN

For a long time, I went to the zendo twice a day to sit. After I was able to do that with some degree of comfort, I started going to *sesshins*, all-day sittings. Sesshins start the night before with a few hours of sitting before sleep. Then everyone returns to the zendo at 5:00 A.M. My first sesshin was brutal. I was in so much pain that I kept shifting my position, but no matter how much I shifted, I couldn't alleviate the pain. The sesshin was supposed to end at around 8:00 P.M., but around five I just went downstairs and out the door, and I didn't come back. I was overwhelmed with humiliation. When I got outside I realized that I was so stoned I didn't know how to find my way home.

It took me a long time to screw up my courage to try another sesshin, but when I finally did, I made it through the whole day without ever thinking of bolting. It was still difficult, but I made it. Once again, my consciousness was altered by the experience, as it always was after every sesshin I undertook, though never again to the extent it was the first time. But each time it led me to a much different apprehension of reality.

Little by little, Mel was trying to take over the garden-apartment building next to the zendo. He wanted Zen students living there in order to build his community and also to ensure that the people in that building wouldn't be making a lot of noise during zazen. When a unit became available he offered it to me and I took it. I had already become one of the most active members of the Berkeley Zendo. During this period Mel would do a great deal for me, but not always in the way that he planned.

Living in the garden apartment I could sleep an extra half hour before getting up to go to zazen. Mel was my teacher, but when I went to weeklong sesshins I went to Green Gulch Farm, where Baker Roshi was the Zen master. It took me a long time to get up my nerve to try a weeklong sesshin. Each time I raised the ante, the last thing I had been doing became less of a struggle. I thought of it as putting another log on the fire. When I started doing one-day sesshins, daily morning and afternoon sitting became easier, and when I started doing weeklong sesshins, one-day sesshins became manageable, even beautiful, no longer terrifying. Everything took on a greater depth and richness. A sesshin was like a leave-taking, not unlike Shabbat, I was to discover later. You'd leave the ordinary world for a designated period of time and go into sacred space.

The first weeklong sesshin I went to was in many ways the most soaring and searing experience I had ever had. It was totally exalting and totally shattering in alternate waves. I really thought I had no business going because I couldn't sit very well. In comparison to Judaism, Zen practice is thought to be egalitarian, because you don't have to have any special education, such as a knowledge of the Hebrew language, to practice it. All you have to do is plop yourself down on the floor and sit. In reality, however, sitting is itself a high art, a very advanced physical and psychological skill, a kind of motionless ballet. It takes tremendous energy to sit still. When you are tired, it is hard to resist moving and shifting around. When I was given the job of walking around with the stick, I often observed periods when everyone was tired and bobbing all around, and other times when everyone was full of energy and able to sit perfectly still.

At this first weeklong sesshin I felt I was uniquely defective in the skill of sitting, that I alone was unable to sit properly, and I would get very despondent. "I can't do this. I'm a failure," I would say to myself. I was very tired because we hardly ever slept. Then during a break I noticed that everyone was lining up for coffee. Even though I was not a coffee drinker, and drinking coffee at a sesshin seemed like a sacrilege to me, I nonetheless tried it and discovered that coffee is one of the strongest drugs on earth. That was when I had my first wave of transcendent visions. I began hallucinating when I sat down again. I saw shadows catch fire. I saw light around every object. I found I could change reality as I looked at it; the shadows on the wall changed their shapes at my bidding.

On the third day of the weeklong sesshin I was brought in for *dokusan*, the interview, with Baker Roshi, the Zen master. This first dokusan was the beginning of our Zen master-student relationship. After that, it was never clear whose student I was— Baker Roshi's or Mel's. Each would try to steal me away from the other. Students are the coin of the realm for gurus and Zen masters.

People were called out of the sesshin for dokusan without

warning, one at a time, in a seemingly random order. It was a formal procedure. Someone came and put a small plaque reading Dokusan in front of where I was sitting to tell me I was next. I was then ushered into the waiting room outside Baker Roshi's office and coached in the ceremonial bowing I was to do as I entered the room. It was a dance that ended with me sitting on the floor opposite Baker Roshi, an extremely tall man, an imposing figure with a large, handsome face and a penetrating glance.

I had been going every Saturday to San Francisco and most Sundays to Green Gulch to hear him talk. He quoted poetry and talked about music. His discussions of Zen practice were full of penetrating insights about the way people behaved and interacted, and how they kidded themselves, and then he would offer Zen practice as a solution. He began each talk with a Zen text, often a passage from the *Blue Cliff Record*, a collection of Zen stories, and he would return to an image from the story at the end. I had tremendous admiration for him.

Now as he loomed over me in our first dokusan, he seemed to me like a mountain in his black robes, and I felt weak, ragged, and hopelessly vulnerable. It was time for me to ask my question. I said, "This week, I've been going from suicidal thoughts to exultations. Is this what's supposed to happen?"

"What do you feel suicidal about?" he asked.

"This sense of failure, of feeling somehow defective," I said.

He gave me no advice, but when I came out of dokusan I felt as if I had been cleansed, as if I had done several years of psychotherapy in ten minutes. The sesshin had brought me to a deep place. He had told me to stop fooling around in Berkeley and to come to San Francisco. He made me feel wanted, and I felt healed.

The sesshin provided me with a strange world where I was insulated from the ordinary suffering of my life, but when I came out of the sesshin, suffering was often waiting for me in concentrated doses, as if I had to make up for the week I had missed. It would turn out there had been some terrible disaster, or Betty would be furious at me for something.

The fact that our marriage was not working out was the source of terrible conflict for me. I hated not keeping my word and I hated the pain it had caused my son. I hated not being always there for him. He stayed with me about half the time, but his room was at Betty's. I thought that money might be part of the problem. Betty had an income from her family. When we had lived in Gualala we had renounced it, and I had felt much better. But when we set out on the road to Berkeley, she had started taking it again. Once when I was at a sesshin I had a revelation. We should be together but live on my money. When I came back I asked her to renounce the money again. We would live in reduced circumstances but we would be a family and not dependent on anyone else, I said, but she didn't seem interested.

And in truth, I really did enjoy being by myself. Next to being with someone you truly love, being alone is the next best thing. Betty and I had never had unqualified affection for each other. There was feeling there, but it wasn't pure, and I constantly felt trapped. She manipulated me and I allowed myself to be manipulated. By now, she had had a couple of boyfriends and I had had several casual relationships. We had separated on an experimental basis, but now I felt I had to decide whether to try to make a go of the marriage or just give up on it altogether, and the pressure to make this decision was starting to weigh on me and get me down.

I told all this to Norman. He sat me down and said, "Suppose you decide you want to stay in the marriage but it turns out to be the wrong decision; well, it won't work out and you'll leave the marriage. Or suppose you decide to leave her and that's the wrong decision. So you'll be miserable and try to get back with her. You think it's all up to you and your decision, but really, it's not. Whatever is right is going to happen no matter what you decide. It's much bigger than you are."

## 17 WHEN PEACE BREAKS OUT, THE FIRST THING YOU FEEL IS THE DEVASTATION OF THE WAR

When Rudrananda's plane went down, he had disciples all over the country. Jason decided to go live in the ashram in Bloomington, Indiana. Once he established residency there, it was easy for him to get into medical school, easier than it would have been in New York. I decided to take Steve and go out to visit him. And because I had no car and no money, I decided that we would hitchhike. This was not an altogether unheard of thing to do at the time. Betty had no objections, and Steve thought it would be fun.

We started out at the bottom of University Avenue on a summer's day with a sign that read East. I had a huge backpack, and Steve, who was seven, had a small backpack. There were some other people waiting for rides with us, holding up their signs as we held up ours while the cars sped past. It was now 1975, and the bloom was already off the hitchhiking lily.

People were becoming afraid of hitchhikers, and hitchhikers were afraid of the people picking them up. No one was getting a ride and we all stood there together for hours. Finally, a large station wagon pulled up and loaded all of us in.

This was still during the S.L.A. period. The driver told us that he was part of the S.L.A., and to prove it, he pulled out a gun from underneath his seat. "There's going to be a revolution," he told us. We all cowered in our seats, terrified, as he raved on and waved the pistol in the air. We didn't know if we were going to get out of this alive, but Steve and I were let off on the freeway just north of Sacramento.

Our next ride was from a guy in a Volkswagen bug who did transcendental meditation. He was calm and friendly, the cosmic opposite of the lunatic in the station wagon. He drove us to Reno. It was getting toward evening and I was beginning to wonder where we'd spend the night. We went to a restaurant for dinner and there were slot machines all over the place. Steve put a quarter into one and suddenly bells started going off and money started pouring out. The owner of the restaurant called the cops.

Apparently, it was illegal for Steve to be gambling. The police came, put us in a squad car, drove us to the outskirts of town, and left us on the freeway. We waited for hours while the cars whizzed past. It got dark and there was no place to lay our sleeping bags. Then a tremendous truck pulled up right in front of us. The driver was a short southerner with a soft heart. "I just can't stand to see a little child by the side of the road like that," he said. So he picked us up out of our despair and drove us as far as Salt Lake City.

We slept all that night in his nice spacious cab, safe, sheltered, and warm. In Salt Lake City, he handed us off to another trucker. All the truckers were talking to each other on their CB radios. The second trucker let us off in northern Utah, passing us off to a truck that brought us to "Little America," a huge truck stop with gargantuan gas stations, restaurants, and a trailer park. I took Steve by the hand and we went over to a man who was getting gas and asked him if he'd give us a ride.

The man was a traveling salesman. His whole life was organized around his car. He traveled all over the country, sleeping in a different motel every night. He had no attachments; he did not even let himself get attached to us. He was friendly, but he kept his distance and he dropped us off in Laramie, Wyoming. It was raining hard, so we slogged our way to the Greyhound Bus Station. There we slept in the waiting room until the next bus left for the East. We rode that bus all the way across the state of Nebraska. When the bus arrived in Iowa City it had finally stopped raining, and we got out. By this time, it had been quite a while since we had slept in a bed or taken a shower. We started to trudge across town to a motel I remembered. Steve was beat and I took his pack for him. A man in a car yelled out the window, "You're spoiling that kid!"

The next day we got a ride almost to the Mississippi River. Our ride dropped us off right on the highway, near a dead possum. "Oh no," I said to myself, "this is a real bad sign." We tried to get away from the thing, but this was the only place we could stand, because the road curved and it was too dangerous to stand anywhere else. Just then a perfectly restored 1955 Chevy drove up and stopped in the middle of the road. He did not pull off onto the shoulder, and he was in the middle of the curve. I knew this was a recipe for disaster. I tried to hurry Steve into the car, when a huge truck came barreling around the curve on two wheels and missed us by a hair's breadth. That, I thought, was the death the dead possum had advertised for us, but it had been averted.

The driver of the Chevy was a happy idiot who had gone out to California to get this car. It was his pride and joy. He was driving it back home to Toronto. He stopped in the middle of the highway again to drop us off on a cloverleaf in Gary, Indiana. Again our spirits fell. It was much too dangerous for anyone to stop here and pick us up, and no one did for hours. Then another softhearted truck driver stopped for us. He drove us all the way to Indianapolis, where Jason came and got us and took us to his ashram in Bloomington.

Bloomington was an archetypal midwestern college town, full of large, leafy, deciduous trees, friendly people, and big houses with deep porches. The ashram was in one of these houses. Here the students would meditate and tremble with Michael, the principle teacher, much as they had with Rudi before him. Because Jason was now a fairly advanced student, his trembling had increased. Like Rudi, Michael watched TV, but he didn't watch *I Love Lucy*; he watched violent detective shows. Michael looked like a thug.

He had been a swimmer, and he was heavily muscled with a thick neck. He was a very strong-willed person, very competitive, and an empire builder. He had a store full of priceless Asian art objects in downtown Bloomington. He sat in his room playing computer games all day. I had never seen computer games before. He challenged me to play with him, and as he was beating me, he told me that it was his meditation practice that allowed him to win all the time. He said if I did his meditation I would learn to function at a much higher level.

Meanwhile, Steve curled up behind the sofa in Jason's room and wouldn't come out. He wouldn't talk to anyone. "Your son's soul has been scarred," Michael said to me. "Can't you see how screwed up you are? You're in a dead marriage, your life is a mess, and I don't know what you're doing in that zendo. You need to come here and join my ashram. I'm the only one who can help you."

I could see Michael was good. He was plucking on all my raw nerves, hitting on all my weak spots—my marriage, my guilt about Steve, my doubts about my Zen practice—all the things I felt most anxious about, but he was being a little too obvious. Of course, I could see very well that everything his people did turned to gold. They had beautiful, thriving restaurants and bakeries making money hand over fist. All his students were getting into medical school and law school. I could even accept that there was something about their practice that made them all so effective, and it really didn't matter if it was just group hypnosis. But *my* meditation practice, Zen, as I saw it, was not about material success. It was about existential truth.

Steve and I stayed in Indiana about a week, then Jason boarded a plane with us for New York. Our sister, Carol, had married while I was in Gualala, and she and her husband lived near our parents now. She came over and we all went out on the lawn. While the family had been growing up, we had periodically taken family portraits out there posed on a rock, dressed in nice clothes. Now we all posed for a picture in the same positions again; my six-foot-tall brother precariously balanced on our father's lap and I kneeling beside them in a goatee and the striped T-shirt I always wore.

Everyone kept asking me, "What's wrong?" I couldn't disguise my despair and confusion. I had set out on a journey to find myself, but all I had found was that I was stupid and lost. I had put myself and my son in jeopardy, and Steve was clearly suffering from the suspended state of my relationship with Betty.

I flew back to San Francisco alone, having left Steve with my parents for his summer visit. As I was sitting on the bus going back to Berkeley, still obsessed and distraught, all of a sudden I had a strange sensation. Something inside me said, "Look out the window and you will have the answer." We were going down Third Street in the industrial section. I looked up. There was a sign covering the whole side of a building. It read, NORMAN S. WRIGHT. Norman is right! Of course, Norman was right! It wasn't all up to me.

I had known what to do all along, because we always know what to do, we always carry this wisdom deep inside us, but our confusion and our fear of making the wrong decision masks this wisdom. Seeing the sign on the wall punctured that confusion and fear now, the way a good laugh releases tension, and the truth of what I wanted was suddenly obvious.

I was overcome with relief. The weight of the decision had been taken off me. I called up Betty as soon as I got back to my apartment and invited her out to dinner. Betty and I had been married in 1965, the year Lyndon Johnson had sent the first marines to Vietnam. We had been separated since 1973, coincidentally the year North and South Vietnam declared a cease-fire. Now, in a friendly way, I said to Betty, "I've come to a decision. I think we should not be together anymore." She was a little taken aback, but she took it reasonably well, and there was no scene. But then she excused herself and left me alone in the restaurant.

I went back to my apartment, feeling as if a tremendous weight had been lifted from me, but I also felt terribly sad. I went into my room without turning on any lights and lay down on the bed. I felt no doubt or ambivalence, but I was overcome with a feeling of depression, of failure and defeat. It was now official. The marriage had failed. As I lay there grieving in the dark, I suddenly heard a clamor in the street. It sounded like a riot. It was coming closer and closer, in waves. And then I realized that people were cheering. The shouts were shouts of joy and triumph because the Vietnam War had just ended and peace was breaking out, and the people of Berkeley had taken to the streets to celebrate.

## 18 THE NEED TO BELONG

One day Mel overheard me playing my guitar and he came in from the next room and said, "My God, that was you! I thought that was a record." He was not generally an effusive person. If anything, he was usually fairly critical. But he saw I was a talented person who had never done anything with his talents, and he continued to work on my case trying to bring out my skills. To that end, he made me the first director of the Berkeley Zen Center.

My relationship with Mel was strangely similar to the one I had had with my father. My father was always taking me outside to "help him" with the household chores, but he would never really let me do anything. I would spend hours watching him chop wood and pound nails, and he would insist that I stay there with him, but he would never trust me with any of the work. Now it was the same with Mel. He would urge me to do things on my own initiative, and then he would undermine me. After I became director of the Berkeley Zendo, I decided to bring speakers to lecture there. Jason's teacher, Michael, was coming out to Berkeley from Indiana, and he had contacted me to see if I could set something up for him. After all, Rudi had had a relationship with the Zen Center, having donated some priceless Buddhas to them. But at the last minute, Mel refused to let Michael talk in the zendo because he wasn't a Buddhist, and he wound up speaking in the living room. I was very embarrassed.

Ultimately, though, Mel really did empower me. He was sincere and relentless in his efforts to free me from the paralysis that seemed to have me in its grip then, and, in the end, he succeeded. He set up a poetry reading for Norman and me in a further effort to bring me out of my shell. He thought I was pent-up and frustrated, literally choking on myself.

I tried to get out of giving the reading at least ten times. The week before the reading, I went into a white fear that lasted the entire week and became a white noise for the last several days before the reading. This was the first time I would be reading my new writing in public, the writing I had been doing directly from life, and I was terrified of exposing myself.

Compounding my fear was the fact that I knew many Language Poets would be in attendance. They were the most interesting writers we knew at the time. For them "meaning" and "narrative" were the enemies. They wrote sentences that made no sense, but were strangely beautiful and seemed to suggest a world of possibility beyond language. They told stories that had no beginning or end—or any point, for that matter—and that opened you to the wide expanses of the mind. Our work had something in common with theirs. Our Zen practice was bringing us more and more into a prelingual world, a world where the-thing-itself preceded the word for the thing. But we were also different from them, especially me. I still loved narrative, and more and more I saw the magical power of it, whereas the Language Poets were becoming more and more doctrinaire by the day. They ridiculed writers who used narrative and poems that made sense. I was sure they would hate my work, which contained both in ample supply.

But as terrible as my apprehension was, that's how wonderful the reading was. Norman and I both received a huge ovation. Afterward, too exhilarated to sleep, we stayed up all night at a local diner. I had allowed myself to expose my soul to the world and to all the poets in the community whom I admired, and I had survived. Mel had, in fact, begun to bring me out of my shell.

At about this time I moved into a cabin, not far from the zendo. The previous occupant had had a fire. There were big holes in the walls, and blackberry vines were now growing through them. Shortly after I moved in, my mother sent me a small TV. I hadn't had one for many years. I hated it because I watched it all the time; I was addicted to it. It tormented me, and one day I prayed to God to take it away.

Throughout my life, in times of need I had made these spontaneous prayers, never thinking to question God's existence. During the fifties, when mainstream organized religion dominated American life, some people believed that God was dead. But the sixties had overturned all the ideas of the fifties. Experimentation with drugs and Eastern religions had begun to reopen the dimension of the sacred for people, and many found God there—not the idea of God, not God as some ultimate puzzle with which all the suffering of the world had to be reconciled, but simply God, the experience of God. My practice, Buddhism, was not a theistic religion. It was not God-centered, but it was not concerned with denying God's existence, either. For me, in fact, it always seemed to bring the sense of the sacred to the foreground. So even though I was a Buddhist, it was a natural thing for me to pray for God to take my TV.

Just then, Mel came over and invited me to go to the movies with him. We went to see half of a ten-hour movie about India by Louis Malle. When we got back, we found the cabin had been broken into and the TV was gone. Nothing else was missing, though my stereo and my guitar were much more valuable. Steve missed it at first, and then he forgot about it.

My bedroom window looked out the back and into the kitchen window of a house around the corner. I had been to the house once to vote. A Jewish family lived there. The parents were a bit younger than my own parents. They had two sons, one in high school and one in college, and when I sat in my bedroom I could see them all eating dinner together. Later, the boys would wash the dishes. They were short and looked like mild-mannered intellectuals, although the mother seemed somewhat aggressive. They reminded me of the family I had grown up in.

One day the woman appeared in my doorway when I was just coming out of the bath with a towel around my waist. She said she was working for the Field Poll and asked if she could interview me. "Okay," I said. "What do you do?" she asked. I knew she wasn't really working for the Field Poll. I had been studying Noh chanting and had taken to practicing it at home. The chanting was a specific combination of deep, resonant sounds, very loud and discordant to Western ears. She just wanted to check out this person who was making these strange sounds when her family was at dinner, to make sure he wasn't a menace.

In those days, I didn't know anyone who was living in a traditional family like hers. The Zen Center I belonged to was a strong, positive community, and the connections between the people were deep and real, but it wasn't a blood connection. There was not the essential and permanent bond that comes with family. I felt this most keenly when I took Steve with me to holiday gatherings at the zendo. Looking through the window at this Jewish family across the way, I experienced a profound and surprising sense of longing.

## 19   EMPTINESS IS FORM

Something very significant happened between the third and fourth sesshin I went to: I figured out how to get through it better. The talks were the most difficult part. The sittings were in forty-minute sessions, but the talks might last an hour. So I started taking the talks as a break, not sitting in real zazen, but just sitting on a cushion in the back of the zendo, shifting and sitting up—in other words, cheating.

But at the fourth sesshin they sat me directly under Baker Roshi. No one said anything, but I wondered if they had noticed what I had been doing. In the middle of his lecture, Baker Roshi looked down at me and said, "Stop fidgeting!" I had to hold on for dear life; I couldn't allow myself to move at all. The result was that my experience was very powerful, and on the last day of the sesshin, instead of counting the minutes, I was flying. And I was able to sit straight effortlessly. It felt as if some magnetic force, the magnetism of the Big Bang, was pulling me through the stars—which were whizzing past me—and I was rushing toward some great release.

What I was rushing toward was *satori*, a spiritual enlightenment. When Baker Roshi saw someone on the brink of this state, he would sneak up on him and smash the floor in front of him to send him over the edge, but I saw him coming, so I never had this great release.

It is a mistake, however, to think that satori is the final aim of Zen practice. It is not. Satori, or any other goal, is just one other thing that pulls you out of the present moment of your experience. It's true that after many years of practice, ordinary mind gives way and a deep apprehension of reality takes its place, but this happens in its own time; it is not something to be desired or sought, or even, necessarily, a good thing.

I knew a woman who experienced it once, complete reality. It was a horror. For her, it was the end of all romance, the death of every cherished illusion. When she went to the Zen master with her new vision, he confirmed it as enlightenment, and she was terribly disappointed. It might well be that your first moment of Zen practice is the best, the one most open, the one with the most possibilities. Suzuki Roshi, the founder of our practice, often urged his students to see things this way.

Once at a sesshin I had a burning question I needed to ask. There was no way to know when I would be called for dokusan, so I decided I would make it happen soon by preparing for it. There was no real preparation, but I thought that if I went through the motions of preparing I would cause it to happen. So during the ten-minute walking meditation, I went and put on fresh clothes and went to the bathroom to wash my face and comb my hair. Then I went back to my place and sat down. Right away, the dokusan stick was placed in front of me.

This is a practice I continued throughout my life after this. If I want something to happen, I behave as if it is going to happen. I realized that I could affect the outcome of something by preparing for it. I understand now that this is a blurring of the objective and subjective. It's the same thing as looking at a wall and making the lines on the wall change. We don't realize how much our subjectivity is involved in shaping reality. When we do become aware of this, the world seems remarkably malleable.

However, there are limits to this. There is a famous Zen teaching that says when you first start to practice, the mountains are just mountains, but after you've been practicing for a while, the mountains aren't mountains, they're something else entirely, something profound, beyond the category of mountain. And after you've been practicing for a very long while, the mountains become just mountains again. The *Heart Sutra* says, "Form is emptiness and emptiness is form." Everyone gets the first part right away. They sense instinctively that there is a reality deeper than form, that the constructs we live by have no substance; they are less likely to notice that the second part of the saying is also true. Emptiness is also form. The mountains are just mountains. This is the great paradox of Zen.

The same is true of objective reality. The world seems empty of form, and when we first start to practice Zen, we feel as if we can make whatever we want of it. We are acutely aware of its emptiness, of the fact that it is a construct that is subject to our own manipulation, but as our practice goes on, we discover that emptiness is also form, and the mountain is really just a mountain. The world has a certain inevitability after all, and we are part of it. In the end, there is nothing to manipulate and no one to manipulate it, just mountains.

## 20 COMPASSION

About this time, Trungpa Rimpoche, a great Tibetan Buddhist teacher who was all the rage among poets and writers, came to speak at Berkeley and I went to see him. The place was packed, but I got a seat on the side. He had been taken from his parents when he was very young because the lamas had a dream that he was the next Rimpoche, a position filled by reincarnation. A Rimpoche was akin to a human deity. When China invaded Tibet he went to England, where he studied at Oxford and developed a taste for Western pleasures: drinking and womanizing. Now he was talking about the moon. "When the moon is half full, we call it a half moon," he was saying. He was perched up on a platform. I could tell that he was dead drunk, because he kept falling off the platform, but some big goons were stationed behind him, and they caught him. Finally, he gave a brilliant dharma talk.

There was a big scandal surrounding him at that time. The word was that he intimidated people and took their girlfriends away. A little while later the Karmopa, the reigning Tibetan religious authority, came to town and the rumor was that he had come to read Trungpa the riot act, to tell him that all this screwing around and getting drunk wasn't real Buddhism. Ostensibly the Karmopa had come to the Bay Area to perform the Black Hat Ceremony, the occasion of a great Buddhist conclave.

The Black Hat Ceremony was very rarely performed. The idea was that when the Karmopa put on a certain special black hat, he became Avalokiteshvara, the Bodhisattva of compassion. Each Bodhisattva is a personification of a kind of Buddhist consciousness. There's one for rigor and one for wisdom, but Avalokitshvera is "the Hearer of the Cries of the World." They held the ceremony on the end of a long pier in a huge warehouse in Fort Mason. Thousands of people with zafus and blankets came. All the different Buddhist groups were there, the various Indian, Tibetan, and Zen sects. Although we got there hours early, we still had to sit halfway back. There was a disappointingly picniclike atmosphere, with many young children screaming. The din was unbearable, in part because of the bad acoustics.

Finally, after hours of waiting, the Karmopa and his monks came out. They reminded me of something I had seen in an old *Flash Gordon* movie serial when I was a kid: clay people who materialized out of the walls of a cave. They were exactly like these people—earthy, round, stooped, gnarled, and primitive, but very powerful spiritually.

The program they had handed out when we arrived seemed to indicate that the ceremony would be very long. But in remarkably short order they did a little chanting and took out a large old-fashioned hat box. The Karmopa was sitting on a platform. He looked like a painted Buddha; he was sitting inhumanly still, high above the monks. Just before they put the hat on him, they began to blow some long, crude trumpets. They sounded like elephants trumpeting. Everyone stopped talking except the children, who were screaming. They took the hat out of the box, a black three-cornered hat, and when they put the hat on the Karmopa, the hall was suddenly filled with subtle but dazzling light. The babies stopped crying. There was a white sheet of sound and light that totally filled me, and I felt as if my mind was going to explode.

Over the years, I've spoken about this event with many people who were there. Not everybody experienced this, but quite a few did. After it was all over, they handed out little strings to wear around your neck. I waited for hours to get one of these strings, as did everyone else. I wore it for a while, until I saw that a lot of other people were also wearing them, and then I stopped.

## 21 THEY DO NOT APPEAR OR DISAPPEAR

Occasionally people would come back to Berkeley after a practice period at Tassajara, the monastery in the Los Padres Mountains, and it was clear that their sitting was much more powerful and intense than ours. To go to Tassajara was the logical next step for me, and I decided to go the following year, the year of the Centennial. Betty agreed to take care of Steve for the period I would be gone—Labor Day to Memorial Day, with a two-week break in the middle dividing the practice periods. It would cost $2,000. I began saving my money and went to have my robes made: a tan under-robe made of a heavy material for warmth (there was no heat at Tassajara), a black outer robe, and a shell collar that made a fresh white border at the neck.

Not long before my departure, I gave a reading at a new coffee house on Haight Street in San Francisco called the Grand Piano. The night of my reading, I looked out into the audience and noticed a striking woman with prematurely gray hair and a very pretty face. She came up to talk to me after the reading. Her name was Claudia. She was an artist.

A few days later, I received a card from her in the mail announcing an opening of her work at a gallery. It was going to be a one-woman, one-painting show. She had spent years on one monumental hyperrealistic painting of a rose. I felt this might have romantic implications. It did. The concentric network of petals pulled me in. I went home with her after the opening and stayed for a week.

One night, after we had been together for a few weeks, she was at the zendo with me when Betty phoned crying, saying she needed me to come over right away. "I'll be back as soon as I can," I told Claudia, but when I got to Betty's, she wouldn't let me leave. Each time I got up to go she begged me to stay, and I didn't get back to the zendo for fifteen hours. Claudia was gone. She had left me a note. "I guess this isn't going to work out," it said.

"This is how it's going to be for the rest of my life," I thought. "Even though we aren't together, Betty is going to keep me from having a relationship." I felt humiliated. Everyone at the zendo who had comforted Claudia while she was waiting for me now knew how crazy I was.

This all happened within a few days of my leaving for Tassajara, and I left for the monastery feeling shaken and disgusted. I got a ride with Norman. He and Kathie, his pregnant new wife (another Zen student whom he had met the night of our reading at the zendo), were also going to the practice period. Driving over the Tassajara road in the dark, I began to talk about what had happened with Claudia and I realized Claudia should have stuck by me. As soon as we got to the monastery and I had settled into my cabin, I sat down and wrote her a long letter. "What happened was terrible, but you should have stood by me. I refuse to let this relationship end," I wrote. I wrote her every day after that and called her from the only phone there, whenever it was working. So the relationship didn't end. In fact, it became wonderful—full of yearning and idealized love. It kept me from being totally subsumed by the monastic life. And the monastic life kept me from being totally subsumed by this relationship.

Tassajara was originally an Indian place. It had been a health resort at the turn of the century, then was abandoned for many years until the Zen Center acquired the property. Its natural sulphur hot springs were known for their healing properties. A long meeting house and a stone dining hall overlooked the creek, along with cabins and a bathhouse. From Memorial Day to Labor Day it was a resort, and the monks were the staff for the resort. I had been there before on brief stints as a work student in the summer, clearing poison oak from the hiking paths. When you were there as a summer work student, you slept in a crowded space in the attic over the dining hall, and the guests got all the nice cabins. During the winter, when Tassajara operated as a monastery, there was plenty of room for everyone, and the monks occupied the cabins. From Labor Day to Memorial Day, when Tassajara was closed to the public, no one could come in or out except those assigned to go for supplies, the Zen master, and his entourage.

As soon as we new monks had settled into our cabins, we started *tangario*,, the initiation at the gate, three days of undifferentiated sitting without any breaks. There was no relief; there were no forty-minute sessions to count on, no ringing bell to anticipate. It was the most grueling experience of my zen career. To add to the intensity, it was miserably hot, and there were hundreds of flies. They hovered in front of my face, but I couldn't brush them away.

The zendo at that time was in the old social hall. It was a long narrow room with a hardwood floor and a platform at one end. They had lined it on either side with zafus and zabutans, and Japanese sitting furniture, small rectangular platforms just big enough for two people. We sat facing the stone walls. The creek outside made a soul-satisfying complex sound, to which the chirping of crickets was added at night.

The stage of the social hall was for the Zen master. The head monk sat there when the Zen master wasn't at the monastery, and the bell ringers sat in the first seats at the foot of the stage. My seat was at the very back, just in front of the head waiter and the dining room staff, because I was from Berkeley, a practice place of low status compared to the San Francisco Zen Center where most of the others came from.

Two days after tangario was over, the regular practice period began with a one-day sesshin. After tangario, it was a breeze. The first morning it was still dark when we came out of the zendo. The air was cool, and the crickets suddenly stopped their chirping. I looked up. A tremendous shooting star was blazing across the sky. It seemed to have all the time in the world to fall through the dark before it disappeared.

The next day there was a ceremony for the installation of Steve Weintraub, the new head monk, or *shuso*. Once you were the shuso, you could give dharma talks. At his installation he had to give a dharma talk, which included his spiritual autobiography and told how he had reached this point in his practice.

Like me, Steve Weintraub had grown up in Brooklyn. His

family had a restaurant, Goodies, on Avenue M, right around the corner from Avenue N, where I lived. His talk was the story of a man who leaves home, goes on the road, becomes part of the counterculture, and then discovers Zen practice. Steve Weintraub was, of course, Jewish. Whenever I came into a room, I checked to see who there looked Jewish. I wondered if anyone knew that I was Jewish, and if they cared. I had been doing this unconsciously ever since we had moved to Pleasantville, but I had just recently become conscious of it. The more I meditated, the more aware I became of the contents of my unconscious mind.

Every morning now I got up at 3:20 A.M., when the bells started ringing and the drums started beating in complex patterns. I would throw on my robes and go to the zendo in the dark. The stars would be swirling overhead. After zazen, we were served breakfast, still sitting at our places in the zendo, usually oatmeal or porridge and eggs, which were served in a highly conscious ritual. The waiters would bow before serving us, and we would bow back and say a chant before eating. Every act was performed in an an elegant ritualized manner.

After breakfast we went to the study hall. You could study anything you wanted as long as it was about Buddhism. I usually wrote poetry, but sometimes I studied Buddhist texts about what life was like in the ancient Chinese monasteries, where in their study halls they were reading ancient sutras about life in the even more ancient Indian monasteries. It was a warm room, and people would often nod off. Afterward, there were another couple of periods of sitting, followed by the work meeting.

At work meeting everyone would stand in a circle. It was like a town hall meeting, where we would discuss work assignments and pass on information essential to the communal well-being, such as, "Don't leave your sandals outside your door because a fox has been coming and taking everyone's sandals." This was the only time when everyone was together outside the meditation hall, so there was always a lot of talking and joking.

At the first work circle they decided that I should be a plumber. Others were gardeners or carpenters or machine shop workers. I thought this was a joke, because I had no knowledge of plumbing. The closest I had ever gotten to it was holding the wrench while my father did a minor bit of work around the house. But it was a Zen idea to cast against type. People started leaving notes for me that read, My toilet isn't working, and I would go to their cabins, open up their toilets, and look inside. I found that if I studied the mechanisms inside the tank long enough, I could discover what was wrong, and to my great amazement and pride, I became good at fixing toilets.

There was a man at Tassajara who really was a plumber and he tried to advise me. We needed to lay some new pipe because there were more people at Tassajara than the water could handle. He couldn't do the actual work himself, because his back had gone out. "Be careful with your pick," the real plumber advised, but I had already broken a main pipe.

There was no water at the monastery for a week after that. Everyone laughed about it, but I felt horrible. Nevertheless, I still had to go about my plumbing. There was a dormitory over the dining hall, which housed more people than the plumbing could handle. It had been an ongoing problem that nobody had been able to fix. I tried everything to get the toilets unstopped—a plunger, a snake—but nothing helped. One day I was up a ladder over the entrance to the dining hall working on the plumbing from the other end, determined to unclog it, when all of a sudden it let loose and all the sewage that had been stopped up came pouring out.

I, the guy who had always been told to just stand there and hold the hammer while others more capable did the important work, had fixed something other people had been unable to fix. All my life I had carried around, bottled up inside, a negative image of myself and what I was capable of doing. Now I could let it go, and as the shit poured out, I had a tremendous feeling of release.

After the work period there was always a brief service and then lunch, followed by a short break when we could do our laundry, which we did all by hand, write letters, or rest. There was work again in the afternoon. We never got a lot done because neither work period was very long.

In late afternoon we would all go to the bathhouse for our daily plunge. It was wonderful to immerse ourselves in the big tubs, which were fed by the hot springs. Soon after I arrived it had begun to grow cold. There was no heat, but the baths warmed us, and afterward our robes kept the heat in and kept us warm for the rest of the night, even when the weather was freezing. Feeling clean and very warm, we would return to the zendo to sit. Dinner was followed by a brief socializing time when people would have each other to tea. Then there was the evening sitting schedule. We'd finish sitting at 9:30 or 10:00 and go to sleep.

This life made me feel very healthy, very awake. On our days off, they'd give us time after breakfast to fix a bag lunch to take on a hike or wherever else we wanted to go. My friend Brian and I loved to run on the rocks down the Tassajara Creek. The creek was high, and we ran for miles. It was dangerous, and had we broken a leg or sprained an ankle, we wouldn't have been able to sit. We also started a football game, which was very controversial for the same reason. Once a week or so, everyone had a day off together. One day, a group of us went up on a hill and told one another our life stories. We all felt very close. There were about fifty people at the monastery, and I came to love many of them.

On days off there were wonderful dinners in the dining hall, and twice these were followed by social evenings. The first was a night of readings, when we were invited to read poetry, either something we loved or something we had written ourselves. Norman and I read our poetry, and after that people looked at us with new respect. There were many attractive women there, some of whom seemed attracted to me, but I wasn't available; I was being faithful to Claudia. Most people at the monastery were celibate. The second social evening was supposed to be a night of comedy. Earlier that week a wave of uncontrollable laughter had gone through the zendo, which had lasted all day, but when they showed us a Laurel and Hardy movie no one was laughing. Laurel and Hardy were trying to move a piano, but they wrecked a whole house in the process. It was a horror. After months of zazen, we were too sensitive to see the wrecking of a house as funny. The film seemed more like a prophecy of the fall of Western civilization than a comedy.

At the end of the first practice period there was a weeklong sesshin. It didn't have that edge of extreme difficulty that sesshins had had for me in the past, because there wasn't an abrupt change between it and what had become normal everyday life. It was the easiest and most pleasant of any I had experienced. One day, during the sesshin, Baker Roshi started talking. This was not a lecture; we were all facing the wall. He said that he was in our minds. Wasn't his voice inside our heads? If we attended to reality carefully, we could see that this was true, and if we wanted to draw on his strength while we were sitting, then we should.

Before we left for the two-week break, there were two ceremonies. The purpose of the first one was to test the acumen of the head monk. Each of us had to ask him a question to try to trip him up. All the old head monks from the past fifteen years came to Tassajara for the ceremony. They tried to grind him down, asking him very difficult questions, challenging him. I spent weeks preparing a very elaborate question that was like a little poem. Many people later congratulated me for asking such a good question, which embarrassed me.

At the second ceremony, everyone had to ask a question of the Zen master. The idea was to reveal yourself to your fellow monks, to ask the Zen master the kind of questions you would usually only ask him in private. A man who had been a lumberjack, the most sincere person I had ever met, asked, "Why am I so alone?" It broke everyone's heart. It was exactly the right question. He had put his finger on the real paradox of his life. When he asked it, he made us realize that we were alone, too.

Philip Whalen, a poet, asked, "I look around, and everyone else is enlightened except me. How come?" This also was exactly how we all felt.

Baker Roshi said to Philip, "Well, if that's how you really see other people, that's wonderful."

Because in the shuso ceremony I had asked a question to get everyone to admire me, and because I was ashamed of that, I now tried to ask a question that no one would admire. So I said, "How can I improve my practice?" Everyone started to groan. Then I saw what I had done. Because I was so involved in my ego, I had given up the chance to formulate the real question of my life.

I got a ride back to Berkeley in a small pickup truck. Looking out of its small porthole, I watched as civilization picked up speed again little by little. I could feel the pulse of life building as we wound up and down the steep one-lane dirt mountain road onto the pavement down to Carmel Valley and out to the highway. First there were no other cars, then there were a few, then hundreds.

So I returned from this mountain fastness. I went straight to Claudia's, but when I got there I found our relationship wasn't exactly what I had imagined it to be when we were writing passionate love letters back and forth. There was something awkward about it, something was off. I really didn't need to concern myself with what it was, however, since this time between practice periods wasn't exactly real life, just a furlough.

Steve joined me at Claudia's and we sat in her comfortable, civilized, elegant apartment looking out at the glittering city. The whole basis of existence began to roll away, to slide away beneath us—the rug going one way, us going the other. "It's an earthquake!" Claudia shouted. We jumped up and ran to the doorways. It only lasted a few seconds, but they went on forever. "I feel nauseous," Claudia said. "Isn't this fantastic?" I said. Since I didn't own any property at the time, I was really able to enjoy earthquakes.

Sometimes, during that two-week break while on the bus going from Claudia's to Berkeley, or in the drugstore, I'd notice that people's faces were filled with misery. My months at Tassajara had left me wide open, with no defenses. It was hard to bear.

One day I got on a bus and went to the Alameda County

Courthouse. During the first practice period I had sent away for a Do-It-Yourself-Divorce kit. Today was my court date. All the other people arriving to get their divorces seemed to be accompanied by lawyers and to be carrying stacks and stacks of papers. I didn't think I needed any of that because Betty wasn't contesting the divorce and we weren't fighting over custody.

"Are you sure you're going to be okay?" the judge asked me, after he had perused the forms I had filled out.

"Yes," I said.

A courtroom is a ritual chamber where reality is altered: guilt is determined, property changes hands, boundaries are moved, and people and money fall in and out of one another's possession.

"Are you sure you're all right?" he asked me again. He seemed to be concerned about me.

"I'm sure," I said. The judge looked down at me with compassionate eyes. The enormous bench on which he sat made him larger than life, as he had to be, since he changed human lives. I felt myself going through an alchemical process. I was standing in a cosmic courtroom.

The judicial process had transformed me. I had walked in married, but I walked out divorced.

# 22  MY NAKED HEART

At the end of the break, I took a bus to Monterey, hitchhiked to Jamesburg, and got a ride in from there. Norman and Kathie had gone to stay at Green Gulch so they could be near a hospital when their twins were born, but it was good to see other old friends. I was assigned a new cabin, which I had all to myself, a great luxury. It was a beautiful cabin overlooking the river, which I kept perfectly spare. In the zendo, they no longer sat me in the back. I had been promoted.

At the first work circle they put me on a team of crack workers to build the new compost toilet. Because of my great success with the plumbing, they believed I could do skilled work. The other people on the team were actual carpenters and contractors. Once again, I became the guy holding the hammer. They also informed me that I was to be the driver—the one who went at least once a week to get supplies. At my poetry reading,

I had read many of my bus driver poems, and that had given me away. Although they usually cast against type, they also needed someone who could navigate the precipitous one-lane dirt road to the monastery, especially in the snow. I enjoyed it, but once I started driving out, I wasn't in a hermetically sealed world any more. I broke the seal every week.

One day Baker Roshi made one of the women there his personal assistant. She was proficient in zendo skills; she had been at Tassajara a long time and had been in charge of the services, ringing the bell and chanting. Now she was to wait on Baker Roshi hand and foot. After one week, she just disappeared. No one ever explained where she had gone. I was completely mystified, and the mystery only deepened a while later when a few of the women staged a quiet revolt. They started expressing their unhappiness at how women were treated at Tassajara. One day one of the women stood up at a meeting and said, "What do you do if you're a Zen student and you can't respect the Zen master anymore?" She was trembling. Baker Roshi laughed.

One night there was a talent show where we were supposed to make up skits. One of them was a takeoff on *The Wizard of Oz*. The idea was that Baker Roshi was the wizard and everything we were doing at Tassajara was a sham. We all laughed so hard we thought we would burst, but when Baker Roshi heard about it later he became very angry. On days off now he would talk all day, telling stories, and everyone would have to sit and listen. But it wasn't really Zen teaching, and I was beginning to wonder why he had to do all the talking.

They asked me to start sewing my *raksu*, the garment you wear at lay ordination, but I procrastinated. When we were all supposed to be doing it together, I simply didn't do it. I cut up Claudia's letters and made them into poems. I wrote a long

monologue in the voice of my grandmother, Bubbe Ida, trying
to capture her breath. I did everything but sew. Why? I didn't
know. Then one day sitting zazen it was clear. With every stich
of the raksu I was supposed to say, "I take refuge in the Buddha." It was something we had said after lectures, about once a
week, but now, saying it with each stitch, I realized how uncomfortable I had always felt when I said it, and how uncomfortable I felt now, saying it over and over for hours. Saying
these words as part of preparation for ordination as a Buddhist
was suddenly very serious. I couldn't say that I took refuge in
the Buddha anymore—I couldn't say it because I was a Jew.

The problem wasn't that I felt I was betraying God. In fact,
when I was sitting in zazen, I often felt more in contact with
God than I ever had before. But I felt I was betraying my soul.
Mine was a Jewish soul. I was betraying myself.

Zen meditation, which focused on the present moment, had
given me a wide, vibrant view of the world. It laid reality bare.
It allowed me to overhear the constant arguments going on in
my head. Now I heard something else, underneath, after all
the veils were drawn back. I confronted my essence, and my
essence was Jewish.

It got very cold. It snowed some. There was no heat, and
days off now became a torment. I would spend them lying on
my bed all day wrapped up in my sleeping bag. One day when I
had my dokusan with Baker Roshi I told him, "When I think of
doing this practice for the rest of my life it seems endlessly
bleak." There is something about Zen that is irrefutably dry.
All the gestures are very mannered, slow, and choreographed.
There is something very solemn and serious about it all: the
shaved heads, the black and brown robes, the bare feet, the
bowing, the terrible need to sit very still. I waited for Baker

Roshi to respond to my question, but all he did was laugh, as if to say, "If that's how you feel, then just stop doing it."

At the end of the practice period most of the Zen students stayed on at Tassajara to work during the guest season, but I had arranged to leave, since I needed to get back to Steve. I was depending on a man named Frank to give me a ride out. But then Baker Roshi started to put pressure on Frank to stay, haranguing him in public, telling him he was crazy and that he needed Baker Roshi to help him. I started to get scared that I would never get out of there.

There was an element of cruelty about Baker Roshi that I had once admired because I thought it showed honesty and directness. One time at a lecture a fat man in the audience asked Baker Roshi how he put his lectures together. Were they spontaneous or did he prepare ahead of time? Baker Roshi said this was not an appropriate question. "You shouldn't be asking this," he said. "You should be asking, why am I so fat?" At the time I thought this was fine, that it was best to just put everything on the table—to say what this person must have known everyone else was thinking but no one else would say. But now I began to think that it had, in fact, been cruel and sadistic. So when Baker Roshi told Frank that he was crazy, and the proof of it was that his cabin was cluttered with things (which was true), I thought to myself, "I'm going to be stuck in Tassajara with this megalomaniac for the rest of my life. I'm never going to get back to Steve, Claudia, or Berkeley."

I spent the last week of the practice period propping Frank up. "No, Frank," I said. "You're not crazy. You can leave," I told him.

I didn't want to have anything more to do with Baker Roshi, but he didn't seem to notice. "We're really going to miss you,

Michael," he said to me. He had forgotten that my name was Alan, but he remembered that I had brought Jason's guru, Michael, to Zen Center once. "And we're especially going to miss your mother," he added. My mother had been sending me care packages the whole time I was there full of macadamia nuts and liqueur-filled bonbons and the like, and of course I had shared them.

In the end, Frank did give me a ride back to Berkeley. In exchange, I agreed to read his writing—an immense, rambling autobiographical moment-by-moment account of his LSD experiences. When I did, I saw he was, indeed, crazy.

I had assumed when I left for Tassajara that I would return to Green Gulch, the Zen Center's community farm, or the San Francisco City Center, so I had given up my cabin in Berkeley to someone named Joe Cohen. Joe had written me several hysterical letters while I was at Tassajara complaining that the cat that went with the cabin was driving him crazy. So I wrote and told him he could give the cat away. Almost immediately the cabin was completely overrun by mice. Now Joe Cohen was even more freaked out. So when he heard I was coming back from Tassajara, he wrote and said, "Please, please, come and take the cabin back," and since I didn't want to live anyplace connected to Baker Roshi, I did.

Berkeley was fragrant and blossoming. My cabin with its walls uncovered by the fire was like my naked heart fresh from the monastery. As I sat upstairs again in the Berkeley Zendo I felt how strong my sitting had become, how still.

One day I went to a sesshin at the Zen Center in San Francisco and decided to go in to dokusan with Baker Roshi. Although in the past I had always asked questions from the deepest place I could reach, this time, since I no longer trusted Baker Roshi, I asked a question from the surface instead, an academic question. Nonetheless, he made a big deal about my question and based an entire public lecture on it during the sesshin. Being at Tassajara had given me rank, and now I discovered that rank mattered more than merit. This rankled me and added to my growing feeling of disaffection. I found myself sleeping in more and more and missing zazen. Slowly but surely, I had begun to dismantle my Zen practice.

Claudia was very happy about this; she had always hated Zen. But we were not getting along very well. She was upset that I had cut up her letters and made them into poems. Our whole relationship had been based on a desire fed by being apart and now that we could be together, that didn't seem so desirable. At least, not to me.

She was angry at me because I didn't want to get married and have more children. "It's because I'm not Jewish," she said. "Don't be silly," I said. "That has nothing to do with it."

One day I got a call from my brother Jason. He told me how miserable he was. He was having a terrible time with his beautiful girlfriend, Lois, who had been sleeping with their teacher, Michael. Michael had explained to her that she had to do it for the good of her practice. One day Michael's girlfriend had walked in and discovered them in bed together. Michael had jumped out the window and climbed down to the street on a fire escape. Jason was crushed when he learned of all this.

Shortly after this, some of the people from Jason's ashram called me. They were really worried about Jason because he was so depressed. "So we decided to buy you a ticket to fly out to Indianapolis to surprise him for Christmas," they said. Jason had moved to Indianapolis for his second two years of medical school. Claudia was furious. Christmas was very important to her. But, of course, it meant nothing to me, so I went.

Jason was living in the ashram's Indianapolis center. When I got there, I was surprised to see that Lois was living in the same house, though not in his room. He had the biggest room, and, as the most advanced student in the house, he was also the resident teacher. "Tomorrow we'll go see Michael," Jason said as soon as I had put my bag down. I was confused.

We ran out of gas on the frozen road between Indianapolis and Bloomington. We had to go to a farmhouse and interrupt a family's Christmas dinner. They were not happy about it.

When we got to Bloomington everyone was twitching as usual while meditating on Michael, who was watching a violent detective program on TV. Suddenly it all seemed quite horrible. Michael wanted to talk with me alone, to show me respect, since I was his student's brother. I wanted to deck him, but I didn't, because he was my brother's teacher.

Jason did not talk about Michael and Lois on the road back to Indianapolis. I didn't know what to say. When we got back to the house we went up to his room. He opened his closet to hang up his coat. It was a huge closet, and I was surprised to see that it was full of clothes. He must have had a hundred shirts in there. It reminded me of our parents' closets.

Our parents were tremendously proud of Jason for becoming a doctor. I, too, felt very good about the path he had chosen. He had always wanted to become a healer, and now he was going to be one. In many ways, I felt that I was the one who had raised Jason. He was seven years younger than me, and when he was little and our father was in the hospital, as he often was, I was the one who took care of him. I taught him all about sports, and we used to wrestle until he got bigger than me. When he grew up, he, like me, had been attracted to Eastern religions and meditation, all of which made us very close. But we were also very different. As a doctor, he would have a real place in the world, which I did not. Looking into his closet I realized just how different the two of us really were and always had been. He had always favored color and opulence, whereas I had always favored simplicity and sparseness.

# 23 HEALING PRESENCE

I hadn't been back in Berkeley long when I got another urgent call—this time from Jeff Linzer's girfriend, Susan, and his ex-wife, Charlotte, in New York. "Jeff's in a coma," they said. "He has triple lobar pneumonia. The doctors say there's no hope. He's going to die. If you want to see him alive, you'd better take the next plane out here before it's too late."

It was snowing when I got to New York. Jeff was in St. Luke's Hospital on Amsterdam Avenue. I went directly there from the airport. Susan and Charlotte met me outside under the green awning, and together we went up to Jeff's ward.

The doctors were standing over his bed. "It's good that you came," they said. "You can say good-bye. He's not going to last the night."

"Please don't say that in front of him," Charlotte said.

"It doesn't matter what you say in front of him. Can't you see he's in a coma?" the doctors said.

It was almost universally assumed in those days that people in comas didn't register anything, but Charlotte, Susan, and Jeff's brother and sister and I, who took up a vigil by Jeff's bed, didn't believe it.

Jeff did not, in fact, die that night, nor the next, nor the next. In the ensuing week, each of us tried to save him in our own way. The doctors kept treating him in spite of their pessimism. Charlotte sat by his bedside and talked directly to him, nonstop. Susan touched him and rubbed him, and said special prayers and chants, which her Indian guru had taught her. I would pull up a chair next to his bed and get into half-lotus on top of it and sit zazen. When I did, I felt he and I were communicating with the fundamental essence of our beings, and, moreover, that this communication was healing. None of us at Jeff's bedside did anything that was particularly Jewish, however, although we were all Jews.

This went on for a week. At night, we all slept in Jeff's apartment on the Upper West Side. One night someone from est called (Jeff had been very involved with the group when he got sick). "He's in the hospital," we said. "He's in a coma." "Well, maybe this would be a good time for *you* to come down and get est training," was the response. We hung up on them.

One morning while I was sitting by Jeff's side, I noticed he seemed to have more life. I've often noticed in my subsequent experience working with people in comas that when you pay close attention to them you can notice subtle changes in their intellectual, spiritual, and physical states. The doctor walked in and said, "He got a lot better last night. It's amazing. Maybe he's going to come out of this."

For the next few weeks it was like watching a time-lapse film of the first several years of infant development. He went through all the stages. First he began rolling his head around uncontrollably, but his eyes were open; he was awake. He started to make nonsense sounds, then words. By the end of the week he was actually speaking. He said to me, "I felt you doing that while I was in the coma." The "that" he was referring to was zazen.

This is how I learned about the healing power of presence.

# 24 CLOSURE

When I got back to Berkeley, I found Claudia was still angry with me. She resented the fact that she was doing all the work in the relationship, she, who was in therapy. She kept insisting that the reason I wouldn't marry her was because she wasn't Jewish. "That's preposterous," I said. "But if you insist, I'll go to therapy, too," and I did.

I went to a therapist recommended by her therapist. He had a small but aesthetically perfect office in Albany, just north of Berkeley. He was very skilled. Even in the first hour he asked many questions that led me to surprising insights about my life, including the overwhelming realization that I didn't want to work on my relationship with Claudia. I wanted to extricate myself from it. Although I had been infatuated with her, I had been using her, albeit unconsciously. I had used her as a hedge against the monastery, and I had used her to get out of my relationship with Betty. She had been quite helpful in that regard. Largely through Claudia's insistence and adroit manipulations, I had, I felt, finally come free of that entanglement. But now the infatuation, the monastery, and the wife were gone, and there was only the hurt we were causing each other escalating rapidly. I saw all this very clearly on my first visit, and as soon as I left the therapist's office, I went straight to a phone and ended the relationship.

I used to have a kind of psychic litmus test for spiritual teachers, a feeling I would get in their presence that told me they were authentic, a kind of radiance I could see in them. I had it with my Zen teachers, I had it with Muktananda, I had it with the Karmopa, and I had it with Trungpa, drunk as he was. After three or four sessions with this therapist, during which he continually brought deep insights out of me, things about my life I had never been able to see before, I had it with him—that same radiant feeling that had always told me I was in the presence of an authentic guru. At first, of course, I thought it meant that this whole business of authenticating gurus was some kind of grotesque projection, some delusion now exposed, but many years later I came to think of it differently. This therapist was, in fact, an important spiritual teacher, even if he didn't see himself that way. Sometimes light comes in unexpected vessels and they aren't always labeled properly.

He helped me see that while, at first glance, Claudia and Betty couldn't have been more different, I had fallen into exactly the same relationship with both of them. Something was off, and it must have been in me. After all, I was the only thing these relationships had in common. I began to see that the circumstances of our lives always repeated themselves until we got

CLOSURE

them right, either because of some mysterious karmic mechanism or because of the simple fact that the unresolved elements of our lives kept bringing us back to the same place until we resolved them.

So now in the therapist's office we examined these unresolved elements, hour after hour, focusing on them over and over again, and finding their antecedents in my primal relationships. My family lived in an elaborately protected knot. At the center of the knot was my father, a heartbreakingly vulnerable man on whom we all depended for protection. And because we knew that our protector was really so vulnerable, we were constantly trying to build him up, to make him seem more powerful, in his mind as well as ours, and the way we did that was to give up our own power, to weaken ourselves so that he would seem stronger in comparison. It was a game only blind people could play, of course, and the game had a terrible cost, especially for me. It cost me my strength, which I willingly surrendered under the cover of guilt. And I played the same game with my mother, and with Betty, and with Claudia. It was the only game I knew. But looking at this game hour after hour in the therapist's office, it began to lose interest for me and, finally, its power over me.

Thinking about my family reminded me that when I left the newspaper ten years earlier to go off to write, I had had a vague but compelling vision of writing a novel based on the sweeping drama of my family's tortuous journey from Europe and our struggle to find a place in this crazy country, but I'd never had the slightest idea how to do it. Suddenly, I realized that I did, that the poetic studies of direct speech I'd been working on recently were simply the sketches, the preparation for this grand

131

project. I could perhaps go back East and record the direct speech of each of my living relatives, weaving this speech together into a great epic poem.

Before my therapy, I could not have willingly placed myself in the cauldron of my primal family for any length of time, but now it didn't seem like such a frightening prospect. It didn't have as much power over me anymore; I felt I could handle it. The therapy had put me in touch with the real story of my family, not just the family myth, and I saw how compelling it was. I had been driving a tour bus for Grayline during the tourist season that year, but I had been laid off for the winter. After giving Betty money for Steve and paying my therapist, I still had enough left over to finance the trip.

Clearly, I was at the end of one era in my writing and on the brink of a new one. I seemed to have sensed this unconsciously, having scheduled a whole spate of readings in San Francisco, Berkeley, and Mendocino County, which, I now realized, was a kind of farewell tour. I decided on one final gesture to punctuate the transition. I would go out on Sproul Plaza with the political ravers and lunatic prophets and read every word I had written so far, starting early in the morning and reading into the night, if necessary. A freelance radio journalist had asked to record one of my readings, so I told him about this plan, and he decided to record this day, instead.

And so it was that I went onto Sproul Plaza very early one morning and began to read my poetry, surrounded by a small radio crew with recording equipment. I read without stopping all day and into the night. Sometimes crowds formed around me, and sometimes I read to an empty plaza, my words bouncing off the concrete and expanding to fill the emptiness. Different parts of my work attracted different kinds of crowds. The work I liked best, the early work I had done when I started practicing Zen, the work I had read at that first reading in Mel's basement, attracted a small but extremely enthusiastic crowd. "Where can I get these poems? Are they yours? Did you write them yourself?" the people wanted to know. Then there were long stretches of writing that hardly anyone listened to, and deservedly so, I thought, after the words bounced around and came back to me. My latest work attracted the biggest crowds, so big that they made me get up on the highest steps of Sproul Plaza so everyone could see me. The crowd on the steps reached its height just as I began to read "Deadhead Miles." "Deadhead Miles" was a long piece that intertwined the speech of a dozen Grayline drivers. Being a direct record of the speech of bus drivers, it was full of scatology, racism, and anti-Semitism, and it was probably these elements that had drawn the large crowd. As I looked out at this increasingly hostile crowd I realized that they didn't know I was reading the recorded speech of other bus drivers; they thought it was me speaking, and they were furious. The worst moment came when I was reading a particularly offensive anti-Semitic piece and I looked down and saw a group of Jewish students staring up at me in great distress. They were deeply offended, and they were clearly trying to decide whether they should rush the steps and beat me up. I looked down into the crowd again. There was my cousin, David Cossack. He carried me off the steps after I finished the poem. I was through.

The next day, I left for the East Coast with my tape recorder and several packages of blank recording tape under my arm.

## 25 FAMILY

Both my grandfathers had already died, so I started the interviews with Bubbe Ida, my maternal grandmother, who was staying in a condo in Miami for the winter. We sat out on the beach in folding chairs. I said, "Tell me the story of your life." "There's nothing to tell," she said. And then she started talking, and she didn't stop until she had told me a story no one in the family had ever heard before. It was the story of her first love, the man she had loved before she met my grandfather Sam. Sam and Ida had been good companions and had taken care of each other all of their lives together, but Sam would often complain that Ida had never quite returned his affections. Once they stopped speaking to each other for several weeks. When the children stepped in to mediate, Sam poured out his heart to them: "Your mother was wearing a beautiful nightgown, and I said to her, 'You look as beautiful tonight as when I first met you,' but she never even looked up from her book."

Now Ida sat back in her folding chair with her knitting in her lap, and looking out at the ocean she began to tell me her story. Ida's father had been a great rabbi who spent only a few days a year at home with his family. The rest of his time was spent teaching Torah, from town to town, all over Eastern Europe. He died late one night in such a village with his head in a book of the Talmud. They found him that way in the morning. Chana, his wife, and his three children, who had been left to fend for themselves while he was alive, were now utterly helpless and impoverished. Chana was reduced to picking rags to feed her children, and she had to move into a tiny shack with a dirt floor behind her brother's house.

Chana's brother was the *shochet*, the ritual slaughterer, in a tiny town called Stantson Malarita. Almost everyone in this town was poor. They all lived in shacks with dirt floors and a few sticks of furniture. All of them, that is, except the *feltcher*, the pharmacist. The feltcher was wealthy. He had a wooden floor in his house, real furniture, pictures on the walls, a samovar. Ida became best friends with the feltcher's daughter, and so it was that she came into his house and met his son, Mischa.

Mischa fell in love with Ida as soon as he saw her, and she loved him, too. But Mischa's mother, the feltcher's wife, was horrified. She had always dreamed of making a grand match for her son. She chased Ida out of the house with a broomstick. "Orphan! Orphan!" she would scream. "You can't have my son. He deserves much better than you." Mischa and Ida continued to see each other in secret. But now his mother was chasing her all around the village. Ida had to take long circuitous routes around town to avoid her. Her life was becoming impossible. Mischa said, "Let's run away to America and get married."

But Mischa's father wouldn't permit it. Mischa had not yet been drafted. If a young man left Russia before he was drafted, the government would take everything his family owned. Most of the people in Stanson Malarita couldn't have cared less. They had nothing for the government to take. When their sons ran away, a man from the government would come and cover their few sticks of furniture with stamps proclaiming that the furniture now belonged to the Czar. They would return each year and cover these stamps with more stamps and then finally they would just forget about it. This in fact had happened when Ida's brother Usher had run away to America to avoid the draft. Chana's few sticks of furniture were covered with layers of stamps, but there was very little likelihood that the Czar would ever come to claim it, and who cared if he did.

But things were different for the feltcher. The feltcher had a great deal to lose. The feltcher had real furniture, paintings, samovars, and beautiful carpets. And the feltcher had money, too, and the government would take it all. So he didn't want Mischa and Ida to run away to America, and he was adamant about it; Mischa was also adamant; and the mother was the most adamant of all. Ida could barely go out of the house without being accosted by this woman and her broomstick and her taunts.

So what to do? Nobody knew what to do. So they did what people usually did in that time and place when they were stumped. Ida and Mischa and Mischa's father got on a train to go to Bresklitovsk, where through Mischa's father's influence, they had managed to arrange an appointment with the great Brisker Rebbe, Chaim Solevetchik. Surely he would have a solution to their problem. The three of them filed into the Brisker Rebbe's study. Ida remembered him as the most beautiful man she had ever seen—a small man with a white beard and a white shirt unbuttoned at the collar, with twinkling eyes and a radiant smile.

The father told his story first: "I love her, I love him, and my wife is crazy, there's no doubt about it. And I also think they should run off to America and get married, but not now, that's all. He'll be drafted in a few years and I'll buy him out of the draft, but if he runs away before he's drafted, I'll lose everything. The government will take everything I have, and I have a great deal."

Then the father sat down and the son stood up. "I don't care about money," Mischa said. "I only know I love Ida and I want to marry her now. Life is precarious. Who knows what will happen if we wait several years. I want to marry Ida, and I want to marry her now, and I don't care about anything else."

Then Mischa sat down and Ida stood up. "I love him, but I'm not going to marry him. I'm going off to America by myself and live with my brother Usher." Mischa and his father looked as if they had just been punched in the stomach. Their jaws dropped and their faces turned white. So Ida explained. "If Mischa and I run away to America and get married, then my mother will be left with that woman. She will make her life unbearable as she has made mine these last few months, and I could never do that to my mother. So I will not marry Mischa though I love him very much. I will go to America by myself."

The Brisker Rebbe, who had been sitting motionless in his armchair listening to each in turn, now stood up, crossed the room, and stood in front of Ida. Then he put his hands on her shoulders and kissed her on the brow. "Go, my child," he said. "God will reward you for what you're doing for your mother this day."

So the three of them returned to Stanson Malarita, and Ida packed up to go to America. Mischa took her to Hamburg and put her on the ship, and after a voyage full of adventure and wonder, Ida finally made it to her brother's house in Pawtucket, Rhode Island. Mischa wrote her every day for months, but Ida never saw the letters. Her brother hid them from her. He didn't want her dwelling on the past. He wanted her to make a new life in America. And sure enough, after a while, she met Sam, my grandfather, at a family picnic in Pawtucket. They had a tempestuous courtship. Sam pursued Ida doggedly, but she literally ran away from him several times. Once she ran away to New York. Another time she ran to Philadelphia. But sooner or later Sam would show up with his hat in his hand to bring her back to Pawtucket. And finally she succumbed, and they were married.

Mischa never married. He was too busy taking care of Ida's mother and sister back in Stanson Malarita. He came to see them every day. He helped them financially as much as he could. Ominous clouds were gathering over Europe. The Nazis came to power. Ida and Usher tried desperately to get their mother and sister out of Europe, and they actually managed to arrange visas for them through HIAS at one point. But the sister refused to go. She was engaged to a young man there and she had seen what happened to Ida, and the mother wouldn't go without the sister. But Ida and Usher pleaded with her until finally she agreed to come, but by this time she had glaucoma, and they wouldn't let her into the United States anymore. Her window of opportunity had closed forever. Mischa continued to take care of her, and in the end, they all died together: Mischa, Ida's mother, Ida's sister, and her young family, as well. The

Nazis came to Stanson Malarita, and they made them dig their own graves, and then they shot them in the back and pushed them in the graves together.

Meanwhile, Ida lived out her life with Sam. They had four daughters together, lived in comfort for years, and then barely survived the Depression. Eventually Sam began to make a good living again refinishing floors, and they acquired some property. All four daughters grew up well, married well, and made families out in the suburbs of New York. Then Sam got cancer. They said it was from the benzene he used finishing floors. He died at Memorial Sloan Kettering Hospital after being sick for only a few months.

A few months later Ida went to Israel, and as soon as she arrived, she went to Tel Aviv, and as soon as she got to Tel Aviv, she went straight to an address she had been saving on a crumpled piece of paper in her purse for many years. She knocked on the door. The door opened, and a woman her age stood in the doorway. It was Mischa's sister—the one who had been her best friend in Stanson Malarita and had taken her into the feltcher's house where she and Mischa had met and fallen in love. She took one look at Ida and started to scream. She screamed and screamed. A man came running to her side, apparently her husband. "She's supposed to be my sister! She's supposed to be my sister!" she told him.

This is the end of the story my grandmother told me that day on the beach. She had been knitting afghans as she told me the story—one for each of her twelve grandchildren—but now her knitting needles were still. A group of Chasidim had come out on the beach in their black caftans. They were preparing to purify themselves in the ocean before the afternoon prayers, and I could feel the secret and sacred shape of my grandmother's life welling up in the humid air. I could feel the unbearable suffering, the loss and the disappointment she had endured, and I could feel the light, the love beneath the suffering struggling heroically to endure, and finally enduring, even when its object no longer existed.

The next day, I left for New York with this story in a suitcase and my new afghan in a shopping bag, and when I arrived, I went straight to my other grandmother, Bubbe Masha. She was already in her dotage, and it was hard to get a coherent story out of her. When I finished the interview she stood up on her cane to embrace me. "The next time you come," she said, "bring me back a woman!"

"I will," I said. I then went to talk to all my mother's sisters and their husbands, and all my father's siblings and their spouses, as well as my parents, my brother, and my sister. Each interview would begin the same way. "Tell me the story of your life," I would say. "There's nothing to tell," was invariably the answer, followed quickly by a great outpouring. As I listened I was struck over and over by the sanctity of each life story. In the milieu I had inhabited for the last several years, stories had not been honored. There was a deep prejudice against narrative in the poetry circles I traveled in. Buddhism uses stories to teach, but it holds that the story of a person's life is an illusion, something that the mind creates that is not really real. But these stories of my relatives' lives seemed very real to me. And every story seemed to have a sacred shape. I always think of this when I am preparing to officiate at a funeral and ask the family to tell me the story of the life of the deceased. When you see the life laid out on the table, it's like standing on a hill and looking down on a body of water and seeing its whole shape— what you can't see when you're on the ground right next to it.

As I interviewed my relatives, I discovered that there is a tremendous amount of suffering in every life. Every life has been shaped by its particular suffering. What makes the various lives different in shape and pattern is where the suffering occurs—at the beginning, the middle, or the end. These stories made me think about my own suffering, and the role it had played in shaping my own life thus far.

The plan I had for the book was to use all my relatives' stories to create a great tapestry. Only my own story would be left out; I was too close to see it clearly. As much as possible, I would try to re-create each relative's breath, leaving a space in the text every time they took a breath on the tape. Naturally, I could only do this for my living relatives.

My grandfathers, who were both dead, would be major characters, but I would have to create their stories out of other people's accounts. I was hearing a lot of good stories about Zayde Sam, especially. (He had died while I was in college.) So many of the stories I was hearing were about him, and I was feeling his absence, so I decided to go out to the cemetery and visit his grave. Just as I drove up to the plot where he was buried, I tuned in on the lyrics of the song playing on the car radio: "We are family—I have all my sisters in me!" It occurred to me that Zayde Sam and all the other dead people might really enjoy hearing this, so I stopped the car, opened up both doors, and turned the volume up as high as it would go.

When I got back to Berkeley I found myself thinking about Bubbe Masha's order to bring her back a woman, and I realized I was lonely. Something obviously was keeping me from finding the woman to bring back to my grandmother. Suddenly I realized what it was: I still felt married to Betty! Our civil divorce had not been enough to break the bond.

Betty and I had had an Orthodox Jewish wedding. On the day we were married, I was taken into a private chamber with two rabbis, one of whom was ninety-nine years old. He had been the founding rabbi of Betty's family's synagogue. They began to conduct the premarital agreements with symbolic exchanges of handkerchiefs and money. They had me pull on a pen, and witnesses signed the wedding contract, the *ketubah*. Then they brought me out and led me to the *chuppah*, the marriage canopy. At one point in the ceremony, the very old rabbi began reading from the ketubah in Aramaic, but after he had been reading for a while, he suddenly paused in midsentence. He seemed to be somewhere else entirely, and he stayed there for a long time. No one moved. It would have been disrespectful to the old rabbi to suggest that the absence of his mind from his body was in any way strange, so no one said anything. He was far away, he was elsewhere. Then after what seemed a very long while, he started reading again, without explanation, picking up exactly where he had left off.

But it was while we were all waiting under the chuppah for the rabbi to return from wherever he was, that I began to appreciate how real all this was. Now all these years later, I realized that this powerful ritual had never been undone. Under Jewish law, a law dating back thousands of years, I was still married to Betty. I needed to get a *get*, a Jewish divorce.

Betty knew a rabbi and made all the arrangements. He arrived at the house with witnesses. In addition to the traditional delivery of the get—which the rabbi places in the woman's hands, and which she holds over her head while walking four steps forward to show she's not being coerced—the rabbi suggested we each make a statement. I said, "Let all the pain be over." In this way, my marriage to Betty was finally and actually rendered null.

Not long after that, I got an invitation to go to a wedding celebration for a writer I had known in Iowa. I was flattered and surprised, because we weren't really close. I didn't think I could go, however, because I was back driving a tour bus for Grayline and I was sure I'd have to work. As it turned out I did—I was given a nightclub tour. But at the last minute I found another driver who was willing to replace me, and I hurried home from the bus yard to change. But then, as I was changing, I asked myself, "Do you really want to go to the wedding? Won't you feel awkward there? You hardly know the bride and groom." But another voice in the back of my mind responded, "Why don't you go? Maybe you'll meet someone," and so I went.

As soon as I got there I saw Bob Grenier, another writer from Iowa. I had been running into him of late in downtown San Francisco because he was working as an attendant in the parking lot of the Hilton, where I often drove my bus to pick up and drop off tourists. Like me, he always seemed to have a real job. "I don't like the fumes in the garage too much," he said, "but the beauty of this job is that it gives me time to think."

"I don't like thinking too much," I said, which was a knee-jerk Buddhist response.

"Oh, I love thinking," Bob said, "because when you're thinking, you're close to God." Just then he introduced me to the woman who had been standing next to him. Actually, I had already recognized her. It was Sherril Jaffe, a writer I admired.

I had seen Sherril read several years before at the Grand Piano. As I watched her that night I thought, "Her writing is really good. She's attractive. I wonder what it would be like to be with her?" More recently, I had actually been scheduled to read with her at the Grand Piano. I put a circle around both our names on the flyer advertising our reading at the Grand Piano and sent it out to all my friends.

But Sherril never showed up for that reading. She had a terrible cold and had to cancel. I was delighted, because she was a much more popular writer than I was, and so I had this good-sized audience that she had generated all to myself. So I was predisposed to like her.

But now as Bob introduced us and I looked into her eyes and we began to talk, I realized that I more than liked her; I loved her. The whole universe, after all, had been conspiring to bring us together. Bob melted away, and Sherril and I chatted about our grandmothers. But beneath the surface of our words were other words—"You will be mine forever. I'm safe now. God does exist. Now life can begin in earnest." Because we were at a party, other people kept coming up to us to talk, but nothing could distract us from each other's gaze. Then finally a woman came up and said, "You've been hogging her all night," and she dragged Sherril away.

I panicked, not knowing what was going to happen. Then I saw Sherril putting on her coat and walking toward the door. She turned then, and came over to where I was sitting. "Here," she said, putting a piece of paper in my hand. It was her phone number.

She lived up in the country, in Sonoma County. The next day I was assigned to take a busload of stewardesses to the Russian River nearby, and I called her from there. But she wasn't home. I called her again from Berkeley that night. Her voice was the most beautiful thing I had ever heard. We agreed that I would come to her house on my first day off. I told the waitress in the coffeehouse I went to the next day that I had found my other half.

When I got to her house in the country, I found Sherril in the garden picking strawberries. She was wearing a red sundress. I stayed three days, then I had to go back down to the city because of my job. She came down to my cabin in Berkeley two days later. It didn't make any sense that we were living in separate towns leading separate lives. "Will you marry me?" I heard myself ask her, as soon as she walked in the door.

"If you want me to," she said. "Yes."

## 27 NARRATIVE

"But who should marry us?" I asked her later when we went out for a walk. Three Buddhists in brown robes passed us on the sidewalk, ringing a bell. "Buddhist weddings are very beautiful," I said.

"And very fashionable," Sherril said. "But I've never been a Buddhist."

"And I'm not really a Buddhist anymore," I said. Now we were passing a little synagogue. It was half a block from my cabin. I had been living there for years, but I had never noticed it before. "We're both Jewish—why don't we get a rabbi?" I said.

"That's right—we are both Jewish," Sherril said, struck by the coincidence. "If we had a Jewish wedding, that would really shock all our literary friends." We had already shocked all of our friends by getting engaged thirteen days after meeting each other. After he heard the news, one of my writing friends took me aside at a bar on the way to a reading. "What I don't understand," he said, "is why you have to get married. Why don't you just live together?" He was extremely good-natured and there was no derision in his question, or any other type of criticism, just genuine curiosity.

"Living together without getting married is like Language Poetry," I told him, "and getting married is like narrative, and you know how I've always loved narrative." He thought this was a wonderful answer. He must have told this story to many people, because several of the Language Poets were inexplicably furious at me for months afterward.

My family, however, was overjoyed at the news, even before they met Sherril, because they could hear the happiness in my voice over the phone. Bubbe Ida sent us a check right away. Steve decided that he wanted to live with us, and we even found a house to rent in Berkeley, which was a nearly impossible thing to do.

Everything was working out perfectly. As soon as we had fallen in love everything had become easy. And then the house deal fell through.

Our first impulse was to fall into despair. How could this be happening? Had our feeling of being blessed been false? No, we couldn't believe it; it felt too real. But if it were true, we reasoned, then losing the house in Berkeley must also be a good thing. How could that be?

The answer was that we could live in Sherril's house in Sebastopol. We hadn't considered this before, because Steve was signed up to go to middle school in Berkeley. But now we discovered that Steve wanted to live in Sebastopol. He liked it there and he was worried that if he went to school in Berkeley he would have his lunch stolen every day.

One day shortly after Steve and I had moved in with all our things, Sherril and I looked in the local yellow pages under "Congregations." The nearest rabbi was in Santa Rosa, twenty minutes away. He was a Frenchman with wild flyaway hair named Leo Abrami. "I'll be happy to marry you. No problem," he said.

So we were married in our house in Sebastopol a few months later, at the end of December. The morning of the wedding, a steady rain began to fall, and it increased in intensity as the day went on. We found out later that it was the heaviest rainfall in the history of California. I was extremely happy that day, from the moment I woke up. When I went out for my morning run through the cemetery, the rain was coming down in great silver sheets, as if the angels were crying great silver tears of joy.

Shortly after I got back from my run, Sherril's mother called. She was upset because she thought the rain would spoil the wedding, but nothing could spoil this day, except, of course, the rabbi failing to show up, which almost happened. He was over an hour late. "I could barely see the road in front of my face," he told my mother, who was furious at him.

The ketubah was signed, and we were married in our living room under a chuppah held up by Jason, Norman, and Sherril's two closest friends. A fire crackled in the fireplace, and our little dog, Muggins, lay asleep on the hearth. Friends and family pressed around, and the rabbi began to intone ancient words in Hebrew and Aramaic. We were married forever. The power of the language made me dizzy. Sherril stood beside me in an antique dress she had borrowed from a friend, her lovely pale skin visible above the neckline.

So it was that she became sacred to me as my wife. The year

was 5740 by the Jewish calendar. We were part of an ancient stream.

People poured into the house to celebrate all afternoon. We had invited many more people to the party than to the ceremony, expecting it would be outside, but now, with the rain, they were all pressed together inside the small house, happily bumping into each other and eating our food.

That night, Sherril and I went to a motel in Bodega Bay overlooking the ocean, but first we went to dinner, one of our last unkosher meals. I ate oysters, dozens of them. Then we went back to the motel and lit a fire in the fireplace.

The next morning when we woke up, Sherril told me her dream: "You and I were in an old beat-up pickup truck driving through the cosmos, and we saw a beautiful young girl with her thumb sticking out, trying to bum a ride. We stopped and she crawled into the cab of the truck. She told us her name was Hannah, and we drove off into the night, singing, 'Oh, we ain't got a barrel of money, maybe we're ragged and funny, but we'll travel along, singing a song, side by side. Oh, we don't know what's coming tomorrow, maybe it's trouble and sorrow, but we'll travel the road, sharing our load, side by side.'

"If we ever have a baby, what do you think of the name 'Hannah' for her?" Sherril asked.

"I like it," I said. "It was my Bubbe Ida's mother's name. She was killed by the Nazis."

Within a few days, Sherril realized that she was pregnant. One of the first conversations Sherril and I had had, after discussing our grandmothers, was about having children. I had assumed that I didn't want to have any more children, which was what I had told Claudia. But as soon as I was with Sherril, it was clear to me that I did. Claudia had said I didn't want to marry her because she wasn't Jewish. I hadn't married Sherril because she was Jewish, I had married her because I loved her, and her Jewishness was part of what I loved about her.

We were happy all through the pregnancy, and I planned for it to be a deeply spiritual event, preparing by doing yoga and planning what music we would play during our home birth. But there were complications, and we couldn't have a home birth. To my disappointment, this beautiful moment was going to have to take place in a sterile hospital. Sherril's labor went on for seventeen hours. The table where Sherril lay was awash with the vivid reds and blues of her blood and the fluids of birth. The colors were so vivid that I had to choose between fainting or turning away. And then the stark delivery room became a luminous sacred chamber. I felt myself entering a larger consciousness, and Hannah came rushing into the world.

I reached out and caught her. Her eyes were wide open. She began turning her head and looking around. We placed her on Sherril's belly. She was covered in vernix and completely beautiful. The nurses dimmed the lights and spoke in whispers for her benefit. When the umbilical cord stopped pulsing, they handed me the scissors and I cut it. My foolish ideas about making the birth into a spiritual event had been swept away by the power of the event itself, like so many chaffs of straw. The impulse for life was powerful and profound, far beyond anything the pallid armamentarium of self-improvement could conjure.

## 28  HOLD ON TO YOUR HAT

On the same day that we went to see Rabbi Abrami to ask him if he would marry us, I asked him several other questions. "I have another favor to ask," I said. "I have a son. He's twelve. He's been taking acting lessons and was recently in a play about children of the Holocaust. The other day he asked me if he could have a bar mitzvah."

"No problem," Rabbi Abrami said. "Bring him here. We will begin to study." It turned out he had recently begun a bar mitz-vah class expressly for kids with little or no Jewish education. "Is there anything else you would like to ask me? Go ahead, ask," he said.

There was something else I wanted to ask now that I saw I could. "I was a Buddhist for many years," I said. "Every morning I would get up very early and go to meditation and then return to meditate in the afternoon also. Do Jews do anything like this?"

"Exactly," Rabbi Abrami said. "Every morning Jews get up very early and go to minyan, where they put on tefillin and pray. And they do this again in the afternoon and evening. On Saturday, Shabbat, we read a portion of the Torah in the synagogue. It takes a year to read the whole Torah, but on any given Shabbat, all Jews all over the world are on the same page, so to speak. Why don't you begin studying Torah this week? The portion for the week is called Tazria Metzorah. Here's a *Humash* you can borrow." He handed me a book that contained the first five books of the Bible, the text of the Torah. The text was broken into *parshiot*, portions that are read in the synagogue each Shabbat, one for each week of the year. Each Torah portion was paired with a selection from elsewhere in the Bible, the *haftorah*, which was also chanted after the Torah portion each Shabbat.

When I got home, I opened to Tazria Metzorah and began to read. It was about leprosy, menstruation, and all the things that made you impure and thus ineligible to enter the Temple. It was about clothing and houses that got leprosy. I had had no idea that Judaism had such weirdness in it. I looked at it with new respect, and I decided I had to go to the synagogue on Saturday to hear what people would say about this strange business. When we arrived at services that Saturday eight people were sitting around in a schoolroom in deep discussion. I had been thinking about the Torah portion all week, and I joined in. Since there were fewer than ten people there, they didn't have enough for the minyan required to take the Torah out. At the end of the service, Rabbi Abrami asked me if I would come the following week and present my thoughts to the group on that week's portion.

It was a long double portion full of fundamental moral teachings and packed with information, and I talked about everything. I didn't know then that a *derash*, or sermon, was supposed to take off from only one aspect of the Torah portion. But each time I attempted it, I learned more about the process. Pretty soon, I was giving the derash almost every week. More people started coming, and we moved from the schoolroom into the main sanctuary of the synagogue.

My talks were informal and not didactic. To write them, I reached into the same place where my Ouija board readings had come from. I structured them like Baker Roshi's dharma talks but referring to the Torah portion rather than the *Blue Cliff Record*, of course. I would spend all week studying. As I carefully read the portions I would notice how intricately constructed they were. I read all the commentaries that there were in English. These included the great modern Torah scholar Nehama Leibowitz's encyclopedic studies, which introduced me to Midrash, Talmud, and modern commentaries. I also read Rashi, Maimonides, the Ramban, and the Talmud. I studied hours and hours every day. Then one night I had a dream. In the dream I asked Rabbi Abrami to show me how to put on tefillin, the phylacteries worn at morning prayer. It was a vivid dream, the kind that stays with you all day long.

I thought about it the next day as I drove to Berkeley for a doctor's appointment. I was going down Shattuck Avenue, still in the pall of this dream, when I looked out the window and saw a sign that said Tradition: Jewish Book Store. I knew Berkeley very well, but I had never noticed this shop before. I pulled to the curb and parked. When I went into the store, and who should I see standing behind the counter but Rabbi Abrami!

I said to him, "I just had this amazing dream, and in the dream you taught me how to put on tefillin."

He reached behind the counter, pulled out a set of tefillin, and showed me how to put them on. I have put them on every day of my life since. You spell out one of God's names—Shaddai—with the straps of the tefillin on your hand, so when you put them on, you are literally binding yourself to the name of God. In my dream I had a yearning to do this. "You'll need a *siddur*, a prayerbook, too," Rabbi Abrami said. Then he sold me the Birnbaum prayerbook and taught me how to pray, which I would do three times a day.

I devised a three-day rotation for my prayers, since my Hebrew skills were poor. One day I would struggle through in Hebrew, the next day I would pray all in English, and on the third day I would do both, alternating lines. It would take me two hours or more to pray a half-hour service, and because it took so long, this prayer practice would change the texture of the rest of the day. I would visualize the words as an energy exchange— the words going up to God and God's attention coming down. Prayer began bringing me to the same place my Zen practice had taken me.

Before I prayed, I would study, in a prayer shawl and teffilin, sitting in half-lotus. Steve had moved into a little room with French doors on the first floor of Sherril's house and was now going to the junior high school in Sebastopol. Every day when he came home from school I would study with him for his bar mitzvah. For my own, I had learned only a little bit of my Torah portion, and I had merely read it out loud without chanting it, but Steve was learning the full *haftorah*, and he was learning to chant it according to the *trope*, the traditional musical notations. Now I was learning all this with him; it was as if I was studying for my own bar mitzvah.

Meanwhile, I was continuing to give the sermons. One day Rabbi Abrami told me that he thought I should go to rabbinical school and become a rabbi. It was the last thing in the world I would have thought of doing before, but soon I couldn't get the idea out of my head.

Rabbi Abrami, who had been a conscientious objector in the Algerian war, was suddenly granted a reprieve, and he went back to France. Now there was no rabbi at the synagogue. I had already begun leading the services, because Rabbi Abrami had taught me to do it from tapes, by rote, and I always gave the sermons, so I continued to do so. After services there was always a lunch, and we were frequently joined by a woman named Candace, who called herself a Nazarite Jew. She often interrupted the services to make speeches about Jesus, and this infuriated some, but most people tolerated her because she was indigent and clearly needed the food we shared with her at lunch. One day she came up to me and put her hands on my head and said, "I have a message from God that you are going to be the next rabbi of this synagogue."

In the meantime, ever since our wedding, Sherril and I had been taking on the *mitzvot,* the laws governing Jewish life, starting with *kashrut,* the dietary laws. We said to each other, let's just try it out; if we don't like it or if it's too hard, we'll go back to the way we were. But it wasn't hard at all. After kashrut, we decided to try out Shabbat, keeping the Sabbath. This was very difficult, however, because my job as a tour-bus driver was primarily a weekend job. I tried to avoid work on Shabbat as much as I could, but there were times when I couldn't. On those occasions I kept Shabbat as fully as I could while working. I wore a *kippah*, a skullcap, under my Grayline cap. When I sat in my bus at Union Square waiting for the tourists, I would study the portion of the week out of a pentatuch. One day one of the passengers saw me. "Look, Herbie!" she said. "The bus driver's studying Chumash!" It was becoming increasingly painful to me that I couldn't really keep the Sabbath. What I needed was a job that would not require me to work on weekends.

I hated being out late at night driving tourists to night clubs, anyway. I wanted to be home with my family. Sherril was pregnant again. I wanted to go to bed when she did at night and wake up when she did in the morning. Then one day a friend of mine who was a librarian at the Jewish Library in San Francisco called me up to tell me he was quitting. Did I want his job? It was a place where I would never be required to work on Shabbat or any of the Jewish holidays.

"But I don't know how to be a librarian," I said.

"Meet me in North Beach tonight for coffee and I'll explain it to you," he said. "You can interview for the job tomorrow."

So that was how I became a Jewish librarian, and, as it turned out, I was pretty good at it. All my studying had made me quite knowledgeable; I loved Jewish books and I was able to answer all the patrons' questions.

Now Sherril and I could really see what it was like to keep Shabbat, now it was possible. The first week we tried it we were as rigorous as we possibly could be. We decided to observe the prohibition against using electricity on Shabbat. We didn't know that it was only turning lights on and off that was prohibited, and that observant people left their lights on all Shabbat or put their lamps on timers, and some observant people didn't even consider turning on a lamp a violation of the Sabbath. In the middle of our first trial weekend, Sherril said, "I wish I could do the laundry." But she didn't. After we came home from synagogue, I went out on the deck to pray the afternoon service sitting in half-lotus, wearing my prayer shawl. Yellow birds came and sat on the branches of the birch tree that was growing through a hole cut in the deck. I saw them every week after that, but only on Shabbat, never on other days of the week. As the day wore on, the house would grow darker and darker, until, after three stars appeared in the sky, we did the ceremony separating Shabbat from the rest of the week— *havdalah*.

The second week we kept Shabbat Sherril said to me, "I'm so glad I don't have to do laundry today!" After that, she never mentioned laundry on Shabbat. We both thought of other things. Time slowed down. We stopped being busy; we just were.

Besides Shabbat, we celebrated all of the holidays. On Sukkot I built a little hut on the deck, and I studied and prayed in there all week long. The yellow birds came every day. The whole world was vibrant and real.

Meanwhile I had been continuing to lead services at the synagogue, and they hired me to be their interim spiritual leader while the congregation interviewed seminary graduates. So Candace had been right; I was the next rabbi of that synagogue, albeit a phony rabbi. When people called the synagogue office now asking to speak to a rabbi, the secretary connected them with me. I was counseling people and visiting the sick, and now I was giving sermons on Friday night as well as Saturday. "You should do this for real," Sherril said. "This is you." I did feel I had found my real work. The problem was, the more I worked at it and the more I studied, the clearer it became to me that I knew almost nothing. And how could we move to New York so I could go to a seminary for six years, even if one would have me, a person with no background?

I had been getting to know a man who came into the Jewish library almost every day to check out periodicals. His name was David Dalin. He was a Ph.D. in history, but one day he confided to me that he was applying to the Jewish Theological Seminary, the Conservative rabbinical school in New York City. He urged me to do the same. I didn't really have any idea what Conservative Judaism was, although my congregation in Santa Rosa was Conservative. I was more drawn to Orthodoxy because it seemed to me more sincere and authentic. Another library patron, a teacher from the Hebrew Academy, recommended that I apply to an Orthodox yeshiva in Far Rockaway, Long Island, and become a rabbi that way. I was inclined to follow his advice. Coming from the rigorous practice of zen meditation, and looking for its equivalent in the Jewish world, it seemed increasingly clear to me that Halacha, or Jewish Law, was the basis of serious Jewish spiritual discipline, and the Orthodox were the only ones who seemed to take Halacha seriously. But now David Dalin raised another possibility. He said that Halacha had always been an important part of the theology, if not the practice, of the Conservative movement as well and that recently, the momentum in the Conservative movement had been toward a more serious embrace of Halacha, a more rigorous sense of spiritual practice. This was especially so among the younger generation of Conservative rabbis, he told me.

One Saturday after services, when everyone was having lunch in the social hall, I walked back alone into the sanctuary and stood before the ark. I began to pray. I asked if this was really something I should do, if I really should go to New York, if I really should become a rabbi. Before I had even finished my prayer, I was filled with elation and an overwhelming sense of affirmation.

I flew to New York the next week. I was going to check out the Conservative seminary, the Jewish Theological Seminary; then the yeshiva in Flatbush; and then Yeshiva University, the Modern Orthodox seminary in Washington Heights. But I never made it past the JTS in upper Manhattan. On the plane I had read books about the ideology of Conservative Judaism, a movement that believed, at least in the ideal, in the combination of rigorous open-minded scholarship and inquiry and rigorous committed observance. I was well aware that this was not the reality of the Conservative Movement at present, but at least it was its mission. As I read, I said yes, that's what I believe.

When I was ushered into the office of the dean of the rabbinical school for my interview I saw a stack of letters on his desk. Unbeknownst to me, the people in my congregation had mounted a letter-writing campaign on my behalf, urging the seminary to accept me as a rabbinical student. I talked with the dean for several hours. He impressed me enormously. He had a clear, open mind and seemed to enjoy challenging outworn assumptions and threadbare pieties. But like me, he saw halachic observance as the basis of a serious Jewish spirituality, and he saw his own movement as not sufficiently serious in this regard. He told me he was trying to gather a group of young rabbis around him who felt the same way so that they could transform the movement together. I felt excited at the possibility of being part of this process. Finally he said to me, "I believe that

159

you definitely should become a rabbi, and that the Seminary is the right place for you. You should begin a course of study as soon as possible, as you're not getting any younger. At thirty-eight you will be the oldest student we have. However, you do not have any background in Jewish studies so I am going to recommend that you begin in the fall with a probationary year. At the end of that year, if you do well, we will interview you for the rabbinical school. Most of what we study here is Talmud, and all the Talmud courses are in Hebrew. Your Hebrew skills are very weak. I'm going to require you to join our Hebrew classes in Israel, which begin in two weeks. Can you do that?"

For the first time in my life, I really thought I might faint. Fortunately, the phone rang then, and the dean was engaged in a lengthy conversation, giving me time to think. I thought about the fact that our daughter Hannah was only twenty months old, and it was only two weeks since Hannah's sister, Malka, had been born. Malka had come into the world easily and happily after only five hours of labor. We had left the hospital an hour later, so that Hannah, off playing at a friend's, would not feel abandoned. "Look what we brought you!" we told her, when she got into the car and saw her baby sister with her perfect moon face. How would we travel to Israel with two babies in diapers? Moreover, there were our jobs to quit, our two old cars to dispose of, chickens in the yard to give away, the house to sell to pay for it all. Steve was already scheduled to move back in with Betty to begin high school in Berkeley. He had done well in the country, walking home through the orchards from school, marching in the Apple Blossom Parade, learning the bassoon. But what would Sherril say? She had told me she believed I should be a rabbi. I saw a door opening. I saw myself standing on a threshold, my wife by my side, our babies in our arms.

"May I call my wife?" I asked the dean as he hung up the receiver. He handed me the phone. "Hold on to your hat," I said when she answered.

# PART II

*God Was*

*in This Place*

*and I Didn't*

*Know It*

## 29 THE FUNNEL

When I got home I discovered that the front door to our house was stuck shut, and I had to go around to the side entrance. In order for one door to open, another door has to close. I believed this, but not quite so literally. As it turns out, God is rather literal-minded and full of little jokes.

We began packing immediately. Within two weeks we were driving down the Gravenstein Highway for the last time, past the orchards, past the fields of soft grasses, and past the fragrant eucalyptus. I was leaving California, the place where I had been reborn, where so much that was significant had happened to me, and now I could see how beautiful, how perfect it all was.

At the airport, as we began pushing our girls in their double stroller down the long hallway that would lead us out of our life in California, we began to hum. We hummed the melody to *Shir Hamalot*, the song Jews sing at table to introduce Grace

After Meals, the Song of Ascent the pilgrims sang when they were going up to Jerusalem in ancient days.

"Jerusalem has always been a holy city," my first teacher in Israel explained to our group as we sat out on the stubble grass of Kfar Goldstein, the youth village in Jerusalem where we were to be housed. "It was holy before there were Muslims, holy before there were Christians, holy even before there were any Jews. It is first mentioned in the Torah as the city of Salem, ruled by King Melchizedek, 'a priest of God Most High.'"

We dragged our suitcases up the stone stairs to our dormitory room. Someone found a rickety crib for Hannah. We pulled a drawer out of the bureau and padded it for baby Malka, and Sherril and I pushed our cots together.

Shortly after we fell asleep, or so it seemed, the sun exploded through the open window, and with it came a terrifying beating of wings. Sherril screamed. But it was only a dove that had come to roost in my straw hat, which I had left upturned on the desk. I took this as a good omen.

Classes began the next day. I was soon leaping ahead in my Hebrew studies. My immersion in prayer while we were living in Sebastopol had put me way ahead of the other beginners. And the readings used in my Hebrew class were giving me more than practice in the language. They were teaching me the common classic Hebrew stories that everyone who grows up learning Hebrew knows but that were all new to me. One was the story of Rabbi Akiba, one of the greatest rabbis in the tradition. Like me, Rabbi Akiba did not become a rabbi until he was forty. Reading this story gave me courage.

Since the youth village where we were living wasn't really appropriate for a family, we found an apartment to rent in Hapalmach, a lovely old section of town with tree-lined streets.

There were many small synagogues in the neighborhood, where I would go to minyan. My favorite was a small Sephardic shul, a plain room with wooden walls painted white, where the people were very welcoming. They prayed in the quavering tones of Islamic modalities.

But on Shabbat afternoon, we would go to the Kotel, the Western Wall of the Great Temple, the only wall still standing. We pushed our girls there in the stroller, through the twisting, narrow streets of the Old City. The Jewish Quarter had not yet been rebuilt, and we would have to pick our way carefully over the ancient rubble.

One evening, shadows were falling as we walked there. The pink Jerusalem stone began to turn white as the sky faded from aqua to magenta. When at last we came out into the plaza in front of the Wall, men in long black coats and broad-brimmed hats were gathering. Soldiers stood with their guns and tourists with their cameras. Children were running in circles.

I went and leaned my forehead against the ancient stones and felt waves of energy coming out of the Wall. Men in black garb were rolling out Torahs on tables from the caves at the north end. Prayer groups were gathering around every table with its Torah, and I heard the sounds of each prayer service starting up one after the other. They came together in a fugue, funneling all the prayers out of the stones and up to Heaven.

# 30 THE KADDISH

We spent a lot of time that summer touring Israel. One day we went to the Diaspora Museum in Tel Aviv, where you can find out about all the Jewish settlements in Europe that no longer exist.

My father had been born in the tiny shtetl of Volchin, a few days after World War I broke out. His parents, Masha and Isaac, had a comfortable house in the middle of an orchard, but the Pale of Settlement was one of the principal battlefields of the war. When the armies approached, the family piled into a wagon and, along with millions of others, tried to keep from being caught in the crossfire, fleeing east to escape the armies of the west, and west to escape the armies of the east. They did this for years, narrowly escaping death many times. There was no food, hardly any water. Masha's breasts were dry as straw; my father, her infant son, was starving.

Masha drank mud from the ditches, but still, no milk came. My father cried and cried. In one village they passed through, he lapsed into unconsciousness, his infant belly distended horribly. The local feltcher gave him up for dead, but after several days, his fever broke, his belly subsided, and he went back to normal, which for him was screaming for food all day long. His mother tried to suffocate him several times to end his torment, but, of course, she couldn't do it. So he survived his infancy, but after that, he was always insatiably hungry. His nickname became *Nachabissle*, a little more, because however much food he was given, he always said, "Nachabissle, nachabissle"—a little more, a little more. He grew up lean and hungry, worked harder and was more ambitious than any of his siblings, and when I was four months old, he came down with Crohn's disease, a terrible intestinal disorder that prevented him from digesting food.

Nonetheless, from that moment forward he began to prosper. He could now have all the food money could buy. But he couldn't digest it; his stomach was shot. He got his first death sentence then, when I was four months old. His doctor said he would die very soon from the condition, but the doctor died before he did. Over the next forty years, in fact, many doctors told him he would die, and he outlived them all. He had surgery after surgery, and each time he hovered near death. Each time the family was gathered together and told by the doctors to expect the worst. During those years he writhed in agony, his personality souring and his temper flaring as the pain in his belly continued relentlessly. And he worked, long hours, six days a week, from collapse to collapse. He would work till he dropped, then he would almost die, then he would miraculously recover and go back to work again. Doctors who were sent his medical records before meeting him couldn't believe it when he walked

in the door. "With a history like this," they would say, "we expected to see an invalid at death's door. You have no business
standing up, much less working the way you do."

We were all convinced that he would never die, that he
would always cheat death, even after he was forced to retire because he was simply too weak to work any more no matter how
hard he tried to force himself. Even then, it never occurred to
us that he might be mortal. But when we returned from Israel,
my father's complexion looked strange to me, and for the first
time I began to wonder.

My mother found an apartment for us on West 113th Street,
between Broadway and Riverside, ten blocks from the seminary. But then both girls came down with scarlet fever, so we
stayed with my parents up in Westchester for a few days before
moving in. We sat at the table with my parents every night,
being served course after course while my mother weighed out
her own food, carefully preserving her perfect figure, and my father argued with me about everything. Whatever I would say,
he would say the opposite, and loudly, especially if it had anything to do with religion.

But one morning I walked into the living room and my father was sitting in the chair he sat in when he read the newspaper. He was not reading the paper. He looked odd, as if he
had been crumpled, and there was a yellow tinge to the whites
of his eyes. In the voice of a frightened boy, a voice I had never
heard before, he said, "I have a favor to ask you. Will you please
say Kaddish for me after I die?"

I was shocked. He had never asked me to do anything for
him before. And he had never expressed anything but con-
tempt for Jewish ritual. He never missed an opportunity to
explain to me that I was basing my life on a fairy tale. There

obviously was no God, and even if there were, He clearly couldn't care less what people did. This had been clear to my father since he had discovered *his* father, the Orthodox rabbi, coming out of a movie theater on a Saturday afternoon, during Shabbat, when it is strictly forbidden to handle money. "I always pay ahead of time!" Zayde Isaac had tried to explain. "I have a deal with the owner of the theater. I just go in there so that I can take a nap, a Shabbos nap. It's impossible to take a nap at home with you and all your brothers and sisters making noise!" But my father didn't believe him. Years later, Zayde Isaac, long divorced from Bubbe Masha, died alone in an old age home, and I'm quite sure that my father, who was allergic to synagogues anyway, never went to shul to say Kaddish for him. And yet, if my father really believed Jewish practice was meaningless, why did he want me to say the Kaddish for him when he died? The only answer there could be was that, appearances to the contrary, Judaism had a deep hold on his soul. So I told my father there had been no need to ask, of course I would say Kaddish for him.

The next day the girls were better and we moved into our apartment on the Upper West Side. I was standing on the sidewalk outside our new apartment building while the movers carried our furniture in, when I looked up the street and realized I was looking at the green awning at the entrance to St. Luke's Hospital. I had passed under that awning every morning during the weeks I sat by Jeff's bedside while he lay in a coma. I marveled at the coincidence, and it occurred to me that there was probably some connection between sitting by Jeff's bedside and finding my life's work.

That afternoon I left Sherril and the girls in the midst of our half-unpacked boxes and went up to the afternoon minyan

at the seminary for the first time. There was a charged atmosphere in the room. Three great Talmudists presided over these
minyans, Dovid Weiss Halivni, Shaul Lieberman, and Israel
Frankus. They were all European, all Holocaust survivors.
Frankus *shuckled* as he prayed, bending forward and back to the
rhythm of the words in the way that Jews commonly pray the
service, but the other two stood perfectly still, as still as Zen
masters sat in zazen, radiating concentration. They each knew
every word of the service by heart. Halivni and Frankus prayed
without prayerbooks and with their eyes closed, but Lieberman,
who knew not only the prayerbook by heart but the entire Talmud as well, always used the prayerbook. He would say, "God
forbid your mind should wander and you should say the wrong
thing." Seminary legend had it that he struck people for making mistakes while leading services. Once, when saying a blessing before the Torah, I stumbled over the words and he rushed
up, grabbed me by the lapels, and shook me.

Despite the summer of study, my Hebrew skills were still not
very good, not good enough for me to study Talmud yet, so they
gave me Bible and philosophy classes. Since a good deal of the
reading in these classes was also in Hebrew, I had to memorize
large portions of the Bible just to pass the exams. No one else,
of course, went to these lengths, and consequently I got the
best grades in these classes.

But the problem concerning my Hebrew skills was not
nearly as daunting as my initiation into critical methodologies.
The basic assumption of this method of text study was the the-
ory that the Bible was written by many people at different times
and in different places, and all the different stories had been
woven together by a redactor, a mere editor, albeit a divinely
talented one. It shocked me to see the Bible torn apart like this,

172

analyzed as if it were any other text. Moreover, they were telling me that Rashi's teaching, which had meant so much to me in Sebastopol, was often inaccurate and wrongheaded because it was based on what turned out to be Rashi's faulty ideas about Hebrew grammar. Intellectually, I was convinced, but this method of study seemed to be putting me at a critical distance from the spiritual suggestions of the text in which I had immersed myself in Jerusalem.

Then Bubbe Ida began to die. She lay in a hospital bed drawing more and more inward. One day when I was standing by her bedside, my mother handed her a check to sign. She took the pen my mother handed her and weakly scribbled her name at the bottom. My mother took it from her hands and gasped. Then she showed it to me. Bubbe Ida's usual signature, which was full of dots and squiggles, had resolved into a single straight line. The heart monitor behind us, which a moment ago had been a jagged red line full of alternating peaks and valleys, flattened into a single horizon. My grandmother was gone.

We sat shiva in her apartment for a week. While we were saying the Kaddish, a lamp flickered on and off, as if she was winking at us. That Shabbat, when Sherril and I and the girls were sitting around the table, a book suddenly fell out of the bookshelf. It was *Ida* by Gertrude Stein.

The next week in class, we were studying Rashi's commentary dealing with the story of Meshach, Shadrach, and Abednego, who went into the fiery furnace and came out unscathed. "Okay," I said to myself, "I have to go into this fiery furnace where everything I thought I believed is challenged. But it's not going to destroy my faith. I'm going to come out unscathed."

"The problem is not critical scholarship; the problem is atheism," Dovid Halivni counseled me. "Any way you study the Torah, the Torah is still sacred. All that matters is the consciousness you bring to it. When you do critical scholarship from a religious point of view, the Torah becomes more powerful, not less. The things that are disturbing about it you can explain better, and it is even more awe inspiring to think that this complex document came into being over thousands of years, mediated by human beings with all their imperfections, than that God simply handed it down to Moses at Sinai." Halivni also told me that every morning he got up and talked to God for half an hour, and the rest of the day, God spoke to him. What he meant was that he prayed at minyan every morning and studied Talmud the rest of the day. If this deeply spiritual man could have his faith deepened by critical scholarship, then perhaps mine could be, too.

Halivni gave a little talk during the service which welcomed Shabbat every Friday night. One Friday my parents agreed to drive down from Westchester to go with us to services and to have Shabbat dinner with us. It had started snowing in the afternoon, and we called them to suggest that they postpone their visit for another time, but my father said that he wasn't afraid of a little snow, and they came. The snow was falling very fast, slowing traffic and covering the sooty despair of the streets with hope as we walked together up Broadway to the seminary. I sat between my parents in the basement of the old library where the entire seminary community came to welcome the Shabbat with fervent singing. Then Halivni began to speak. He spoke of how beautiful the snow was, falling all around us, bringing the world to a halt just as Shabbat fell, so that everyone now would be forced to experience the great peace of the holy Sabbath and acknowledge that there was a will in the world greater than their own.

When we left the synagogue and began to walk back we realized that this was no ordinary snowstorm; this was a blizzard. The snow was piling up on both sides. We stumbled over the drifts to our apartment, and all during dinner we could see the snow still falling. The world was wonderfully silent. There were no traffic sounds, no sirens, no car alarms. As soon as we were finished eating, my father stood up and said to my mother, "Come on, let's go. Get your things."

"You can't drive back in this!" I said.

"Of course I can," my father said. Halivni's words about the snow forcing everyone to observe the Sabbath had apparently been fighting words to my father. My mother looked nervous, but he was already helping her on with her coat. "It's only snow," he said. Reluctantly, I went out and helped him dig the car out.

At one in the morning, our doorbell rang and there stood my parents, looking sheepish and asking if they could spend the night. They had only gotten two blocks. And my mother had fallen and injured her back.

Masha, my father's mother, died shortly after this. It was odd to me that both my grandmothers should die as soon as I moved back to New York. Had they been waiting for me to get here with my wife and two babies? I was grateful that I had been able to see each of them in these last months, and grateful to be going through the mourning rituals with the rest of my family.

The semester ended, and I had all A's. I loved studying, spending endless hours up in the old library reading Torah and Talmud, Heschel and Herberg, with the sun pouring down through the tall casement windows. I had not yet been officially admitted to the rabbinical school, however. It would all finally be decided at my interview. I watched as other candidates came out from their interviews in tears, which really worried me. Then the door opened, and they motioned me in.

Five rabbis were sitting around a table. Three were professors, one a dean, and the last, a pulpit rabbi. They grilled me for an hour, and in the course of the discussion it became clear to me that after my experience in Santa Rosa I already knew more about the reality of being a pulpit rabbi than did any of these professors, sheltered in the ivory tower of the seminary. The next day, Joel Roth, the dean of the rabbinical school, called me to his office. "Congratulations!" he said. "You're in." I was overjoyed. Only five and a half more years of study and I would be a rabbi.

My joy and my triumph were short-lived, however, because shortly thereafter I got a call from my mother. My father was in the hospital. Could we come right up? Someone would meet us at the train.

My father was lying on a bed surrounded by nurses. His temperature was going through the roof. They were piling ice bags all over him. Sherril and I stood on either side of him, each clutching one of his hands.

"Why are you holding onto me so tightly?" he asked us. "I'm not going anywhere." But then they came and rolled him out of the room, rushing him to surgery.

We waited with my mother, my brother, and my sister for what seemed like hours, but they didn't bring my father back to the room and no one came to tell us what was happening. I couldn't bear the look of terror on my mother's face. Finally, I said, "I'll go upstairs to see if I can find anything out."

I took the elevator to the highest floor. The hospital was a T-shaped building, with the elevator at the point of juncture. To my left, now, was intensive care. In the corresponding hallway to my right, behind a big red door, was surgery. There was a small glass window in the red door just at eye level.

I pressed my eye up against the pane, searching for some sign of my father. On the other side, doctors and nurses glided silently in and out of rooms. I felt that I was peering into a counterworld, a place where everything was the reverse, the mirror image, of this world. At the far end of the corridor I was peeking into was a large window, framing a tree. It must have been a very tall tree to reach up to this window on the top floor of the hospital. The sky showing through its branches was silver. I felt a storm brewing as the branches of the tree soundlessly began to sway. I knew then that my father was going to die.

They returned him to his room later that day, and he woke up with his family around him. We went every day to visit him there. Hannah, who was not yet three, sat on his bed and shared his food. Malka, at eleven months, took her first steps in his room. He was very yellow. "Some God you've got there! Don't talk to me about God!" he said to me. I let myself be drawn into these arguments, and then I would be overcome with shame. I knew he was in tremendous pain.

One day, after a month had passed, he was taken upstairs to intensive care, at the end of the T opposite surgery, and he died there, his bed facing the tree in that other world I had glimpsed through the little window in the red door. My sister screamed in protest, in disbelief. My father had gone to the edge of the abyss countless times before, and he had always come back.

Just before the funeral, we got a call from the mortuary. They wanted someone to identify the body to make sure they were burying the right person. "I'll go," I said. I was the eldest son. I was now head of the family. They led me into the chapel. The casket was open. My father was wrapped in a shroud. I had insisted that they give him a traditional Jewish burial. Since he had died on a Friday, he couldn't be buried until Sunday (you can't hold a funeral on the Sabbath). The weather was warm, and they had had to ice him, since embalming is forbidden by Jewish law. Rigor mortis had set in and his face had contorted into a terrible scream.

The image of his expression haunts me still. In it I felt his reproach for the horror I had submitted him to—the horror of being iced—all for the sake of my stupid religious ideas. Never mind that icing is gentle compared to embalming, which creates the illusion of peace on the face of a corpse. In shock, I performed the first funeral in my career as a rabbi, the funeral of my own father.

Hundreds of people came. Hundreds came to the house after, and for the next week. All my teachers and peers from the seminary came to my apartment every morning for minyan. I felt buoyed up and protected. Every afternoon, we drove up to my mother's house, where the atmosphere was almost partylike. Everyone who had ever attended her parties over the years was there. My mother walked around in her stocking feet, without her lipstick, and with a look of terror in her eyes.

I said Kaddish three times a day for the eleven months of mourning. According to Jewish tradition, in the year after you die you are undergoing judgment by the heavenly tribunal. The idea of judgment after death is a universal religious belief, but in Judaism, what you are being judged for is not exactly clear. Some say it is for admittance to *Olam Habah*, the World to Come. During this year of judgment, whatever your mourners do that is good—giving *tzedakah*, charity, or performing any other religious act, such as leading services—accrues to the merit of your case.

Most people, however, do not know enough Hebrew to lead services. This has been true throughout Jewish history, and this is how the Kaddish, which has nothing to do with death, became the prayer for the dead. The Kaddish occurs at every point of transition between the various parts of the prayer service and is not in Hebrew, but Aramaic, the language Jews spoke when the Kaddish originated. Since it was in the spoken language of its day, it was the one prayer in the service everyone could read, so reading it became a way mourners who did not know Hebrew could fulfill the obligation of performing a religious act in order to accumulate merit for a dead relative.

Of course, it is far better for a mourner to lead the whole service. During the year of mourning for a parent, a sibling, a child, or a spouse, you have a higher *chiuv*, religious obligation, to lead the service than other worshippers (except for those observing a *yahrtzeit*, the anniversary of the death of a parent, sibling, child, or spouse). Jewish law recognizes a hierarchy of obligations. In this case, the person with the highest obligation to lead services is the one with the most compelling need to do so.

So I, with my elementary Hebrew and rudimentary synagogue skills, was suddenly called upon to lead services, to *daven*, before perhaps the most expert congregation of daveners in the world, the minyan at the Jewish Theological Seminary. To say I was intimidated is an understatement, but the community supported me, and Joe Brody, the dean of students, though a very busy man, spent many hours working with me one-on-one, word by word, until I had the intricacies of the service down.

I was so involved in getting the service right that I hardly thought of my father as I led the prayers and repeated the Kaddish. The words of the Kaddish glorified God; they did nothing, as far as I could see, to remind me that my father was, in fact, dead. But even though the Kaddish did not originate as a prayer for the dead, there are some after-the-fact explanations for how, in a subtle way, it nonetheless actually is. One *midrash*, one Jewish legend, explains that whenever anyone dies, God is diminished, so when you say *Yitgadal* . . . , magnified . . . , the words are working to address this loss, to increase God, as it were. Another midrash points out that the death of a loved one is precisely the moment you want to curse God. The words of the Kaddish, which affirm God and God's role in the world, help to put a brake on this anger. Indeed, that is exactly the way my sister had reacted when our father had taken his last desperate labored breath. She had cursed God, crying and screaming. But I hadn't cried. I hadn't cried at all.

What I had done was set out punctiliously to follow the laws of mourning. In the eleven months of mourning, I did not miss a single day of saying Kaddish for my father, though I rarely thought of him while saying the words. And then the last day of mourning arrived. It was then, as I began to say the Kaddish for the last time, that I saw my father at the beginning of the prayer, asking me to say these words for him: *Yitgadal v'yitgadash* . . . All these months, without my noticing it, we had, in fact, been holding on to each other inside these words. Now the end of the words was coming into view—*aleinu v'alchol yisrael*—the moment when I must bow farewell, to the left and to the right, and step back out of this prayer where my arms were around my father and his arms were around me. I had to let go.

They led me sobbing from the bimah.

# 31 STUDYING TALMUD

I loved studying Talmud, but not because it taught me great
spiritual truths. It didn't; the content was completely mundane.
For example, we studied the history of the laws about how to
*kasher*—to make kosher—a knife that you had bought from a
gentile. There were many variables to consider; for instance,
had it been used for hot, cold, or pungent food? Should you
bury it in the ground? Boil it in water? Bring it to the point of
white heat? There were dozens of treatises on this subject written over hundreds of years, and reading them was like listening
in on a conversation that took place in some timeless realm.
But each of the commentators came to a completely different
conclusion about how to kasher this knife, and this threw me
into a crisis. If the rules of kashrut really reflected the will of
God, how could it be that there were so many different answers
to this question? This crisis was resolved when it finally dawned

on me that what was important was not any particular result in itself, but rather the sincere effort to determine the will of God and to live by it; it was the process of trying to figure out how this could be done that was sacred. Studying Talmud began to change my thought processes, making them more precise. I realized then that my friend Bob Grenier was right: thinking is a spiritual activity. It does bring you closer to God. This is, in fact, one of the basic axioms of the Kabbalah. But it was all new to me and my Zen sensibility.

Every Saturday afternoon I would study Talmud in the seminary *beit midrash* purely for pleasure. Just before the evening service, I would put down my book and go outside to the park. The world would be alive, the trees radiant in the attenuated light. Going through this process of trying to uncover the will of God through the study of Torah and Talmud, and then trying to live by it, was putting me into a completely different universe.

The Conservative Movement differs from the Orthodox Movement in that Conservative Jews believe that the *halacha*, the body of Jewish law, is subject to evolution, that it is alive. The Orthodox, on the other hand, see it as a fixed and unchanging code. When Jews lived in the hermetically sealed ghettoes of Europe, whatever changes occurred in their lives took place within this seal; they were Jewish changes and no one questioned that the halacha should evolve with these changes. But after the Emancipation, when Jews became citizens of the nations of Europe and no longer lived in self-contained communities, this idea came into question. Orthodoxy rose up and said, "Now that Jews are living in the larger world, we can't trust halacha to be evolutionary any more." Reform went the other way. It said, "We'll accept changes even if we have to give up halacha, if that's what it means for us to be able to live as citizens of the wider world." The Conservatives came along after the other two and said, "No, you can't have Judaism without halacha or halacha without evolution. Halacha means 'the going.' It's a process. It has to incorporate social change even if that change isn't purely Jewish anymore, as if it ever was. The fact is, Jews have always incorporated ideas and practices from the larger culture. The seal around the ghetto wasn't as hermetic as we sometimes imagine it to have been." Intellectually, I believed in the Conservative position, but part of me wondered if there wasn't something more authentic about the Orthodox, so on Thanksgiving I went with a friend to 770 Eastern Parkway in Brooklyn to a *farbrengen*, to see the Lubavitcher Rebbe, the spiritual leader of Chabad, the largest Chasidic Movement in the world.

It started at eleven at night. We soon found ourselves crowded into a huge room, like a gym with a big dais at the front, where the Rebbe sat surrounded by dignitaries, politicians, and rabbis. The Rebbe spoke in Yiddish, but there were headsets available for translations in several different languages—English, Hebrew, Spanish. We sat in the bleachers, which reached up to the ceiling. On the back wall was a bunker: the women's section, sealed off with glass and concrete. Not far from me I recognized someone I had known vaguely in Berkeley—the number-two man in the macrobiotic movement. Apparently, he had become a *ba'al teshuvah*, a kind of "born again" Jew. He was dressed head to toe in black. My friend and I were among only a few who weren't dressed all in black. It was a sea of long black coats, hats, and beards. Hundreds of people were there, packed in like sardines. Once we were wedged into our places and I realized I couldn't move, I began to get scared that I would be crushed or suffocated.

The Rebbe gave a series of seven talks, finishing at three in the morning. In between the talks there was the ecstatic singing of *nigunim*, Chasidic melodies without words, which built up a spiritual head of steam. The speeches, however, seemed simplistic and obvious to me, like Kabbalah for the masses. The Rebbe was drinking glass after glass of schnapps, continuously toasting people as they called out to him that he was the Messiah. When they did, he would smile and hold his glass up to them. He seemed to be encouraging it.

I had already had my fill of gurus and Zen masters, so there was no chance that I was going to leave the seminary to don Chasidic garb. Still, I had begun to wonder if the seminary was really the right place for me. There was a lot of rancor there at that time because of the issue of women's ordination. The three major Jewish denominations had been pretty well defined by their response to women's issues in recent years. There was a consensus in society at large that the change in the status of women, which had been gradually penetrating American society over the past generation, was both a good thing and a permanent one. Orthodoxy said, "This is all well and good, but it has nothing to do with us. The halacha is fixed and unchanging, and is under no obligation to respond to social change. The role of women can change all it wants in the marketplace, but it's not going to change in the synagogue." For them, the ordination of women as rabbis was unthinkable. The Reform Movement, which does not see itself as bound by the halacha, simply said one day, "Okay, we'll ordain women as rabbis," but for Conservative Jews, it was a much more complex issue, and they had been wrestling with it for ten years.

Halachicly, the ordination of women was not a single problem. It raised several different legal issues. Could women lead religious services? Could they be counted in a prayer minyan? Could they read from the Torah? Could they be called to bless the Torah? Traditionally, women had not been permitted to do any of these things. But Conservative halachic scholars had succeeded in reinterpreting the tradition to solve these problems, all except for one: the question of agency. It was inconceivable that someone could be a rabbi without being able to lead services, but the person who leads services is a *sheliach tzibur*, an agent of the public who says the prayers for those who cannot do it themselves, so that they can fulfill the obligation. But in order to be somebody's agent, you have to be at least as obligated as they are. If you are less obligated, you can't do it for them, and women were not obligated to do the daily prayer service because they were exempt from all time-bound commandments—presumably because of child-rearing responsibilities. Although there was a great deal of support for women's ordination among the students, the three great Talmudists were against it. They couldn't find any way to surmount these halachic obstacles. It was whispered in the hallways that it would never happen while Shaul Lieberman, especially, was alive.

Lieberman was perhaps the world's greatest living Talmudist. My mind would soar when I would read his analyses of rabbinic texts like the *Mishna* and the *Tosefta*. But most people were afraid of him. Students avoided getting into an elevator with him because he was famous for suddenly quizzing them as they rode down. On the other hand, he had authored the "Lieberman Clause" to the ketubah, the Jewish marriage contract. Before this clause, a Jewish divorce could only be granted at the initiative of the husband, and, if the husband refused to do so, the woman could never remarry. There were women in this predicament in virtually every traditional community. The rabbis would cajole and sometimes even picket the recalcitrant husbands, but no one could force them to grant a get, and their abandoned wives were doomed to spend the rest of their lives alone. The Lieberman clause said that if a man refused to grant a get, then a rabbinical court could do it for him. The clause showed that Shaul Lieberman was deeply offended by cruelty to women. Still, he was not ready for the whole social order to change; he was not ready for women to be ordained as rabbis.

Then, just before Passover, Shaul Lieberman flew to Israel, and when the plane landed, they found him dead in his seat. According to tradition, if you die in Israel it is a sign that you are a *zaddik*, one of the righteous. But where did Lieberman die? Had he died in the air or after the plane had landed? This mystery seemed to express the ambiguity of Lieberman's life. Was he a zaddik or was he a brilliant man with a mean streak? One thing became immediately clear, however; the seminary faculty would now vote to accept women to the rabbinical school.

Joel Roth, who was dean of the rabbinical school and on the Talmud faculty, wrote a treatise, a *teshuvah*, on the issue of women's ordination. (A teshuvah is an answer to a *she'elah*, a question.) Women were asking if they could be rabbis. Roth's teshuvah was long and scholarly, citing many precedents. Since the problem was that women did not have the same obligation as men to pray, he first asked, "Can a person take on a *mitzvah*, a commandment, voluntarily?" He then asked, "If you take on a mitzvah voluntarily, does it then become obligatory?" His answer was yes to both, and he backed this up with many sources as well. He then asked, "Once such a mitzvah becomes obligatory, is the obligation equal to that of one who has had it from the beginning?" Again, he said yes, but here he could only cite a few sources, and none of them was exactly on target. His argument for this last point was not as persuasive as the others and relied largely on the momentum that the previous arguments had generated.

Frankus wrote a brief response, saying that no one argued with any of the points Roth was making except the last—the only one that mattered—and, quite simply, he was wrong on this one. There was a clear hierarchy of obligation, so that even if a woman voluntarily took on the obligation of praying each day, and this obligation became binding on her, it would still be a lesser obligation than the one a man was born to, and, consequently, she could never lead prayers as his agent. Moreover, in a public speech, he accused Roth of intellectual dishonesty.

I didn't know what to do. It was clear to me that Frankus was right, but ever since beginning my studies there, I had been following Roth's interpretations of the tradition, for example, the laws of ritual purity, *nidah,* which require a husband and wife to abstain from sexual relations during menstruation. The Torah requires seven days of abstention, but the Orthodox practice is to wait another five days to be certain the period is over, and then for the woman to go to the *mikvah,* the ritual bath, before relations can resume. Roth said the extra five days were unnecessary, arguing that the whole purity cult didn't have any meaning anymore after the destruction of the Temple. We still continue to observe the laws of nidah, but only because of their secondary benefits. The practice of nidah brought sexuality, one of our strongest impulses, into the religious arena. It enhanced the marital relationship, giving the partners a chance to relate to each other in a way that was not based on sexuality during the period of abstinence. Then it gave them the opportunity to feel like teenagers again as soon as it was over. Since it

187

wasn't really based on the impurity of the blood, Roth reasoned, it should only be necessary to abstain for the biblical seven days, and men should go to the mikvah, too.

Men could only go to the mikvah in our neighborhood by appointment. It was run by the Orthodox, so there was no point in trying to explain to them why I needed to use it. However, Rabbi Roth had located a mikvah up in Washington Heights where one could go at any time during the day without an appointment. I took the subway there and got off with some of the scariest-looking people I had ever seen. We all pressed into huge clanking elevators that brought us to the surface, where I made my way through the dangerous streets to the remnants of the German Jewish community that had once flourished there, and to a small synagogue. I went in the back door, down the elevator to the boiler room, and through a door in the back that led to the mikvah. It was not very clean, but I had it all to myself.

One day after one of these adventures, when I was heading back to the subway, I ran into someone I knew from the Modern Orthodox seminary, Yeshiva University, which was nearby. He was also connected with JTS and knew how upset I was by Roth's teshuvah on women's ordination. He had suggested that, since I was in the neighborhood, he take me up to YU to see about switching.

The first question they asked me when we got there was why my hair was wet. After I explained, I knew the interview was over. I could tell how crazy Roth's idea of ritual purity sounded in their ears. "You can't just think anything you want," they told me. "There's a right way to think and a wrong way. That's what 'Orthodox' means—'the right way to think.'" That was the moment when I realized once and for all that I could never be Orthodox. I was too far gone. It was an easy, even a desirable, thing for me to accept limitations on the way I behaved, but I could never accept limitations on the way I thought. I returned to JTS, realizing that if I quit, there would be nowhere else for me to go. As I walked past the chapel, I saw Rabbi Roth praying intensely before the ark. The vote on women's ordinartion was in progress.

As it happened, the faculty voted to accept women's ordination, but not on the basis of Roth's teshuvah. Feminists who felt the Roth teshuvah was too traditional had joined with those on the right, who were angry that the issue was being treated as an administrative rather than a halachic issue, with low-level Hebrew teachers having as much to say on the matter as the great halachists on the Talmud faculty. Later, when I went out into the world, I saw how naive and idealistic I had been at the seminary. Halacha wasn't really the basis for most people's objections to women's ordination. Out in the congregations, those opposed to women's ordination were, by and large, people who wanted to defend their power over women, or people who were simply afraid of change. They didn't live the rest of their lives by the rules of halacha, and most of them were only using it to justify the status quo. Once out in the congregations, I would become a staunch advocate of women's ordination.

But now the word was that Halivni, accused of being a misogynist, would leave the seminary. The truth was, he had no animus against women; he simply had an exquisite sense of halacha. So next year he would not be speaking at Kabbalat Shabbat services and this beautiful Friday night service, with the entire community gathered to pray in the basement of the old library building, would fragment into two groups: egalitarian and traditional. I had a great deal of sympathy for the women, but I had staked my life on the Conservative Movement being sincerely halachic, sincerely spiritual. Now it seemed not to be, and I fell into a depression.

One day, when I came home from class, I went into Hannah's room where the girls were playing with a tea set, and I lay down next to them on the floor. I was very tired, and my back hurt. Steve, who was now fifteen, had been visiting all week, and I had been taking him to jazz clubs every night after dinner. I had discovered jazz in high school. It had become a consuming passion, and now I was sharing it with my son. The next day the pain was acute, and every day thereafter it got worse until, finally, it was so bad I could hardly stand. I felt hot one minute, then cold; I had the shakes. Sherril piled the blankets on top of me and took my temperature. It was 105.

As Steve helped me in under the green awning of St. Luke's Hospital, I remembered how I had marveled when I saw that awning the day we moved into our apartment. I thought then that I understood its significance in my life, that there must be some connection between what I had done to help Jeff recover and my becoming a rabbi. But now that significance was changing. Now my own illness was part of the equation. Trying to understand it was like studying a page of Talmud. That first moment when I had stood in front of my new apartment expanded in my delirium until it was large enough to contain not just what I saw at that moment I glanced up at the awning, but what I felt then and had forgotten until now—a cold wind that suddenly rose up, causing a chill to run through me. That wind had come from the future. It was here, now, as I passed under the horrible green awning, shaking with fever.

THE HOLOCAUST

I had full body sepsis and was in the hospital for two weeks. Steve went back to Berkeley, my mother came and stayed with the girls, and Sherril sat with me every day. I was happy then, somehow, simply reading the Torah and praying, alone in my hospital bed, or sitting holding my wife's hand without talking. It was good to rest, to do nothing, to simply let the world exist without me.

It wasn't clear to anyone what had made me so sick, although I wondered if I hadn't picked up a bug from the dirty mikvah up in Washington Heights, and I promised Sherril I wouldn't go back. After I had been in the hospital for a few days, a Jewish chaplain came in to see me. He started making small talk and asked me what I did. When he heard I was a rabbinical student, he said, "What? You're too old to be a rabbinical student." Then, after a long uncomfortable pause, he said,

"If you're a rabbinical student, you can say a prayer for your-self." He put down his card and walked out of the room. It was a pity, because I could have really used a rabbi just then. Were all chaplains so burned out and useless? Here was a situation where someone with a bit of talent and compassion could do some real good for people who were suffering. This was a time when people were really open to thinking about God.

Gradually I recovered and was allowed to go home. One day, a few weeks later, I was sitting in the seminary dining room and Mortie Liefman, the dean of the cantorial school and the semi-nary specialist in doing good works, sat down next to me. He told me he was going to start an internship for chaplains at Sloan Kettering Memorial Hospital and asked me to partici-pate. Within a week, I found myself following behind Pesach Krause, the head chaplain at Sloan Kettering, as he made his rounds. Unlike my chaplain at St. Luke's, Pesach would go for broke with everybody. Sometimes he was so direct people would kick him out of their rooms, but many more times they would connect with him immediately. I trained with a psychia-trist, who would have me write "verbatims" of what happened when I visited a patient. This was not a matter of memorizing what was said but rather of listening with complete attention, the better to recall it all later. When you listen to people in this way, it brings very deep things out of them, and it enables you to intuit how to respond.

Shortly after I started at the hospital, there was a conference on dealing with cancer victims, which featured a psychiatrist named Lawrence Lashan. He had treated people with cancer for many years with a great deal of success. His first point was that patients needed to take up a spiritual practice; spiritual discipline healed, and the lack of it was unhealthy. Next, he felt it was important to try to help the patient identify what might have triggered the cancer. He believed that cancer ensued five to ten years after the patient had experienced some trauma or loss—losing a job or a spouse, moving, and the like. But his main thesis was that a leading cause of cancer was not living out your destiny, not doing what you were meant to do with your life. He told several stories to illustrate this point. One of his patients was a man in his sixties who finally realized that he had always wanted to be a doctor, but he was now too old to go to medical school. Lashan asked him what it was about being a doctor that appealed to him. He said, "All day long you sit in an office and people come to you and ask you questions and you give them information that they really need." The next year Lashan went to visit this man in his new job. He was working in an information kiosk in Florida. People came to him all day with questions, and he gave them the information they needed. He was happy, and his cancer was in remission.

The next story he told was about a man who had been the leader of one of the biggest gangs in New York, but he had outgrown this life. His fellow gang members were all either dead or too old for gang life anymore. Suddenly he came down with cancer. Lashan asked him, "What was it about belonging to this gang that you loved the most?" "It was the rhythm of the life," the man said. "There were short bursts of intensity when your life was on the line, followed by long periods of just hanging out with the guys and talking about these moments, savoring them. And I loved the complete love and trust you had with the other people in the gang—you had to have it because your life was in their hands. If the guy in front of you and the guy behind you didn't do exactly what they were supposed to do, you were dead." After Lashan heard this he figured out that this man should become a fireman, which he helped him to do. It wasn't easy to get a former gang member without a high school degree into the fire department, but he did, and the man became a great fireman. His cancer stayed in remission for ten years, and then he experienced another crisis. They wanted to promote him to a desk job, which paid better pay and was less danger-ous. No one, neither his wife nor his superiors, could under-stand why he didn't want to take the job.

Another story Lashan told was of a woman who had always wanted to be a ballet dancer. She was now elderly, too old to dance, so instead, she devoted her time to the study of ballet and wrote books about it. She died in the midst of this work, a flower who died in full bloom, for even though she died, she had healed. Healing is not necessarily measured in years of survival.

The medical people at the conference did not like Lashan's theories, fearing they might lead to patients blaming them-selves for coming down with cancer, but I found them very compelling. I didn't take them as literally as the doctors did. To me, Lashan's stories were like poems, which expressed a deep truth about the soul's needs. I became a convert. Now when I sat with patients, I wondered about the traumas they had suf-fered.

One of my patients was a very bright woman in her eighties who had never married and had no children. She had spent her life as a social worker and had reached the conclusion that none of her work amounted to anything. Full of Lashan's ideas, I was absolutely determined to help her find the meaning of her life. She was equally determined to resist any such attempts on my part, and she was a lot smarter than I was. Whenever I would suggest that she might have done some good in her life, she would explain in no uncertain terms that not only had she done no good at all, she had probably done more harm than good. But one day, in the middle of one such futile exchange, she suddenly looked up and said to me, "You really are sort of a dope. You come in here every day trying to find some meaning in my life, but there isn't any. Still, you keep coming, and I'm beginning to think there's meaning in *that*."

We interns got credit for the number of people we visited, but I stayed so long with each patient that I had a very low count. At first the brain surgery floor was a godsend, because nine out of ten people were comatose. I could stay just for a minute, leave my card, and get credit for a full visit, but this lost its thrill after a while, for I soon realized there was some good in just being with people, whether they were conscious or not. I started staying by their bedsides for an hour at a time. It was like a meditation. I learned to "feel" people without talking. In fact, I wouldn't leave the patient's bedside until I had "felt" them—felt in contact with their presence, picking up subtle communications and even detecting when they were coming out of their comas.

I realized that this kind of "tuning in" to patients was an important aspect of what went on in all successful interactions with patients, even those I *could* talk to. One of my patients was a young college girl named Karen, who was dying of cancer. Her mother and father had had a bitter divorce and there was a great deal of tension between them around her bedside. It was as if they were competing for the right to say what her life had been about and why she was dying. When the time came for her to die, Karen seemed to take control of her own death, carefully calibrating the timing of it until everyone who was important to her had arrived at her bedside. I could feel her consciousness growing as her death approached. As soon as everyone was there, she died. Her parents immediately started screaming at each other over her body. They blamed each other for her death. They said terrible, hurtful things to each other. Suddenly, it came to me to say, "Her life was perfect as it was." Both of her parents collapsed and stopped screaming. They put their arms around me and started crying. I did the funeral, and hundreds of young people came.

Another patient I visited was very angry all the time and would always insult me. I had to force myself to go into his room. One day I just couldn't face him so I walked past his room, but he came out into the hallway to insult me. I understood then that he really needed to express his anger, to put it onto someone else. It was hard for me to take, but I realized this is one way a chaplain can be useful to people.

Sam Klagsburn, the psychiatrist I trained with at Sloan Kettering, tells a story about a patient he treated when he first began working at a hospice in Philadelphia. The staff had asked him to drop in on a particularly difficult patient who had been abusing everybody for weeks. Sam went to see him, and the patient spent the entire hour abusing Sam horribly, yelling and cursing him at the top of his lungs. "Oh well," Sam said to himself as he was leaving. "You win some, you lose some." But the next week when he returned to the hospice, everyone came running up to him. "What did you do with that guy? He's been a changed person." So Sam continued to see him every week, and every week he continued to abuse Sam horribly, and soon his cancer went into remission, against all reason and against all the expectations of the doctors. Finally, he left the hospice and went home. About a year later he came in for a check-up and Sam bumped into him on an elevator. "You look terrific!" Sam exclaimed. "Yeah," the man said. "No thanks to you."

As in all hospitals, but especially at Sloan Kettering, the children's floor was the hardest one to work. Most of the chaplains would just race through it, and the parents would often complain about this. Soon I, too, wanted to race away from this floor. The suffering was unbearable. With kids, it wasn't about finding the meaning of their lives. You can't deal with a child as if he or she were a single unit. Kids are part of a family, a communal consciousness. You had to talk to the whole family, and invariably these families were in agony. I tried my best, but it was torture.

In the Talmud, the death of a child is taken as proof that there is such a thing as meaningless, irredeemable suffering. Whenever one rabbi tries to see meaning in suffering, some hidden benefit or a course correction when we've gone astray, another rabbi will bring up the death of a child, which the Talmud takes as an unassailable refutation that suffering could have any meaning at all. Suffering is just suffering. According to Buddhists, suffering is the first noble truth, and it is relentless. We can never escape it or explain it away. I never understood this so thoroughly as when I was working on the pediatric ward at Sloan Kettering. I never felt the impulse to run away from suffering as strongly as I felt it there. In the end, I didn't run away. In the end, I sat by the bedsides of these children and in the waiting room with their parents. I sat until I got past seeing my own children and their vulnerability in these children. I sat until I realized the great truth that Rabbi Yochanan came to at the end of the Talmudic discussion on suffering: Our attempts to understand suffering and to give it meaning are futile and empty, and the death of children proves it. Suffering is an irreducible and inevitable mystery and can only be met by a mystery of equal force—the power of simple human presence to heal. Rabbi Yohanan sat with the dying, young and old, tried to explain their suffering to them, and when he failed to do so, he simply sat with them in silence, held their hands, wept with them, and that seemed to work, that brought healing. So I sat with these children and their families day after day, praying that Rabbi Yohanan was right.

This internship was the first real "place" in the world I had ever had. It was thrilling for me to put on my badge on the way to the hospital and to eat my lunch in the big staff dining room with all the doctors. On most floors, doctors and nurses gave patients only a few minutes a day, and the patients were left terrified in their rooms the rest of the time. The doctors seemed to regard us as a competing priesthood. I would be deep in conversation with a patient, and a doctor would walk in without so much as an "excuse me" or "hello" and interrupt our conversation to say what he had to say.

Every time I'd leave a room, I'd force myself to say a *misheberach*, a prayer for healing, even though most of the patients I encountered weren't religious. They didn't belong to congregations or have rabbis of their own, which is why they needed me. They would usually say to me, "Okay, we can talk, but nothing religious." So it took some moxie to offer to say the misheberach for them, but I felt it was important; I felt it was what I was there to do. Once in a very great while someone would say, "No thanks, I've lived my whole life without God, and I'll die that way, too," but this was exceedingly rare. Most people would make a joke of it. They'd say, "Okay, I might as well cover all the bases," but then, when the ancient Hebrew words of the prayer began to fill the room, they would cry or squeeze my hand. It made them feel as if they were part of a larger community of meaning, just as the meaning of their individual lives was being threatened. These moments taught me a great deal about what prayer was, what Hebrew was, and what healing was. Hebrew was the medium of expression that connected them to a continuity of meaning larger than their own. This was tremendously healing. All of this taken together is what Jews have always understood as prayer.

One Friday night, on *Yom Ha Shoah*, Holocaust Remembrance Day, I went to the seminary for the *Kabbalat Shabbat* service. (This was before Lieberman's death and Halivni's departure.) Israel Frankus's son Yossi had just become engaged to a young Talmud student. Frankus was the shyest and the least acclaimed of the seminary's three great European Talmudists. Halivni would talk every Friday night, Lieberman would leap up to the bimah screaming whenever anyone made a mistake, but Frankus rarely spoke, and never in public, except when he was teaching Talmud, when his passion for Talmud possessed him and he would dash around the classroom reciting the intricate Talmudic arguments at breakneck speed. But when someone passed him in the hallway, he was so shy he rarely even said hello. You knew he was a survivor because you could see the numbers tattooed on his forearm when he rolled up his sleeve every morning to put on tefillin. Since it was Yom Ha Shoa, Halivni spoke about the Holocaust, which he had also spent in concentration camps. Although it was Shabbat, when unpleasant things are traditionally kept at bay, Halivni evoked the full horror of the Holocaust with a few strokes.

I remember almost nothing of what he actually said. His speech was like something from a deep dream, a hallucination, another dimension, which vanishes as soon as it comes into this one. What I do remember is the effect his words had on the congregation. We were devastated. People had their heads in their hands. People were weeping. Finally, he said, "I don't see why we should remember it at all," and walked off the bimah.

You could have heard a pin drop. Most speeches about the Holocaust were about how we should never forget it to ensure that it would never happen again. Halivni seemed to be pointing out how simplistic, how inadequate this response was. If we *really* remembered the Holocaust, there would be no way to contain the horror.

After what seemed a very long time, the service started up again, and we managed to limp through to the end, but with none of the joy and exuberance with which we usually greeted the Shabbat. Then the *gabbai* (the one in charge of the minyan) stood up to make the announcements as he always did. Whenever he announced that someone was engaged, everyone would sing *Simin tov u' mazel tov* with great enthusiasm, and this night he was to announce the engagement of Israel Frankus's son Yossi. We were still sitting in stunned silence when he made the announcement. No one knew what to do. We didn't want to slight Dr. Frankus and his son, but it seemed obscene to sing *Simin tov u' mazel tov*, with Halivni's horrifying words still hanging in the air.

The silence continued uncomfortably for what seemed an eternity. Suddenly Israel Frankus astounded everyone by leaping to the bimah. This was the same Frankus who rarely said hello in the hallways, but now he was standing at the head of the congregation shaking his finger at us accusingly. "You better sing *Simin tov u' mazel tov!*" he said. "Don't you understand? The whole point is, they tried to finish us off, and they failed. I'm the only one left in my family, and now my son is going to get married and have children, and my family will continue. You better sing *Simin tov u' mazel tov!*" And so we sang—at first softly, then louder and louder and with a deep sense of joy that encompassed all the tragedy and all the triumph of the Jewish people.

A few nights later I left the apartment after dinner to go to a night class. The entrance to St. Luke's was lit up, and suddenly everything became crystal clear. The purpose of my own hospital stay in St. Luke's as well as all the hours I had spent by Jeff's bedside there had been to prepare me for working at Sloan Kettering. My work at Sloan Kettering had also been my grief work, helping me to come out of the depression I had been in since my father's death. I took a deep breath, feeling the life inside my body. A man was singing to himself in front of the gates to Columbia University. The moon was high in the sky, and then I saw another light. It was the light on top of the seminary tower, like a beacon that guides ships in the night. I climbed the steps leading into the seminary courtyard, and as I did, I read the words engraved in the entry for the first time, though I passed them every day. Tonight they spoke to me: "And the bush was not consumed."

## 33 PRAYER

JTS required rabbinical students to spend one year in Israel, and we decided to go the following fall. One day, shortly before we left, Norman was in New York for a visit and decided to come to minyan at the seminary with me. He had often told me about the intensely Jewish life he had led as a boy. He had been his rabbi's favorite and had prayed and studied with him every day. When he was eleven years old he had vowed to himself that he would always remain faithful to Judaism, and, as far as he was concerned, he had never broken that vow. He never missed High Holiday services, and it was only because of him that I had begun to celebrate Passover seders again. He had never felt alienated from Judaism, and he did not see his involvement with Buddhism as posing a conflict to his Jewish identity. In fact, in a way that was often difficult for me to understand, he saw his Buddhist practice as the fulfillment of his Jewishness.

In the fifteen years that Norman and I had been close friends, I had never been in a synagogue with him, and I was shocked when he walked into the minyan and threw on a set of tefillin as if he'd never missed a day in his life. He picked up a siddur and began to daven with great fluency and passion, shukkling mightily backward and forward. After the service was over, there was a radiance on his face I had never seen before, not even after a sesshin in Tassajara. "Now that I've done Zen meditation," he said, "I could do this for the rest of my life and it would be enough. I wouldn't have to do anything more. But if I'd never done Zen meditation, I wouldn't even know what this is," he said. I knew exactly what he was talking about. I had felt exactly this way so often in my own prayer life, as if Zen meditation had opened me to the great richness of ordinary Jewish prayer, a richness that was no longer apparent to most Jews.

Norman had been rising in the ranks at Zen Center. He had gone to Japan to receive transmission. He was now a Zen master, and soon I would be a rabbi. We were each other's path not taken.

The apartment we rented in Jerusalem was built out of chalky pink Jerusalem stone that gave off an odor of old bones in the heat of the day. It was in Talpiot Mizrach, a magical neighborhood of new apartment buildings winding up and down a mountainside where the old U.N. headquarters used to be before 1967. From our living room we could see the hills of Moab and the volcano-shaped Mount Herodian. Spread out beneath our building were beautiful Arab villages. Their cobalt blue windows warded off the evil eye. Loudspeakers on the top of a minaret broadcast the Moslem call to prayer. It woke us up before dawn every day, when it was still cool.

We soon learned to shop at Rafi's, a corner grocery store with a four-sided counter where people of every description crowded around on all sides. We bought our milk there in plastic bags, while Rafi ran back and forth dispensing items and making change in Hebrew, Arabic, French, English, Russian, and Yiddish. We had a community center in our neighborhood where Hannah took ballet lessons. There was a Calder sculpture of a red heifer in front. Across from it was a supermarket where all the food was kosher. Sometimes, we would see Bedouins on camels or donkeys in the courtyard. In the bomb shelter—every neighborhood in Israel has a bomb shelter—there was a Conservative synagogue. Religious politics being what they are in Israel, it was hard for a Conservative congregation to have a regular synagogue. That is where we went to pray on Shabbat. There were a lot of Conservative Jews in this neighborhood, many of them Conservative rabbis. But they didn't have a daily minyan. For that, I went to a little Orthodox shul in a geodesic dome across the street.

Orthodox shuls in Israel are a lot like filling stations. Unlike American synagogues, they aren't "community centers." They don't have adult education, folk dancing, or board meetings. People just come, pray, and leave. You go there to fill up your tank every morning, and that's it. In America, going to synagogue is more about being Jewish than about prayer, but in Israel, being Jewish is taken for granted. What happens there in the morning prayer services is almost a biological event, like bees sucking nectar out of flowers.

Real prayer is a fundamental mindfulness activity. The basic thing you're trying to do is concentrate on the text of the prayer service, but, inevitably, your mind is carried off by other thoughts or distractions, and when you become aware that you are distracted, you gently bring your mind back.

People complain about the speed of the Jewish prayer service. They say it's too fast for them to understand the words, but it's that very rush of words that works as a kind of anti-language. It wipes your mind clean of language and conceptual thought even though it's made out of language and conceptual thought. Daveners who have had strokes that affect their ability to speak are still able to daven because prayer is a nonverbal activity. Even though it uses language as a medium, it comes from the nonverbal center of the brain.

Still, language is language, and it often happens that a particular word or phrase will unexpectedly take on new meaning during the prayer service. In the midst of praying, a phrase will suddenly assert itself and rise out of the jumble of sounds the way a particular sound or sensation can race to the foreground of one's consciousness during mindfulness meditation. Certain phrases divorce themselves from their obvious context and take on a new meaning, or seem to be speaking directly to you. The prayer service hovers on the boundary between the verbal and the nonverbal.

In fact, though the prayer service uses language, this language describes a nonverbal event, an exchange of pure energy. I often felt this most intensely during the *Amidah*, the centerpiece of the service. During the Amidah, we pray for various personal concerns—healing, material well-being, spiritual redemption—and, toward the end of the Amidah, we pray also that our voices will be heard and that God will be pleased with our prayers. Standing silently with my hands clasped to my chest, I would often feel that these things we were praying for, and the prayers themselves, were ascending and descending like the angels on Jacob's ladder: divine energy coming down to heal us and redeem us, and a divine consciousness to meet the energy of our voices and our prayers as we raised them to heaven. All content, all imagery, verbal or otherwise, would sometimes fade away altogether as I said the Amidah, and I would feel myself to be in the presence of a formless transcendent radiance, which I always took to be the presence of God.

Before reciting the Amidah, one steps first backward, then forward, in a gesture that came from the ancient protocol for approaching a king. The stepping back and then forward is a physical reinforcement of the belief that one is entering another space, a sacred space in which one can encounter God. This is not just an idea; it has a physical reality; it is something we do with our bodies. The prayer service is full of gesture: bowing at specific moments, covering the eyes as the *Shem'a* is recited, and gathering and kissing the fringes of the prayer shawl at various points. Jewish prayer has a physical dimension. One prays each day from the same physical space, from the same seat in the synagogue, and each time we return to this seat and move through these choreographed gestures, the experience of encountering God is triggered in our bodies.

The Amidah begins by invoking the names of our ancestors—taking us out of our individual egos so that we can experience something larger—the stream of our consciousness as a people beginning with Abraham, Isaac, and Jacob, the source of this stream. All the prayers are in the "we" form, even the prayers we say silently to ourselves. When we pray, we stand at the nexus between self and other.

And it is a powerful thing to begin each day addressing God

for thirty to forty-five minutes. Prayer can evoke a radiant, luminous sense of being in God's presence, which carries over into the rest of the day. Hours after minyan I often notice that I have been experiencing the radiance of trees and the holiness of strangers on the street.

There was a deep joy to being in Israel and studying Torah in Jerusalem. I had the familiar sense of coming home, which every Jewish tourist describes upon visiting Israel and especially Jerusalem—a kind of heartsick yearning for the very stones of the city. Living in Israel seemed meaningful to me in a way that living in America never had. Just being there I felt myself taking part in the destiny of the Jewish people. Yet the truth was, I had no real role to play in Israel. My talents didn't seem needed there. The last thing anyone in Israel needed was another Conservative rabbi, and I often had the sense of being out of place, of being unsure of the language and misreading the culture.

Every day I would ride the bus up to Hebrew University on Mt. Scopus, pressed against the other passengers, with Israeli pop music playing softly on the radio. When the news came on, everyone would fall silent, united in attention, and I strained to understand what was being said. I still felt I understood less Hebrew than the neighborhood dogs.

At the university, I was studying biblical prose prayer with Moshe Greenberg. Greenberg had noticed that there were several hundred texts of what seemed to be spontaneous prayer embedded in the text of the Bible. When people were facing some terrible crisis or their hearts were full with either gratitude or the need to confess to some grievous wrongdoing, they simply unburdened themselves of a prayer to God right on the spot. But when Greenberg extracted these prayer texts from their biblical contexts and compared them, he found that they weren't as spontaneous as they seemed. In fact, they followed specific patterns, and they followed them very closely.

There were three basic prayers: supplication, thanksgiving, and confession. The supplicatory prayer, for example, always contained an address to God, a description of the supplicant's distress, a motive clause (why it would be in God's interest to grant this prayer), and the prayer itself, the supplication. There were long prayers and short prayers, and not every prayer contained all the elements of the pattern—sometimes other elements were added—but the patterns were remarkably consistent nonetheless. When people prayed, they were not just randomly pouring out the contents of their hearts; rather, they were pouring their personal feelings into a form provided for them, not unlike jazz musicians improvising on a standard.

So Greenberg proved that in its earliest context, prayer occurred at the nexus of the self and the communal consciousness, and this continued to be the case as Jewish prayer evolved over the centuries. In Talmudic times, only the *chatimot*, the blessings that sealed each prayer and named its central concern, were fixed. The body of the prayer itself was to be improvised. If the prayer was about healing, then you were to improvise a prayer about the particular healing that you needed and then seal this prayer with the same blessing for healing that everyone used. As time went on and the diaspora became widespread, the Jewish people became more and more fearful of improvisation, and the services became increasingly fixed, although even now one can still feel the vestige of this primal aspect of Jewish prayer. We begin and end each prayer together, but every individual reads the body of each prayer alone and at his or her own speed. According to the *Shulchan Aruch*, the guide to traditional Jewish observance, we should pray in a voice loud enough so that we can hear ourselves but not so loud that we can't hear all the other voices as well. So it is that we are still groping for the nexus between the self and that stream of spiritual consciousness from which Jews have been addressing God for thousands of years.

One Shabbat in the spring of our year in Israel, I was walking out of the Conservative synagogue in the bomb shelter and ran into the rabbi from the Orthodox synagogue where I went to pray every morning. He looked at me with shock. "I'm very disappointed in you," he said. He was writing me off because he had discovered that I was Conservative, and if I was Conservative, he could no longer respect me. I felt hurt, angry, and humiliated, and I became increasingly uncomfortable at his daily minyan in the geodesic dome. But this wasn't the reason I eventually stopped attending this minyan altogether. There was something else at work, a syndrome that many observant Jews experience when they first come to live in Israel. In the diaspora you sometimes come to believe that Judaism is such a tenuous enterprise that if you miss one day of minyan the whole thing will collapse, everything rests on your shoulders. But in Israel this clearly isn't the case. Judaism is in the drinking water, and it will go on very nicely no matter what you do, so you go through a period when you tend to become a little lax in your observance. First I stopped going to minyan every day, then I never went. I started praying alone at home instead, and then I watched in horror, as if from outside myself, as finally I stopped praying altogether.

Then my mother and Steve came for a visit. I took them touring all around, and one day we went up to Yad Vashem, the Holocaust memorial. I had been there several times, but this time an exhibit caught my eye that I had never noticed before. It was about the many ways Jews had continued religious observance in the camps—using potatoes for Hanukkah menorahs and shoelaces for tefillin—and, in spite of imminent starvation, fasting on Yom Kippur. There was a picture of a scrap of a page of a prayerbook prisoners had used to daven with.

The next day, I went back to the daily minyan. It took me several months to figure out why. It wasn't, as I first suspected, because I felt shamed by these heroic examples. It wasn't because I thought, "If they could pray at Auschwitz, I certainly should be able to pray in Israel." It was something much deeper. When I saw that exhibit at Yad Vashem, I realized that all the Jews who had ever davened the traditional Jewish service were in that service. They had put themselves in every word.

Most of us can understand that we are changed by the words we use. What is harder to understand, but equally true, is that we change the words as well when we use them, the way the shoe of a small child begins to express the shape of that child's foot when it's well worn. My great-grandfather, who had prayed this service every day of his life with great passion and fervor, had managed to insinuate himself into the words of the service. That was where he was now. In fact, that was the only place on earth where he was, and all the Jews who had used these words with heart and sincerity were in them, too, and when I prayed the service, when I said the words, I was there with them.

The great koan of prayer, the present-day paradox, is that this prayer service works so well, and the particular text of the prayer service—every word—derives a tremendous sanctity from all the Jewish souls who have said these words for several thousand years. But the plain fact is, 99.9 percent of Jews alive today find this prayer service completely inaccessible. They don't know Hebrew, but they think they should understand what the prayers mean. They have short attention spans, and the Jewish prayer service is long and subtle. People today are always trying to change the prayer service, to make it shorter, more relevant, more overtly spiritual. There's no doubt that these things need to be done because, unfortunately, Jewish prayer is an opaque and empty experience for so many Jews. But if we start lopping off phrases, if we start abbreviating and digesting, what will become of all the souls embedded in the words? What will become of the incredible richness of a two-thousand-year-old continuity of liturgy?

Sherril and the girls returned to New York before I did; she had a summer teaching job at the New School to get back to, and I had to stay to take my final exams. On my last Shabbat in Jerusalem I walked to the Kotel. We had come here only occasionally during this year, a far less romantic time than our first visit had been, one in which we had been trying out real life in Jerusalem. The city was no longer a romantic fantasy to us. The Kotel was like the Statue of Liberty to New Yorkers; a comfortable icon we never visited. Still, on this Shabbat, I decided to go. Who knew if or when I would ever return? I realized as soon as I approached the wall that for all my supposed sophistication, I still had the feeling that the men in their black hats and black coats praying there were the real Jews and I was not. I joined a minyan at one of the tables in the plaza, which was being led by a tall Chasid about my age. At first I felt the same sense of intimidation that I had always felt from such men, but I had been studying Hebrew for three years now and it was soon apparent to me that he was butchering the service, stumbling over every word and pronouncing most of them incorrectly. Suddenly the scales fell from my eyes and I realized that I knew him from Sproul Plaza in Berkeley! The long ponytail that he used to wear then had migrated around the side of his head and had become sidelocks.

He was a middle-class Jewish kid from New Jersey. Sixteen years ago he had been pretending to be a native American; now he was pretending to be a Chasid, but it was all the same thing. It was *avodah zarah*, the worship of the exotic, the urge to be something other than what you are, the urge to run away from your actual circumstances, from your real experience. I recognized this because the same impulse was partly responsible for my involvement in Buddhism. I had loved dressing up in robes, I had loved the drums, the gongs, the little bells, all the exotic ritualized bowing. Now I realized that it was possible to practice avodah zarah in a Jewish context just as easily.

I went back to our apartment and began to pack. Toward evening, I walked out on the hillside opposite our building and looked out at the golden dome rising above the Old City. A Bedouin shepherd was following his herd of goats, counting them by placing stones into a little leather pouch called a *tsaror*. Every time a kid was born, he would add a stone, and when one died, he would take one out. People often ask me why it is the custom after visiting a grave to put a stone on the headstone. When they do, I always think of this shepherd, because part of the prayer that is said at a grave is *tsaror b'tsaror ha chaim*, bound up in the bond of life.

Shortly before Sherril and the girls left, we had rented a car, and one day we had gotten lost and found ourselves in the Arab village looking up at our apartment complex. From that perspective, we could see how the buildings dominated the hillside. We had been looking out of a picture window from a huge twentieth-century monolith onto a seventh-century arabesque idyll. The Palestinians, I now realized, had been looking up, helplessly, at the encroaching beast of the twentieth century, a strange and monstrous civilization that had suddenly appeared in their land without regard for them. There was a Palestinian girls' school in the Arab village, and the girls had always practiced their English on us, somehow knowing that we were Americans, but recently they had stopped speaking to us, and the Palestinian children had started throwing rocks at the children going out to recess in Hannah's kindergarten class. A few weeks before, hundreds of Palestinian prisoners had been released in exchange for two Israeli pilots captured in Lebanon. They were greeted in their villages as returning heroes, which infuriated the Israelis, whose friends and loved ones the Palestinians had been accused of murdering. There was a new tension in the air, and fights began to erupt on the streets, fights that would eventually grow into the Intifada.

Now the shepherd looked at me with suspicion. I turned for one last time in the direction of the Western Wall, trying to get a fix on where I was. The tinkling of the little goats' bells receded over the side of the hill. I stepped backward and then moved forward to address the King, to enter the nexus point between myself and others. If I was not for myself, who would be for me? And if I was only for myself, what was I? And if not now, when?

## 34 SERVICE

The first great chancellor of the Jewish Theological Seminary was Solomon Schecter. He made the seminary into a world-class center of Jewish scholarship. Around the turn of the century, he was on a tour of the ancient Rambam Synagogue in Cairo, which had not had a congregation for many years, and was shown the *genizah,* a place, often a bin in the wall of a synagogue, where books or papers bearing the name of God are discarded. According to Jewish law, the name of God must never be haphazardly destroyed, so these books and papers are stored in genizahs until enough have accumulated to be buried. Sometimes they are buried in caskets like human beings, and sometimes they are buried with rabbis and scholars. After Zayde Isaac's funeral, they wheeled his casket down the streets of Borough Park, and men came out of all the little yeshivas and synagogues with worn-out Torahs and prayer books and put them in his coffin.

The Cairo Genizah was full of old scrolls and fragments of scrolls, so when Solomon Schecter saw it, he reached in to see what was inside and pulled one out. He quickly realized that he was holding in his hand a version of the Book of Esther that we didn't know existed, and he happened to be one of the few people on earth who knew enough to recognize it. Then he reached back into the genizah to see what else he could find. This genizah had not been emptied for thousands of years, and during this time, much of Jewish literature had been destroyed because of the widespread persecution of the Jews. We knew that great poetry had been written during the Middle Ages, the golden age in Spain, by Ibn Gabriel, Yehudah Halevi, Ibn Ezra, and Shmuel Hanagid, for example, but no one had ever seen it. Now Solomon Schecter began to pull all this lost poetry out of the Cairo Genizah, which turned out to be as great as it had been reputed to be. Next he pulled out different versions of biblical books, Talmudic manuscripts, and interpretations of the Talmud that had never been seen before.

Many of the manuscripts were practically intact. He sent some of the material to Cambridge University, where he had come from, but many he brought to the Jewish Theological Seminary when he became its chancellor. During his tenure at the seminary, a whole generation of Jewish scholars would make their reputations by piecing together fragments of the Cairo Genizah. Graduate students at JTS are still writing theses on how to piece together these fragments, which are stored in envelopes and housed in a temperature-controlled room on the top floor of the seminary library.

Among the constellation of scholars who came to the semi-nary was Louis Finkelstein. He became the next chancellor after Solomon Schecter. He was an aggressive, powerful, and successful leader. He was also a leading historian of the rabbinic period, and he maintained the seminary as the world center for Jewish scholarship, but his greatest contribution was that he brought the seminary into the mainstream of American reli-gious and political life. He is famous for having said, "You can't be an American rabbi unless you know baseball."

When I arrived at the seminary, Finkelstein was in his late eighties and so feeble it was difficult for him to leave his apart-ment, so a Torah was brought to him and a minyan was held there on holidays and Shabbat, and this is where we went for services after we returned from Israel. There was an old-world European flavor to the services at Finkelstein's. The furniture was old, with the springs popping through. I became the gab-bai, and one of my duties was to pick Louis Finkelstein up out of his seat at those times in the service when it was required that one stand, since he was too weak to stand on his own and too stubborn not to stand at these times. His apartment was on Riverside Drive overlooking the Hudson River. It had not been painted in many years, and shards of paint wafted from the ceiling. Clearly the apartment would have been impossible to paint, as it was stuffed with too many books to move. They were in floor-to-ceiling bookcases on all the walls, and stacks of books higher than my head were piled up all over the floor. Sometimes when I was davening there, my eye would light on an interesting title—a wonderful book I'd never seen or even heard of before—and I'd pull it out of one of the stacks sur-rounding me and start to read it on the spot.

No one ever gave a sermon at these services; only once did

Finkelstein himself give a very short talk. This was at sundown on the Saturday afternoon between Rosh Hashana and Yom Kippur. Finkelstein talked about the description in *Mishna Yoma* of the elaborate preparations the High Priest had to make before he could enter the Holy of Holies in the Great Temple on the day of Yom Kippur. He had to study diligently to make sure he did everything correctly there, and he had to undergo a rigorous course of ritual purification. If he entered the Holy of Holies in an impure state, or if he made the slightest mistake, he would die and Israel would be doomed. According to the *Mishna*, just before he entered the Holy of Holies, the High Priest wept.

"Why does he weep?" Finkelstein asked. "There are many explanations posited by the rabbis in the Talmud," Finkelstein explained, and he went on to enumerate them. He was sitting in the window, and as he spoke, the sun began to sink behind him. Suddenly, the slanting rays of sunlight illuminated the framed portrait on the wall of Dr. Finkelstein's beautiful wife. She had left him years ago to become a Christian Scientist.

The sky outside now began to turn red, and a red glow began to fill the room. Dr. Finkelstein was a completely white person—his skin was white, his shirt was white, and he had a long white beard, but now he was turning red with the sunset. "Why does the High Priest weep before he goes into the Holy of Holies?" Dr. Finkelstein asked again. "The answer is simple," he said. Now he was turning magenta with the sunset, now purple. "He weeps because he is afraid. He is afraid that when he enters the Holy of Holies, God will take him. He weeps because he is afraid of dying."

These were my first High Holidays since we had returned from Israel, my sixth since I had started practicing Judaism. I had been studying the liturgy intensively for four years now and I was beginning to know something about it. I knew the structure of the service and I knew the liturgical poems and the historical circumstances out of which they had arisen, from the Talmud through medieval poetry. The intensity of my studies had deepened my connection to the prayers. At the seminary most people would talk about prayer only from an intellectual point of view, and there were few conversations about the emotional or spiritual side, which would trouble me. Still, really knowing the prayers did have a spiritual impact. It was like knowing the names of birds and flowers. It made you more intimate with them; it made them more accessible to you. That year, for the first time, every word of the High Holiday services was working for me. Every word took me to a particular place in the great three-thousand-year-old stream of Jewish spirituality. Every word was heartbreaking. For the first time, I was experiencing the High Holidays in their full perfection. As I realized this, I knew also that precisely because of that perfection, this experience was probably over for me. I would never simply pray again. Next year I would, most likely, have a student pulpit, and it would be my job to facilitate the services for others. As Finkelstein spoke of how the High Priest wept, I felt the tears welling up in my own eyes, for all this perfection, all this beauty, that would soon come to an end.

We were now out of money, and I had to get a job. I applied for a student pulpit. I was only going to do it in order to earn enough money to make it through rabbinical school. Although the desire to become a pulpit rabbi had been the original impetus for coming to the seminary, rabbinical school had disabused me of that notion. There was enormous disdain for pulpit rabbis at the seminary. The life of a pulpit rabbi was seen as a life of compromise. Outside of the seminary community, out in the field, it wasn't possible to live the rigorously observant life that everyone lived inside it. People, and even some rabbis, drove to the synagogue and used electricity on the Sabbath. Moreover, the only teaching a pulpit rabbi could do was perforce at a low level, the level of congregants: simple explications of the Torah, but little or no Talmud, much less the intricate beauty of the Talmudic and biblical commentaries. When I first discovered how much I loved studying, I decided that I would pursue a career in academia. Then, when I did my internship at Sloan Kettering, I decided that I would be a chaplain. Both these paths would allow me to stay in the seminary community. I would just do a little pulpit work now in order to get by.

The first pulpit work I found was in Bridgeton, New Jersey. To get there, I had to take the train to Philadelphia, then a bus south through the Pine Barrens, almost all the way down to the Delaware River, and then transfer to another bus that took me across town where a member of the congregation was waiting to pick me up. The scheduling was very tight, because it was December, when dark comes early. Once it was dark, it would be Shabbat, and I wouldn't be able to travel. But I arrived in good time and the man who met me drove me to the rabbi's empty house. He was very friendly, telling me what a fine place the town was, what a good place to bring a family to. It was an old farming community, depressed now because of the decline of independent farming in New Jersey. The Jewish community of shopkeepers and professionals had once been vibrant, but it, too, was shrinking, and they hadn't had a full-time rabbi for over a year. This man was obviously courting me, encouraging me to consider coming there on a regular basis, but he said that if I did, I would have to get a car because it was too hard for him to come get me at the bus. After showing me to the empty house, he went back to work, leaving me with directions for how to walk to his house, where I was invited for Shabbat dinner later.

I sat down at the little table in the kitchen and went over the sermon I had prepared for that weekend. It began with the question of why we light eight lights at Hanukkah, one for each night of the holiday. According to the Talmud, when the Jews reclaimed the Great Temple from the Assyrians, there was only enough oil to burn for one night, but miraculously, it lasted for eight nights. But as the rabbis pointed out, this only made seven nights of miracles. Since there was enough oil left for one night, the first night wasn't a miracle. So why, they asked, do we light candles for eight nights? Why do we celebrate eight nights of miracles? There were many theories to explain this in the Talmud, but the mystery was finally solved by Shaul Lieberman who, poring over an early version of the Talmud found in the Cairo Genizah, discovered that what was actually said was that there was *not even* enough oil for one night. The flame had flared up out of practically nothing. So not only were there really eight nights of the miracle, but the miracle was greater in kind as well. It wasn't just the beating of great odds; it was the renewal of the Jewish spirit out of nothing at all. Then I was going to tell the Jews of Bridgeton how the same thing had happened to me, how the flame of my Judaism had flared up out of absolutely nothing when I was sitting in a Buddhist monastery in California.

It was now way past dark and time for me to walk to my hosts' house for dinner. Though somewhat dilapidated, Bridgeton seemed to be a town with integrity. Old Victorians and tall trees, now bare, lined the streets. As I walked I noticed, to my surprise, that almost every house had a menorah burning in the window. Were there so many Jews in Bridgeton? Then I realized that these weren't actually menorahs but candelabras—this farming town's old-fashioned traditional Christmas lights. How lovely they were, and how universal, I thought, was this urge for light at this, the darkest time of the year.

My hosts' house was a pleasant though unremarkable middle-class house. The husband was a businessman. The wife took my coat, and while she was hospitable, I could tell she felt somewhat put upon to have me to dinner. Apparently, theirs was one of the few houses within walking distance of both the rabbi's house and the synagogue, and since I didn't drive on the Sabbath, there was no other house I could go to for dinner. Their divorced daughter was in the living room with her two young children, who seemed a bit out of control. I could sense some tension between the daughter and her parents. Suddenly, the husband said, "Now that you're here, we can light the candles," and he nodded to his daughter. She put a scrap of lace on her head, stepped up to the silver candlesticks set out on a small table, and struck a match.

I was horrified, because it had already been dark for hours, and therefore it had already been Shabbat for hours. By the sensibility that prevailed at the seminary, it was a desecration of the Shabbat to make a fire after dark. Candle-lighting time is always twenty minutes before sunset, to make extra sure that you don't violate the Shabbat. What these people were about to do seemed to me an abomination.

The match touched the wicks and the flames flared up. The daughter circled her hands about the flames. Then she covered her eyes with her fingers and said the blessing. I closed my eyes, also. When I did, I realized, to my surprise, that a feeling of pure holiness was filling the room. The tension between the daughter and her parents and between me and my hosts was melting away.

Harmony and peace descended. When I opened my eyes, there was the Shabbat table set with a gleaming white cloth, china, and silver. The flowers in the bouquet on the mantel bent forward and opened. The candles flickered then, shooting flames through the cut-glass decanter into the red wine in the kiddush cup. It was an old silver cup, dented and polished to a high sheen until it reflected everything at the table, all of us in the room, and the whole world in which we floated.

Louis Finkelstein had once said, "Judaism is very difficult. It demands more of its lay people than most religions demand from their priests. Many people complain that today's Jews don't do enough, that they aren't observant enough. But I think it's a real miracle that they do anything at all. After all, who's holding a gun to their heads?" I stood now in the presence of that miracle. The members of the family opened their eyes. They said "Shabbat Shalom" to each other and kissed each other, and we all went to our places at the table.

WHY THE MESSIAH DOESN'T COME

Bridgeton was a once-a-month pulpit. I needed more steady work, and when a small synagogue in Monroe, New York, advertised for a weekend rabbi, I applied for the position. The name of the congregation was *Eitz Chaim,* the tree of life. The synagogue was in the country, in the middle of a meadow. After my interview, I walked up the hill behind it. When I turned around and looked down at it, I saw it was shimmering and aglow with fiery light. Because of this vision, I was sure that I was meant to come to this place to be their rabbi. They offered me the job, which I took gladly, and we bought a tiny used Toyota to commute in. Our girls loved going to the country on the weekends. They loved climbing trees and hiding in the grasses. Often kids from the congregation would stay to play with them after services on Saturday afternoons. We were all glad to be out of the city with all its misery. When I stood davening on the bimah, I could see the wind in the trees shimmering and dancing, and I began to feel happy. In Monroe I began to remember why I had wanted to be a rabbi in the first place. It was a tremendous privilege to have such an intimate connection with so many souls. I came to know each family's sorrows and joys, and this was a constant reminder to me that each human life is utterly sacred.

The girls went to Sunday school in Monroe on Sunday mornings before we headed back down to the city. They didn't need to, because they went to a Hebrew day school in Manhattan, but it was another way for them to socialize with the youngsters in the congregation. One week their teacher assigned each student to make a *tzedakah* report, which the kids presented at a Friday night service.

"Tzedakah is the Hebrew word for charity," a little boy in a bow tie began. Then, one by one, the children described how they had collected money for the American Heart Association or the Cancer Society or some other charity. Then Hannah, who was seven, read from her report.

"I want to talk about a girl named Tina," Hannah said. Because we lived in New York City, Hannah saw beggars every time she left the house. Tina was a young girl—maybe sixteen—whom we often saw in our neighborhood. She always asked me for three dollars, saying that was what she needed to get an identity card, and Hannah always made me give it to her. One day after seeing Tina on the street, Hannah made me take her back upstairs to get her little purse full of pennies, and she brought it back down to the street and gave Tina half. "Tina and I are friends," Hannah said.

I remembered seeing Tina one day with a hospital bracelet on. "They put me in the hospital because I peed on my leg and I got all these sores," she said to Hannah. "Please spare me three dollars so I can get me my identity card."

Hannah's report was rather shocking to the other kids. Living in a suburb, they never saw homeless people, but we could never leave our apartment without being besieged by dozens of them, many caked with dirt and some raving.

It was always a struggle to get out of the city on Friday afternoons, and as soon as we would get to Monroe the phone would start ringing off the hook, which never left me enough time to prepare for services on Friday night. I'd always tell a story to the kids then.

Judaism has a rich culture of folktales from which to draw. For this particular week I had found one by I. L. Peretz. In the story, Eliahu Hanavi, Elijah the Prophet, comes to bring seven years' good luck to a man and his wife. He comes in disguise— as he always does—this time in a green hunting suit. According to legend, Eliahu is the only mortal who has ever left this earth without dying. He went up to heaven in a chariot of fire, and so he is able to come back down to earth and bring humans information about God. There are many stories in the Talmud about Eliahu Hanavi appearing and telling humans what God thinks about various subjects. Throughout Jewish history he has been reappearing in different places and in different guises, unrecognized, and usually when people are in desperate need.

Since he is always in disguise, anyone, any stranger, any homeless person, might be Eliahu Hanavi. It is said that he is the harbinger of the messiah, and the implications of this are that the way we treat strangers, even the most debased and helpless, has an impact on the coming of the messiah.

As I was trying to memorize this fairy tale to tell to the kids at the service later, the phone rang. The man on the line identified himself as a Seventh Day Adventist. He said they had found a wandering Jew and didn't know what to do with him. "He's an old man," the man on the phone said. "He was hitch-hiking. But he says he's a religious Jew and doesn't want to travel on the Sabbath."

Annoyed because of the lateness of the hour, I put on my coat and picked up my wallet, checkbook, and keys. Then I went down to the church where I found an old man in a green camouflage suit carrying a bedroll. I took him to a motel and got him a room for the night, then gave him money to eat at the restaurant nearby.

"You should have brought him back with you," Hannah said when I came back and told the family what had happened. "He could have slept in the schoolroom. He could have had dinner with us."

"But there's a big bar mitzvah here tomorrow," I told her. "I don't think the people would like to have a homeless man crashing their party."

"Maybe the homeless man is Eliahu Hanavi," Hannah said later that evening after she had heard me tell the Peretz story. "You said he was wearing a green hunting suit. Maybe he was Elijah the Prophet. You should have treated him better."

Although I loved the work, the pay at Monroe was extremely low, which meant I had to get another job to supplement our income. I became a part-time chaplain for a hospice in the Bronx. The Toyota was useful for commuting to this job, too, but it had also introduced a major complication into our life, the nightmare of alternate-side-of-the-street parking.

Every other day we had to double-park our car across the street for a few hours for street cleaning. As soon as the time was up, we had to race our car back across the street in order to get a parking space. If we missed by even a few seconds, all the parking spaces would be gone and we'd have to circle the block like the Flying Dutchman, waiting for someone to pull out, but no one ever would.

A parking space in Manhattan was simply too valuable a commodity to give up, and very few things were worth the risk of losing one. Gainful employment was difficult under these circumstances. One had to always be on the alert for the critical hours when the laws of the parking universe were suspended and everything was at risk. I found myself arranging my whole life around alternate-side-of-the-street parking. My work at the hospice in the Bronx, for example, was meticulously timed to fit into this schedule. I would leave for the Bronx exactly as these critical hours were beginning and return just in time to get my space back.

One day I drove up to Co-op City in the Bronx to visit an old couple in the hospice program. They were both Holocaust survivors and seldom wanted to talk, so I figured I could see them and one other client who was an in-patient and still make it back in time to get a parking space. But when I got to their apartment, they started talking about the Holocaust for the first time. It was a real breakthrough, as if the floodgates had opened. They talked on and on, and it seemed to be very healing for them, which I was very happy about. But as the minutes sped by I began to wonder if I was going to make it back in time to get my parking space, since I still had one other client to visit. When I finally was able to disengage myself from the old couple, I rushed to the in-patient facility, praying that the client I was scheduled to see wouldn't be there when I arrived. Then I could race back home and park, and nothing would be lost—when it suddenly hit me. "Do you realize what you're praying for?" I asked myself. "There is only one reason he wouldn't be there when you get there—and that is that he'd be dead. You're praying that somebody should be dead so that you can get a parking space." I pulled up to the hospital and ran inside, this time praying fervently that I would find my client alive.

He was, though barely. I stayed with him a long time and we had a good conversation. I wondered what other foolish imaginary needs held me in their thrall, pulled me out of the present moment, and left me insensitive to the suffering of others. When I finally got back to my neighborhood, there was nowhere to park.

## 36 DEATH

My second year in Monroe I took over the running of the religious school, and now I traveled up to Monroe on Tuesdays as well as weekends and holidays. But we needed even more money to live, so I quit the hospice in the Bronx and took on a more substantial position as chaplain of the Jacob Perlow Hospice, which was just starting up at Beth Israel Hospital in lower Manhattan.

The manager of the hospice had previously had the same job at a Catholic hospital, right across the street, and I asked her once if there was a difference between a Catholic and a Jewish hospice. "The Jewish patients are much more aggressive consumers," she told me. "The Catholic patients always do what you tell them to do, but the Jews are always asking for second opinions and asking you to make exceptions to the rules for them." When she told me this, I realized that this behavior came out of a halachic tradition. According to the halacha, you had a sacred obligation to find the best medical treatment you could and to follow through on it.

The other important halachic tenet is to choose life at all cost. And because Jewish law placed such a high premium on preserving life, Jews were very late coming to hospice, which required giving up on efforts to prolong life. The vast sea of the Talmud, the twenty-four immense volumes filled with law and lore, are almost entirely devoted to this life and say very little about what happens after, and what little it says is ambiguous.

One of my first clients at the hospice, Sam Greenblatt, was an old Jewish man who had spent his life manufacturing clothing and living with his wife in a small apartment on the East Side, where I went to visit him. Sam and his wife had married very late and had had no children. Now they were both in their eighties and Sam was dying. He was a small man and his cancer had made him gaunt and had drawn his white skin tightly over his bald skull. He asked me questions all the time, impossible questions: "Why do I have to keep living? Why doesn't God just take me?" Although there were no answers to these questions, I felt somehow responsible for answering them anyway. It took me a long time to realize that it wasn't my job to answer such questions, only to listen to them, and the truth is, I never did learn it completely; I would have to keep learning it over and over again.

One day, Sam asked me another unanswerable question: "What's going to happen after I die?"

"Judaism has many answers to this question," I told him, "but many of these answers cancel each other out." What I didn't tell him was that in the Bible, there is a very literal belief that life goes on through our descendants, so that dying childless was the ultimate catastrophe. It meant that death was permanent, that your life was cut off forever. It was a catastrophe they tried to circumvent with a legalism called *yibum*, leverate marriage. According to this, if a man died without offspring, his brother was obliged to take his widow in marriage, and their offspring was considered to be the child of the dead man. If the brother refused to fulfill this obligation, he had to undergo a ritual of humiliation called *halitzah*, which entailed taking off his shoes and waving them over his head at the gates of the city when everyone was gathered there. Then the obligation of yibum fell to the next nearest of kin. Such were the lengths to which the ancient Israelites went to keep a soul "alive."

This was the biblical view, but I didn't dwell on it, given Sam's childlessness. Instead, I hurried on to what the prophets said in the latter pages of the Bible—that we would all come back to life at the end of days, that we would sleep and then be resurrected in our bodies at the end of time. That is why Jews don't do cremation or autopsies, unless absolutely necessary. In the Talmud we get the idea of the "World to Come" for the first time, a counterworld where all the inconsistencies of this life are resolved, where virtue is finally rewarded and evil punished, and where the righteous enjoy the light stored up for them since the beginning of time. The rabbis made a few feeble attempts to reconcile these two disparate ideas—the resurrection of the dead and the World to Come—but clearly, they don't go together, nor do they go with the idea of reincarnation, which is also found in the Jewish tradition, especially in its mystical branches, Kabbalah and Chasidut, where it's called *Gilgul Hanefesh*, the rolling of souls.

"So these are the things our tradition says about what happens after death," I said, "and your guess is as good as mine about what's going to happen. In fact, your guess is a lot better than mine, Sam. You're a lot closer. What do you think is going to happen?"

Sam looked stunned. It hadn't occurred to him that he was already beginning to experience directly what it meant to die. Then a calm came over his face and he closed his eyes in concentration. "I feel like I'm standing on the edge of a great sea," he said.

Once when I was visiting patients at the hospice a family came into the waiting room to talk with me. "We can't get our father to talk about the fact that he's dying," they said, "and we don't know what to do about it."

"Listen very carefully to what he's saying," I suggested. "If he gives you an opening, if it seems like he's trying to talk about the fact that he's dying, ask a leading question. If he wants to talk about it, he'll take your lead. If not, let him be. Denial can be healthy. It can be like a scab. If you rip it off too early, it can make you sick. On the other hand, you don't want to give people the message that what they're going through is so horrifying that you don't want to even talk about it."

They said, "Could you come into his room and show us what you mean?"

I said, "Sure." We went into the room.

"I'm so scared," the man said, as soon as he saw us.

"Don't be scared," the family said, in unison. "You've got nothing to be scared about!" But their faces were clouded over with terror.

"What are you scared of?" I asked him.

"I'm afraid I'm going to die," he said.

"What is it about dying that frightens you?" I asked. "Is it the pain?"

"No," he said. "It's not the pain. It's just not *being* anymore. Being nothing."

So I said, "I see how that could be really scary."

Now the family began to crowd in on him, arraying themselves all around his bed. They stroked his gray hair and rubbed his thin shoulders and kissed the pale white skin of his brow. I could see relief welling up in him. The lines on his face began to relax, and his lips, so taut and tense a few moments before, were now opening into a contented smile. He felt better, partly because he had been able to express his great terror, but much more because with his family now pressing close to him, he felt sure he would not, in fact, disappear into nothingness but would continue in them.

I began to notice that people tended to die exactly the way they had lived. There was one woman who was always finding excuses for the hospice team not to visit her. She was obese and had spent a lifetime avoiding people, telling herself that the situation was temporary, that she would go back out into society as soon as she got her figure back. Now it made her very bitter to know that she was going to die fat.

Another man, similarly, had always planned to finish his life's work, a long scholarly book, but he had never quite gotten around to it. When he told me this, I thought in fear of my own unfinished book, the book about my family. I had spent months in Sebastopol transcribing the tapes and rendering the material. I was hundreds of pages into it, but nowhere near completion. I had put it aside when I went to rabbinical school, but realistically, I wondered if I ever would have time to finish it, if this would end up being the tragedy of my life, too.

This man, whose name was Martin, was a man of ideas, a Jewish intellectual with a beautiful wife from Nebraska twenty years his junior. He had spent his life in public relations, always successful but moving frequently from job to job, working for one firm, succeeding brilliantly, starting one on his own, and then somehow, letting that go, too—always doing distinguished work but never quite finishing it. His great unfinished work was a philosophical meditation in which he asked all the deepest questions. He asked them of me when I came to visit him. He would also ask me questions about his own death. What would happen to him, he wanted to know. What would happen to his wife? But he would withdraw from these questions almost as soon as he had asked them. "I'm too tired to talk about this now," he would say, or he would just change the subject and start making small talk. His book was a series of brilliant fragments, disconnected, going nowhere, but brilliant in each of its particulars.

When his wife realized she couldn't be buried next to him because she wasn't Jewish, she decided she wanted to convert, but only on her terms. She wasn't willing to go to the mikvah, she wasn't willing to study, she wasn't willing to be interrogated by rabbis. "I've been married to a Jewish man for forty years," she said. "That ought to be enough." I said I couldn't convert her under those circumstances, so she found a rabbi who would, an Orthodox rabbi who agreed to convert her for a large sum of money and no other requirements. She did, however, trick me into participating in her conversion ceremony. Since there was no mikvah involved, it took place in her apartment, in Martin's bedroom. She asked me to come by one day. When I arrived, I found a rabbi already there and the ceremony about to begin. The rabbi, who was perfectly aware of how wrong it was to be doing what he was doing, was noticeably upset to see me, and I did my best to make him as uncomfortable as I possibly could, but I did nothing to show my disapproval to the family. Afterward, Martin vacillated between being tremendously pleased with his wife's conversion and seeming to understand that it had been meaningless. A few days before his death, he called me into his room. "I've been trying to write all my life, and my life's been a waste of time," he said.

"Do you really feel as if your life's been a waste of time?" I asked.

"I'm too tired to talk about it now," he said. He died before he had a chance to speak again.

I noticed that people near death were often able to express the essence of their lives in a single heartbreaking sentence. Their statements reminded me of the questions we were always striving to formulate at Tasajara: "Why am I so alone?" When finally letting go of their denial of death, people let go of their denial of life as well, and they began to see their lives with unforgiving clarity.

"I married the wrong man, and I lived without love all my life," Helen told me from the hospital bed that had been set up in the middle of her living room. Her husband, hard of hearing and half mad, was standing a few yards away. I prayed that he hadn't heard her, but I was never sure if he had or not. The living room was a malodorous chaos, a perfect picture of the growing disorder in her husband's mind. He had once been a good provider, a civil service engineer, and they had lived in this apartment in the garment workers' union co-op on the Lower West Side since they had been married. They had one daughter, now estranged from her parents, especially her father. The disorder of the apartment was one of the issues between them. She felt humiliated to bring her friends there, to show them the insanity in which her parents lived. Her father, on the other

235

hand, was terribly hurt that she never brought her friends to see him, a conflict now centered around her new boyfriend. She was well into her forties and had never married, partly, she believed, because she'd been so crippled by her relationship with her parents. She was finally serious about someone, more serious than she'd ever been before, but she was terrified to bring him to her parents' house, and they were furious with her for never having brought him.

When the mother died, the crisis became, where would the shiva be. The daughter couldn't bring her fiancé to this humiliating mess of an apartment. She was sure it would end the relationship. She would have the shiva at her place. But the father refused. "We must have it here," he said. "This is where she lived, and this is where she died. There's something terribly wrong if a daughter can't come to her parents' apartment for her own mother's shiva."

"Look," I told the daughter. "We'll arrange to have the place cleaned up. We'll hire a cleaning service. We'll clean the place up the best we can, and we'll have the shiva here. Under the circumstances, I'm afraid it's the best we can do." Reluctantly, and with terror in her eyes, she agreed.

The man from the cleaning service arrived at nine the next morning. For three hours it was an exercise in futility. These people had never thrown anything away. Sheets covered all the furniture, and piled on top of the sheets were shopping bags full of unopened mail and newspapers as well as unopened packages of paper towels and toilet paper piled in heaps on top of each other. The carpet was scattered with layers of foul-smelling throw rugs from the spills from the bedpans used by the dying woman. The man from the cleaning service moved bits of this immense mess from one part of the apartment to the other, and at twelve o'clock, he gave up. The half-crazy old man slumped in his chair, his head in his hands. I had a terrible headache and a feeling of black despair. My plan wasn't working. The daughter was going to bring her fiancé into a trap, the terrible mess that would reveal the ugly chaos at the secret heart of her family's life and end her chances with him for good.

"I'm going to have to call for reinforcements," the man from the cleaning service said. Within the hour, a wiry black man in his sixties arrived. His name was Esau. Esau started sprinting around the apartment like a dervish. I watched in wonder as slowly but surely the original apartment began to be uncovered. Underneath the bags, sheets, and throw rugs was the most beautiful apartment I had ever seen. The furniture was handsome, the Persian rug priceless, and the art on the walls magnificent. After all the debris had been cleared away, Esau got out a bottle of furniture polish and went to work on every wood surface in the place—the wainscoting on the walls, the big oak surface of the dining room table, the legs of the antique sofa and chairs in the living room. The place began to shine. It was in perfect order, perfectly beautiful, suffused with soft warm radiance. It reflected the order and grace that had prevailed in the family before the old man's mind had begun to go. I looked at my watch. Dusk was beginning to fall. It was getting dark. I suddenly realized that it was the first night of Hanukkah. I had just witnessed the miracle of Hanukkah, the miraculous rebuilding of the house, the miracle of light arising out of nothing in the darkest time of year. The daughter came to the shiva, bringing the fiancé. "Rabbi, I think I like that boy," the old man told me.

Another client, Morris, was lousy with rabbis. He remained close with the rabbi he'd grown up with in Brooklyn, and the

237

two rabbis from the Lincoln Square Synagogue, which he had helped make into the shining success of Modern Orthodoxy, also came to see him, as did the rabbi of the synagogue he had helped to found after he had become dissatisfied with Lincoln Square, and his brother-in-law, a prominent Conservative rabbi from Chicago, and now me, the rabbi of the hospice he had just joined. Whenever I went to see him, I had to stand on a line of rabbis, but none of us was doing him any good.

Morris's terror at his impending death was so intense that almost every day he imagined he was dying of a heart attack, or a stroke, and demanded to be taken off to emergency rooms all over the city. He had to keep changing emergency rooms, because one by one they each became tired of his hypochondria and refused to take him in anymore. On one such occasion he called me from the emergency room of Columbia Presbyterian, where he had been taken in an ambulance with an imaginary heart attack. This was his third such visit to Presbyterian that week, and shortly after I arrived, they became so exasperated with him that they put him out in the street in his stocking feet. It was snowing, hard. I hailed a cab and wrapped his freezing feet in my scarf. I understood how the doctors felt. He exasperated me, too. I found myself wanting to say to him, "What are you whining about?" forgetting that he really was dying of cancer.

One day he called an ambulance and had it rush him to the emergency room at Roosevelt Hospital, where he fell into a deep coma. This time he wasn't faking. Roosevelt was between my apartment and the hospice, so I would stop over every morning on my way to work to sit with him, to pray for him, to feel his presence as a human being, each morning perhaps for the last time. On the fifth such morning, I found him sitting up in bed, wide awake. I could see from across the room that there was something strange about him. As I came closer I saw what it was. He was weeping, and he was completely drenched in his own tears. His pajamas and his bedclothes were sopping wet. I had never seen anyone weep like this before. "Morris, why are you weeping?" I said, when I got to his side.

"Four days ago, I found myself slipping into what I was sure was my final coma, and now, look at this!" he said, and then he swept his arm across the room like a magic wand. It was a big ward room, an old room, with eight or ten beds and high vaulting windows that stretched all the way up to the ceiling. Following the sweep of his arm, I could see what he was seeing: large shafts of sunlight streamed in through the windows, and dust motes spun in spirals up and down, like galaxies dancing. Nurses glided silently across the linoleum floors like angels.

Years later, I would read about an almost identical scene in the Talmud and would understand it instantly because of Morris and his weeping. In this scene, Rabbi Eliezer is dying, and Rabbi Yohanan comes to visit him. Eliezer is weeping, profusely, and Yohanan demands to know why. "Is it because you failed to learn enough Torah? Don't worry, it doesn't matter how much or how little you learned, only how sincere you were in your studies," Yohanan says.

"That's not why I'm weeping," Eliezer replies.

"Is it because you were poor all your life? " Yohanan asks. "How can you complain about that? You had Torah, and not everyone gets to eat at two tables."

"That's not why I'm weeping, either," Eliezer answers.

"Is it because of the children you lost?" Yohanan says. "How can you complain about that? I lost ten children," Yohanan says, pointing to the bone of his tenth son, which he wore around his neck as a talisman.

"That's not why I'm weeping, either," Eliezer replies.

"Then why are you weeping?" Yohanan says, indicating a willingness to listen for the first time.

"I'm weeping *l'chol hai shufra d'balai d'afra:* for all this perfection which is fading into the earth, for the perfection of human experience which we never seem able to apprehend until the moment before we lose it."

Morris reached up and grabbed my hand with frightening intensity. "Rabbi," he said, "this is religion." He swept his arm around the room again. I assumed he meant that all that time with all those rabbis, including me, was not religion, next to this direct experience of the sacred in the world, and, of course, he was right. He died a few hours later, at peace with himself and the world. I think of him all the time.

It was a rule of hospice that patients had to acknowledge that they were dying in order to be admitted to the program, but we bent the rules for one woman who didn't seem to be in control of her faculties. We didn't think she was capable of processing the information, and we were wary of frightening her because she was quite volatile. She was Hungarian, laden with jewelry, the rooms of her apartment heavy with perfume. Her floors were covered with many vividly patterned Oriental rugs with mad swirling shapes. She had a certain innate elegance to her, but at the same time she was like a little child, helpless. Her doctor was also European. He believed that hope was very important in the healing process, and that no one should tell her of the severity of her illness. Therefore, she was left to process the fact that she was dying unconsciously.

One day she told me that she had had a dream she wanted to tell me about. In the dream, someone is writing on a white sheet of paper, and the paper turns black. Then the fingers of the hand that is writing turn black, and then the hand. And the arm—the arm hardens into lead.

Her daughter wanted us to help her mother confront the fact that she was dying, so I asked the woman if she had any idea about what the dream might mean. "No," she said, in no uncertain terms. And she didn't care to speculate about it. The woman's Orthodox doctor thought that we on the hospice team were ghouls. In the Orthodox tradition, you don't mention death when someone is dying, the philosophy being that only God decides when someone will die, and you must never give up on people. In hospice you were not allowed to do intravenous feeding or hydration, which, after all, was just shooting sugar water into a tumor without any real medical value, but the Orthodox saw this withholding as halachicly impermissible. They thought it was comparable to starving people and therefore hastening their deaths.

One day I was in the apartment of one of my clients making a shiva call when I started to notice that I wasn't feeling very well, myself. There was a problem with the air conditioning, and the apartment was stifling. The deceased had kept cats and, fearful that they would jump out the window, he had sealed the windows shut.

I was feeling tired, but I couldn't rest because I had to drive up to Monroe to visit Joe Gibbs, one of my congregants in the hospital there, and from there go to the airport to pick up Steve, who was coming for a visit. Steve had dropped out of college after one year at Reed. Now he was living in Portland, Oregon, driving a pizza delivery truck and playing music in various bands. We were looking forward to going around to all the clubs in New York and checking out the music scene. Ever since Betty and I had broken up, I had carried tremendous guilt in my heart for what it had done to Steve, tremendous worry about how the split had affected him. For his part, he had never shown any anger toward me; he was always sweet. Sherril adored him, and his little sisters, Hannah and Malka, worshipped him. I worried about him all the time, however, especially now that he had dropped out of college and was pursuing a career creating music so avant-garde it would never be popular. He was not interested in material success, only art. He reminded me of myself before I had found my path.

But it was very difficult for me to go out to jazz clubs late at night every night. I was exhausted. One night there was a second show, which started at midnight, that Steve wanted to catch. Though it hurt me to do it, I told Steve no, I couldn't, I was just too tired.

The next day at work I found that I was having trouble standing up. I thought my back was giving out. The manager of the hospice offered me her office so I could sit down for a while. I went in and lay down on the floor. While I was lying there in pain I suddenly realized why all my hospice patients were always so anxious to die. When I got home, I crawled into bed, and Sherril took my temperature. It was 105. It was happening again.

The phone rang, and it was my mother. I heard Sherril making an excuse to get off the phone so as not to alarm her. My mother had been phoning quite often lately. She was still in a deep depression over the death of my father, though he had been dead almost five years. She dreamed about him all the time. In one such dream he begged her to come be with him on the other side, but she told him she couldn't come; she needed to stay here for the kids. I had always told her that my father wasn't really gone, that love lasts forever, that the love they had shared was so great and so powerful that it would never end. And in some very real way, it still continued.

Now, in my fevered state, these words of comfort I had offered my mother seemed to hover before me. I leaned toward them until I was so close up against them that I was looking into the spaces between the letters, which grew larger and larger. The words began to break up into little fragments. I couldn't make sense of them any longer. There was only a vast and profound emptiness.

Sherril was piling blankets on top of me. "Steve is going to take you to the emergency room at St. Luke's," I heard her say. I felt Steve lifting me up. The blankets were swaddled around me. He held me under the arms. I saw Sherril diffused in the doorway, sheltering Hannah and Malka in their pink footed-pajamas. Her hair was a radiant cloud of spun gold framing her face. "I can't come with you," she said. "I have to stay here with the girls."

## 37 TESHUVAH

The emergency room at St. Luke's was the same as it was the last time we were there: the TV up on its mountings, the Coke machines against the wall. I sat in the same cold metal chair, and there I waited all night to be seen by a doctor, in exquisite pain and shaking all over, but an endless succession of people in seemingly more dangerous condition kept being brought in and kept being taken before me—people with gunshot wounds and knives sticking out of their backs. I made Steve go home, and then, finally, I was taken in and examined by a doctor. Dawn was just breaking. "Oh, this *is* quite serious," he said, and I was taken upstairs and once again put in a room with an IV.

I had full body sepsis again, but they never did determine what caused it. Every night for two weeks I woke up with my bed soaked through with sweat and my teeth chattering. There was a crazy man in the room next to mine who kept screaming that he wanted a TV, but he didn't have any money. So I secretly arranged to pay for him to have one. The next morning I opened my eyes and saw a huge, angry-looking man standing over me. "Thanks for getting me the TV," he said. After that, I was able to get a little rest, and eventually I was able to sit up in a chair and study Torah.

The parasha for that first week was the story of Joseph. Joseph was his father Jacob's favorite, which made his eleven brothers extremely jealous. One day Joseph's brothers were in a field near Dothan tending the family flock, and Jacob sends Joseph to find them. Along the way he encounters a stranger who tells him which way to go. Bit players like this stranger are exceedingly rare in the Torah. Rashi identifies this figure and his meaning with two Hebrew words: *Malach Gabriel*, the Angel Gabriel.

No one in our life is superfluous; everyone who appears has something indispensable to teach us, without which our life could not go forward. I could think of several bit players in my own life who had utterly changed my life's course. There was the stranger who was looking for someone to sit the house in Gualala; there was Julian Harzel, who introduced me to zazen. And there were countless others. So it was with this unidentified *ish*, this man Joseph came upon in the field when he was lost. This man averted the course of Joseph's life, the life of his family, the history of his people, and the fate of that whole part of the world at that time, because all these things depended on what would happen to Joseph next, and what would happen to Joseph next could not, in fact, happen until he found his brothers in Dothan.

Why didn't the Torah just have Joseph find his brothers on his own? Because then the inevitability of what happens to him next would not have been so clear. What happens next is that Joseph's brothers throw him into a pit and leave him there for dead. Then they daub his coat with animal blood and take it back to Jacob and tell their father that Joseph has been eaten by wild animals. Only Reuven and Judah seem to understand that what they are doing is wrong, but the most they're willing to do at this point is to prevent their brothers from actually killing Joseph. They sell him to traders instead, and he is carried off to Egypt where, through a miraculous and intricate series of coincidental events, divine intervention, and just plain talent, Joseph becomes the ruler of Egypt and saves the region from a famine that would have killed everyone in it.

When Joseph's brothers come to him in Egypt for food, which he wisely had stored away in preparation for the famine, Joseph recognizes them immediately, but because he is now dressed like an Egyptian prince, they don't recognize him. Joseph brings them up on trumped-up charges of espionage, takes their brother Shimon hostage, and says they won't get him back unless they bring him their youngest brother, Benjamin. The brothers go back to tell their father what has happened.

Their father refuses to give up his youngest son. After all, he has already lost his favorite, Joseph, and now Benjamin has become almost as dear to him as Joseph had been. If he lost Benjamin, too, it would kill him. But the famine continues, and eventually the family runs out of food again, and Jacob's sons prevail on him to allow them to take Benjamin with them to Egypt to ask for food.

The brothers return to Egypt, but Joseph concocts new charges against them and seizes Benjamin. Now Judah steps forward and makes a truly noble speech in which he speaks at

great length of the pain the loss of Benjamin will cause his father, and in which he offers himself up as surety for Benjamin.
This speech breaks through Joseph's defenses, and he collapses
in tears, confessing his identity to his astonished brothers.

His brothers are terrified, of course. They think Joseph will
want to take revenge on them for having thrown him in the
pit. "Don't worry," Joseph tells them. "You may have meant me
harm, but God sent me here to save many lives."

The Torah is ambiguous, even mysterious, concerning Joseph's responses and motives in this story. Why did he con-
ceal his identify from his brothers? Was he angry at them? Was
he trying to exact revenge? Was he irrationally still afraid of his
murderous older brothers, even though now he was the King
of Egypt? Whatever his motives, his behavior has the effect of
bringing his brothers, and particularly Judah, back to the precise moral moment they had occupied when they threw him
into the pit. Now a second brother, their father's favorite, was
in danger, and their father's well-being and happiness were
once again being threatened. Would they betray both their
brother and their father again, or would they learn from their
past experience and behave differently?

When Judah places himself in jeopardy to save his brother
and his father, it is clear that he has undergone a profound
transformation. According to the Rambam, this story is the
prime example of *teshuvah gemorah*, complete repentance, of
being brought back to the exact same place where you went
astray so that you can get things right at last.

As I read Joseph's story, I thought of my own. Twice, now, I'd
collapsed during a visit from Steve. Twice, it had fallen on him
to take me to the hospital, in mortal danger of my life. What
was this all about? What mistake was I making regarding Steve?

Why did life keep bringing me back to this strange and deadly place, to the emergency room at St. Luke's hospital with its hard steel chairs, aching to the marrow from a deadly fever?

During the period when I was considering attending rabbinical school, I thought I could overcome all the difficulties—getting the money, learning Hebrew, my age—except for the one obstacle that had seemed insurmountable: leaving Steve. But then Steve came and said he wanted to go back to Berkeley for the rest of high school; Sebastopol's little country high school was boring. And Betty, who had also remarried, was now saying she wanted Steve back. So since it wasn't a question of me abandoning him, but he and Betty freely deciding on their own that he would live with her, it suddenly seemed possible to go to New York, and so we did.

But although it was possible, it was never comfortable to be that far away from him. I missed him all the time. He would come to visit, but a visit is not the same as daily life. When he was with me, we would have intense conversations in which I would try to do condensed parenting. It was killing me to have him three thousand miles away.

After an indifferent high school career, he had been accepted by Reed College. When he decided to drop out after a year, we began to argue. It bothered me that he had dropped out of school just to be a musician.

So we would argue about this, and I would say, "You have to do something that contributes to the world, that you can give yourself to completely." I was filled with guilt and frustration because I didn't seem to be able to influence him. I felt I had lost a handle on his life. But on top of the guilt and the psychological toll this was taking on me, there was also the physical fact that I was pushing it to the hilt in my life: hospice, going to

Monroe midweek for the school and weekends for the pulpit, being a full-time student—not to mention trying to meet the needs of Sherril and the girls. When Steve came, he didn't understand all this. All he wanted was for us to spend some time alone together, and the traditional vehicle for us to do this in New York was to go out late at night to hear jazz, and of course, I was too riddled with guilt to say, "Look, Steve, I'm just being torn in four directions, and I'm on the brink of exhaustion, and I simply cannot go out to listen to jazz until 2:00 A.M. every night and then get up early in the morning and go to work." So I got sick.

The first time I was sick, a big part of the trauma was that my family was back in the hospital just a few months after my father's death. I could see the pain of it in my mother's face. Shortly after my father died, when we were all trying to think of what would be good for my mother to do, my cousin Larry came down with Crohn's disease, and I took my mother to the hospital to visit him. She could tell him a lot of useful and reassuring things about the disease. So I said to her afterward, "Mom, this is what you should do now—volunteer to work with patients who have Crohn's disease. You can make a real contribution because you really connect with people, and you probably have more firsthand knowledge of Crohn's disease than anyone else on the planet."

"I've had enough of Crohn's disease, I've had enough of hospitals, I've had enough of caring for the sick to last several lifetimes," she said, and I realized what a horror her life had been. She had thrown herself into my father's and my sister's medical predicaments so wholeheartedly, reading up on their conditions so thoroughly, that the table conversations in our house always sounded like people boning up for a medical school exam, and she had visited my father and my sister and every-one else she knew who was sick so faithfully that no one had guessed how hard it was for her, how thoroughly she detested the whole business of medicine and hospitals and the people she loved being dangerously ill. So when I was hospitalized and she came to visit me in the hospital—and I was deathly ill—her anguish was fathomless.

Over and above her concern for me was her concern for her-self. Would she be stuck in this nightmare forever? Would the people she loved always be dying? And would she always be rushing to one hospital or another to be at their side?

Why were we all retracing our steps in this crazy way? Why had I chosen Steve's visit to collapse again? Why was my mother being made to relive the nightmare she had gone through with my father and sister, and now again with me? Why had I taken my father's place—frightening my mother to death, trying to shape my son's life, collapsing and threatening to die as my father had always done? What was the mechanism that seemed to have us all in its thrall? What was I supposed to learn from all of it? I hadn't the vaguest answer to any of these questions, but the sense that we were all caught in something mysterious that must, in fact, make sense somewhere, in some universe if not in this one, was abundantly clear.

When I was released from the hospital two weeks later, I told the congregation in Monroe that I just couldn't come up mid-week any more. Then, when I felt a bit stronger, I took a trip out to Portland to see what Steve's life was really like. I was gratified to discover that he truly was dedicated to his music, that he wasn't just fooling around. His band, Slack, had already cut a record, and they had begun to tour. I stopped feeling that Steve's life depended on my getting him to do what I thought he should, and I realized he was going to succeed in making his own way through the world.

That spring I was finally ordained as a rabbi, and to my surprise, the day of ordination was one of the happiest in my life. My graduation from Penn had been a stupid event that had turned into a nightmare. My family had arrived late, and my father had dropped the rest of them off while he went to park. But after he parked, he wasn't able to find them. Throughout the ceremony, I could see my mother, looking desperate, walking up and down along the top of the huge amphitheater where the graduation was being held. The whole thing meant absolutely nothing to me. It was their achievement. My parents now had a son who had graduated from an Ivy League college. It was all about them. But JTS had been *my* choice. I had succeeded at something I had wanted to do, and I was ecstatic.

The speaker at my ordination was Shimon Peres, the prime minister of Israel. I felt a certain kinship with him, having often passed him on the street when I changed buses in front of his residence the year we lived in Israel. I was one of two valedictorians, and to top everything off, when I opened the program I saw that I had won several major awards—homiletics, philosophy, and best student. My bad graduation karma was thoroughly cleansed. And now I was a rabbi.

Now I was a rabbi like my Zayde Isaac. Isaac had come to America leaving his wife and nine children back in Europe but hoping to raise enough money in America, the *goldena medina*, the land of gold, to bring them over in a short time. But he found he was barely able to support himself in America, much less save anything for them. A year passed, and he was in despair. He was beginning to think he would never see his wife and children again.

One day a friend said to him, "You should come out to the cemetery. You can always make an extra buck out there. The rich German Jews pay good money for rabbis to sing 'El Mole Rachamim.'" This is the prayer that is said for dead loved ones when people come to the cemetery to remember them.

So Isaac went to the graveyard, and as soon as he arrived, a wealthy German approached him and asked him to say "El Mole" for his dead mother, and as soon as Isaac started chanting the mournful minor notes of the prayer, he thought of his wife and his nine children who he might never see again. His eyes filled with tears and his voice began to tremble.

Afterward, the German hugged Isaac and said, "That was the greatest 'El Mole' I ever heard! Such passion! Such sincerity!" He stuffed several dollar bills into the pocket of Isaac's waistcoat. "You come back next Sunday," he said. "I have many friends in need of your services." So Isaac returned the next Sunday and every Sunday after that, and within six months' time he had made so much money singing "El Mole Rachamim" for the rich German Jews that he was able to bring his wife and nine children to America.

The first time I had said "El Mole Rachamim" in the cemetery was at my Bubbe Ida's unveiling. The unveiling of a headstone is the ceremony marking the end of the first year of mourning. I was only a second-year rabbinical student then, and I performed the unveiling awkwardly. I stayed by Bubbe's grave long after everyone else left. While I was standing there, a group of about fifty Russian émigrés approached me. They had come to the cemetery expecting to find a rabbi to say "El Mole Rachamim" for their dead relations. "Are you a rabbi?" they asked me. "Could you please say 'El Mole Rachamim' for us?" They dragged me from grave to grave. My Hebrew still wasn't very good, and I had to really concentrate to transpose the prayer from the masculine to the feminine, from the singular to the plural, but I sang the prayer for them over and over again, and as I did, the Russians began to stuff dollar bills into the pocket of my waistcoat. Suddenly it hit me with great force: I was reliving my grandfather's life. My family history was hammering me into place. There was no escaping it.

## 38 THE LINEAMENTS OF THE DIVINE ENCOUNTER

After I became a rabbi, I needed to find a full-time job. The people from my student pulpit in Monroe called me up. "We've decided to go full time," they said. "We don't want to lose you. We want you to be our first full-time rabbi." I had been expecting this, but I had been hoping to find a more substantial place to go to instead. I had the family to support, and besides the tuition we were paying to send the girls to a Jewish day school, I now had my student loans to pay off. I was very fond of the community, however. It reminded me of Mel's community at the Berkeley Zendo. Sherril had made some very good friends among the congregants and the girls loved it there. I lay down on the bed to think about it. Both girls climbed up and straddled me. "We won't let you up until you agree to go to Monroe," they told me, and I finally gave in.

And so we moved out of our apartment in Manhattan and

up to Monroe. We rented a little summer house on a lake to stay in temporarily. They planned to build us a house in the meadow behind the synagogue eventually, but while we were waiting for this to happen, we could continue to sleep in the apartment in the synagogue on Shabbat and holidays.

What was appealing about Monroe was that, although most of the congregation consisted of less observant young families, there was a small energetic group that really took observance seriously and who had formed a community centered around Jewish practice. Even their social lives centered around Jewish events—they met for Purim feasts and to break the fast on Tisha b'Av. Observant like us, they nonetheless challenged some of my basic assumptions. I had always thought that in order to be seriously observant you couldn't drive on Shabbat. That was why we still stayed in the apartment in the shul on Shabbat, a twenty-minute drive from our lake house. The "driving teshuvah," the statement by the Conservative Movement that it was okay to drive on Shabbat if you drove just to synagogue and nowhere else, had always bothered me, as it did many of my peers at the seminary.

Dean Joel Roth had attracted students like me to the seminary who wanted Conservative Judaism to be a halachic movement in practice, which it hadn't really been before. It had been a movement of people who liked things "Jewish style," people who liked to hear Hebrew in the synagogue but who were not otherwise observant. But now the predominant conviction in the rabbinical school was that the Conservative Movement should be a halachic movement with a historical sense of evolution. A woman donning tefillin, no longer an unusual sight at the seminary's egalitarian morning minyan, perfectly expressed this idea: tradition and change. But the driving teshuvah was seen as an abomination for which no seriously halachic argument had been offered. The purists hated it and regarded it as the fatal wrong turn the movement had taken, and I agreed with them. Once people got into their cars, there would be nothing to stop them from going to the gas station, the supermarket, and the bank, nothing to stop them from continuing to desecrate the Shabbat. But the shul in Monroe was in the country, and unless you slept in the place, the way we did, there was no way to get there without driving. To my surprise, I saw that this determined group of observant Jews had the discipline to follow the driving teshuvah to the letter. They drove to shul, but nowhere else. They didn't even turn on the radios in their cars.

The Shabbat services in Monroe were truly meaningful for me. When I prayed with this enthusiastic group, the meadows and trees shimmering through the windows all around us, I experienced extremely intense feelings. In the particular place on the bimah where I would stand to pray, I always felt the presence of God enveloping me. Often during the week, when I was alone in the synagogue and felt the need to be in touch with God during the course of the day, I would go to my place on the bimah.

I spent my days visiting the sick and counseling people. Some people were endlessly in need, and I counseled them endlessly—those who lost their jobs, whose children were killed in accidents, who had debilitating illnesses, whose marriages were drying up, who felt desperate because their children were taking up with non-Jews.

It was now the late eighties, and people who in their younger days had run from anything remotely resembling mainstream religion were now returning in various ways to check it out. People who hadn't set foot in a synagogue in years—former sixties people from the nearby town of Warwick—came for a class in spirituality I decided to offer. It was in the process of preparing for this class that my ideas about Jewish spirituality started to coalesce. I had begun to see an archetype of the spiritual experience in the biblical encounter with God.

Although generations of rabbis—particularly American rabbis—had labored mightily to make the Torah into a running social and political commentary on our own times, as I immersed myself in the text in preparation for reading from the scroll each week, it became ever more apparent that while the Torah did in fact have many useful things to say about contemporary life, it was primarily a spiritual document, preoccupied with the divine encounter and its implications. The overwhelming number of stories in the Torah were stories about how, when, and why human beings encountered God, and what happened as a result. When I put these encounters alongside each other, certain shared characteristics emerged, a kind of archetype of the divine encounter.

The most pronounced of these was leave-taking. Every encounter with the divine is preceded by leaving home and all that is familiar. The story of Abraham, which includes several encounters with God, begins with the words, *Lech lecha*, you must certainly leave the land of your birth, your father's house, and go to an unknown destination. Your journey is completely open-ended. Similarly, Jacob's first great epiphany begins with the words, *Vayetze*, "And he left," followed by, "And he went to Haran." The Torah, which never wastes a word, tells us "he left" because the *leaving* itself is extremely significant. It's the prerequisite for the divine encounter that will follow. In order to encounter God, one must be vulnerable, one must be open, one must have left one's habitual way of being in the world.

Jacob's second great encounter with God also takes place on the road. The first one, "Vayetze," took place while he was running away from his brother Esau, who had threatened to kill him after Jacob had stolen Esau's birthright. He spent the next twenty years with his Uncle Lavan, and now Lavan wanted to kill him, too, and Jacob had to flee back toward Esau. Now, after fleeing the place that was home for twenty years, his isolation and vulnerability are emphasized even more as he leaves all the members of his household and crosses the Jabok River alone in the middle of the night. *Vayivater Yakov levado*, "And Jacob was left alone." Thus begins the biblical account of Jacob's second great encounter with God.

Moses' vision of the burning bush, his own first great epiphany, is the consequence of another leave-taking. He, also, flees for his life. In this case, the Pharaoh wants to kill him, so he runs away from Egypt and lives among the Midionites and becomes a shepherd. His shepherding takes him away from the Midionites as well, to Ahar Hamidbar, the farthest reaches of the wilderness, and it is there, now twice removed from his home in Egypt and as far away from human society as it is possible to get, that he sees the burning bush and hears the voice of God.

Nor is it insignificant that each of these divine encounters takes place while the protagonist is running for his life. Jacob is running from Esau, Jacob is running from Lavan, and Moses is running from Pharaoh. The divine encounter does not come as the result of a technique but as the result of leave-taking, as well as desperation. It comes when our backs are to the wall, when we are running for our lives, and it transforms us.

Transformation is the second great leitmotif of the divine encounter. The Torah always tips us off as to the nature of this transformation through the device of the name change. To be able to name something is to be conscious of it, and a change in name denotes a transformation of consciousness. In Jacob's first theophany, the vision of the ladder rooted in the ground and reaching up to heaven with messengers from God running up and down—a perfect representation of the human spiritual condition—Jacob exclaims: "God was in this place and I knew it not." This encounter has transformed his awareness of his surroundings. He suddenly sees them as being suffused with the sacred, a condition of which he was previously unconscious. This transformation is reflected by his changing the name of the place where it occurred. He calls it *Beit-El*, the House of God, and *Sharei Shamaim*, the Gate of Heaven.

In his second encounter with God, Jacob's wrestling match with the mysterious *ish*, the dark stranger who grapples with him until the break of dawn, it is Jacob himself who is renamed. "Your name will no longer be Jacob," this man declares, "but rather, 'Yisrael,' because you have struggled with God and you have prevailed."

The name "Yakov" is derived from the root *ekev*, which means heel. Jacob comes out of the womb grabbing onto the heel of his twin brother, Esau, trying to supplant his older brother even at the moment of their birth, and this is his characteristic mode of being for the rest of his life. He is devious, driven, given to whining. We don't like him very much. No one else seems to like him, either. Esau tries to kill him. Lavan

tries to kill him. But Jacob likes himself even less. He seems uncomfortable in his own skin, always trying to climb out of his
own reality, out of the present moment of his own life, into
something else. He seizes his brother's birthright, tries to marry
Lavan's younger daughter instead of the older as custom would
warrant, and he favors his own youngest son, driving his older
sons into a jealous rage. But here, in this encounter with his
own dark side, Jacob learns that the very thing he couldn't
stand about himself, his refusal to accept the way things are, is
his divine name—the name God has given him—*Yisrael*, "He
struggled with God."

This is perhaps the most profound psychological transformation it is possible to undergo: the realization that the very thing
we can't stand about ourselves is our divine name, our unique-
ness, the way God has made us, the quality that gives our life its
shape and meaning.

In Moses' vision of the burning bush it is the name of God
that is changed, because in this theophany, it is Moses' consciousness of God that is transformed. The burning bush is the
light of God. Moses takes it to be a bush on fire, but when he
sees it isn't being consumed, he realizes that the light is inter-
nal, and then he hears the voice of God telling him to take his
shoes off because he's standing on sacred ground. Eventually,
Moses will ask God God's name, and God will reply, *Eyeh
chasher eyeh*, "I Am That I Am," or "I Will Be What I Will Be"
(the tense is not clear), and then later, simply *Yud-Hey-Vov-
Hey*, the verb "to be" in the present tense. The name of God is
the only way to express present-tense being in the Hebrew language; you cannot say "I am tall," you can only say "I tall." Only
God can be in the absolute present tense; humans can only approach this state. Even when we are present, mindful, flush

with our experience, there is still a synapse of milliseconds between the experience itself and the time it takes our nervous system to process it. So we are never really in our experience, just watching a movie of what happened several milliseconds ago, but the closer we get to being present, the closer we get to God. Being present is God's name, all breath sounds, no consonant stops—"Yuh. Heh. Wuh. Heh"—all process and flow, no stopping points, absolute being, absolute becoming. Thus, in the story of the burning bush, it is God who is transformed; God receives a new name, or, more accurately, Moses' consciousness of God is transformed.

So these are the three kinds of transformation of consciousness that occur in the biblical encounter with God: an enhanced awareness of our surroundings (God was in this place and I knew it not); a deeper consciousness of ourselves (the very thing we dislike about ourselves is our divine name); and an intensified consciousness of God (God is "Yud-Hey-Vov-Hey," absolute being in the present tense).

Encounters with God are also experiences in which the protagonist finds the meaning of his life, his mission. It is here in the encounter with God that Moses learns that he is to lead the Israelites out of Egypt to the promised land, and that Jacob learns he is the spiritual heir to the covenant between God and his ancestors, Abraham and Isaac, and that his seed will become a great nation locked in a covenental relationship with God.

Finally, the divine encounter is always a fearful one. "How fearful this place is!" Jacob exclaims upon awakening from the dream of the great ladder. And God opens his conversation with Moses with the words *Al tirei*, "Don't be afraid." This is God's standard opening line to human beings—"Don't be afraid." This puzzled the rabbis greatly, and in each case they tried to find some reason that the person encountering God would be afraid, but in doing so, the scholars overlooked the obvious: they were afraid of God. God is totally *other*, the "mysterium tremendum," in Rudolph Otto's phrase, the fearful unknown. This was why leave-taking was necessary to encounter God. God was not to be found in our ordinary experience, not in comfort or security or habit, but beyond all these things, and whenever we go beyond these things we feel fear.

So these were the basic lineaments of the biblical mystical experience. Our Tuesday night group traced the evolution of this experience as it appeared in the rest of the Bible, in the Talmud, and in the Kabbalistic and Chasidic traditions as well. We studied all year, and by the end of the year there was a remarkable cohesion in the group. When I announced that the course was over, it refused to disband. "This isn't a class," someone said. "This is a spiritual practice group." Fine, I thought. And that is how I embarked on my first experiment in Jewish meditation.

Many members of the class claimed to have had experience with meditation, so, I thought, why not turn the group into a Jewish meditation group? I would teach a brief text, a pointedly spiritual text from Kabbalah or Chasidut, at the beginning of each evening, and then we would meditate together for the rest of it. I had meditated on my own intermittently ever since leaving Zen Center, but not since then with a group. But what kind of meditation would we do? I, of course, had been trained for ten rigorous years in the art of zazen, of just sitting, just inhabiting the present-moment experience of breath and body and mind. So we would sit this way, I thought. After all, it was what I knew and what I could teach. But what would be Jewish about it? Well, I knew of a meditation on the name of God, the "Yud-Hey-Vov-Hey," developed by a great mystic, Yitzak of Akko, back in the fourteenth century. Perhaps we could sit a half hour or so and then shift our focus to the four sacred letters. But if they were going to meditate on the "Yud-Hey-Vov-Hey," they would need to see the letters as they were meditating, at least at first. This would mean photocopying the name of God on sheets of paper and placing them before them as they sat.

The very thought of doing this filled me with dread. One does not take the name of God lightly. Once there had been a tremendous controversy in New York because a photograph of a book bearing the name of God had appeared in a newspaper. Observant Jews all over the world shuddered to think of the name of God lining a bird cage or being wrapped around fish and finally being discarded along with the flotsam and jetsam of the universe. I had a very bad feeling about doing it.

We held our first session just before Pesach. I had just read an extremely penetrating explanation of the prohibition against eating *hametz*, leavened bread, on Passover by Ibn Gikitilia, a medieval Spanish Kabbalist. It affected me profoundly, but what I sensed in it was so deep that it was beyond articulation, and when I tried to present it to the group I failed miserably. Then we came to the meditation part of the evening, already feeling confused and disappointed. When it came to meditation, they had all talked a good game, but now as we tried to sit, it was quite clear that I was the only one in the room who could sit still for more than a few minutes. There was constant fidgeting, moving, coughing, changing of position all around. Compared to this, my presentation of Gikitilia was beginning to seem like a great success. We never even got to the contemplation of the "Yud-Hey-Vov-Hey." The group just kind of dissolved after twenty minutes or so, as people got up and wandered out. There never was a second meeting, which didn't surprise me in the least.

So that chapter closed. This group, which seemed to naturally grow around me in such a lively, successful manner, had now disappeared into thin air, and my first attempt to meditate in a Jewish setting had been thwarted by God. I felt this as clearly as I'd ever felt anything in my life.

## 39  KABBALAH

On *erev* Pesach, the first night of the seder, we had a small minyan at the synagogue to usher in the holiday, as we did for every holiday. Only the regulars came to these services, and even with that, we usually had to make a few calls to ensure a minyan. There was a respectable group that evening, but at the last minute, an apparition walked in and sat down by himself way off in the corner of the sanctuary. He was tall and thin with a long black beard, stately, in a simple dark suit, graceful, with an erect back and long, slender fingers. He wasn't the sort of person who usually came to our synagogue. He seemed Ortho-dox, and we all assumed that was why he sat in the corner by himself. We had no *mehitza*, no division between a women's side and a men's side as is required by Orthodoxy, and some-times Orthodox people would pray with us but separate them-selves informally by going off into a corner.

After services he stopped and spoke to me briefly. He barely spoke English, so he spoke in Hebrew. I had given a brief sermon at the service. He told me he had found it quite moving. He was staying in Kiryas Joel, a large community of Satmar Chasidim, which was walking distance from my synagogue. He had come to spend Pesach with his son, who had joined this sect, but he couldn't stand the Satmar. He found them too fanatical, too simpleminded, too fundamentalist, and he had refused to daven with them. He had gone out looking for some place to pray outside the village and had stumbled upon us.

Russian by birth, he had immigrated to Israel at a young age and found his teacher, a *mukbal*, an authentic bearer of Kabbalistic teaching, in Jerusalem. Now he lived in a housing project in Williamsburg, Brooklyn, studying and teaching Kabbalah day and night. He had thousands of students and dozens of close disciples. With fierce, penetrating eyes fixed on me, he now began to discuss the Kabbalah drawing circles in the air with his expressive hands, conveying surprising depth in spite of the language difficulty. Something quite profound began to pass between us. After services on the second night of Pesach, he came into my office and made the following confession, in Hebrew and halting English: "I'm going home tomorrow morning. I couldn't understand why I came here. I hate the Satmar, I resent my son for joining them. He's invited me to stay with him a hundred times before, and I always refused, but this time, I came, and I had no idea why. Now I know why. I came to get you. You will be my student."

We started that evening. He began to explain the basics of his teachings. He drew radiant circles on blank pieces of paper with a ballpoint pen. I was mesmerized, although I understood very little of what he was saying. Over the next several weeks, I

received several calls from his students, encouraging me to join
them as a disciple of this man. They were all very bright, with
the same gentle but energetic tone to their voice. They could
have saved themselves the trouble, though, because I had already decided that I would study with him.

Years earlier, when I first started reading about Kabbalah, I
read somewhere that you can't go looking for a real teacher of
Kabbalah; when you're ready, your teacher suddenly appears.
Back then, I prayed that mine would. Now my life was different. It had been a long time since I had prayed for such a thing,
yet here he was. How could I decline? Williamsburg was very
far away, but one of his disciples lived nearby, in New Jersey. He
was a man named Lenny, a brilliant physicist who worked in ar-
tificial intelligence for the Bendix Corporation. Unfailingly
kind and gentle, he was quite a bit younger than me. He was divorced and lived alone in a small house in Fairlawn, but his
children were always with him when I and other students came
to study with him, and our studies were usually delayed, sometimes by an hour, as he put them to sleep, tenderly and with
great patience. Then he would come down and we would begin
to study.

We studied the *Eitz Chaim, The Tree of Life*, by Chaim Vital,
one of the great teachers of Kabbalah who lived in Safed and
studied with the Ari, Rav Yitzak Luria, the seminal figure of
Kabbalah in Safed. The *Eitz Chaim* was Vital's reduction of the
Ari's teachings. It was like a physics of the supernal world, a
strange antiscience, which endeavored to explain how the universe was really put together under the materialist surface of
the world. It was dense and difficult. Nearly all the other students and disciples of the teacher, whom I will call "X," were
mathematicians and scientists, and they all had advanced Ju-

daic skills. I now came to understand that the old chestnut—that to study Kabbalah one had to have mastered the Torah and the Talmud and be over forty years old—was not some sort of prescription for balance in one's life, as was generally supposed, but a statement about the prerequisites for this kind of study. It was simply impossible to study Kabbalah without a high degree of study skills, particularly in Talmud. I had studied Talmud for six years at JTS, and I was one of the best Talmud students there, able to negotiate pretty well through the minefield of technical language, encoded abbreviations, and inferences drawn from the sparest hints imaginable that constituted a Talmudic text, but Kabbalah presented another degree of difficulty altogether. It seemed to begin where Talmud left off, and I found myself struggling for dear life to keep up. Still, there was something extremely compelling about this study. Even though I could barely keep up with it, I could hear it calling me, pulling me magnetically toward its center.

A strange idea popped into my head. Summer was coming. What if I devoted the entire summer to studying Kabbalah? I was now working constantly at my pastoral duties, from early in the morning until late at night, six and often seven days a week. But what if I simply stopped all that and just did Kabbalah? I would still show up for services, for funerals and hospital visits as the need arose, but I would stop scheduling appointments, stop attending meetings, stop counseling, stop teaching. I would only study Kabbalah.

So this is what I did, and no one seemed to notice. I studied Kabbalah all the time, night and day, for four months. The forms I was studying began to fill my mind, and then my mind became these forms, and I was profoundly altered. I became the *igulim*, the infinite progression of concentric circles that ran from the *Ain Sof*, the endless, impossibly powerful, undiluted, undifferentiated presence of God, down to our material being. My mind became the *kavim*, the lines of energy that drew the divine light from the *Ain Sof* down through the *igulim* to this world, and I became an infinite progression of body forms radiating out from my own body to the immense and primal form of *adam kadmon*, the primordial man. The world had melted away to nothing. Only these forms remained. I now lived in a world of such forms, and it was the most vivid world I had ever occupied, but in my brief excursions back into this world I began to notice some disturbing things.

I began to notice, for instance, that Lenny wasn't the only disciple of my teacher who had left his wife. Many of these disciples had been married, and they had all left their wives, and, in several cases, their families as well. They had left jobs, too, good jobs, jobs as teachers and research scientists. They had discovered, as I was beginning to, that Kabbalah only worked when you gave up everything. It left no time to spare for anything or anyone else, although to say that we discovered this would be misleading. Rather, we were drawn into this, pulled deeper and deeper into the Eitz Chaim, the Tree of Life, by a mysterious magnetism.

I got by all summer by improvising sermons from my studies in Kabbalah. The forms in my mind were so richly suggestive that this was not difficult. The shape of a circle or the relationship between the various spheres in this strange new universe I was inhabiting would suggest deep truths, truths about the spiritual path, about the nature of life. I'm not sure what the synagogue regulars made of these sermons, but then, I had never been sure of what the regulars made of my sermons anyway. In any case, no one said anything and the summer passed without incident in spite of my spending so little time in my work at the synagogue. But as the High Holidays and the beginning of the school year approached, I knew I wouldn't be able to get away with giving so little to my job. I had reached a crossroads.

The new realm I had entered, the realm of Kabbalah, was one of the most intense spiritual places I had ever inhabited. But it had come too late. I wasn't prepared to give up my life, not my work as a rabbi, and certainly not my family. "I did this once already," I explained to Lenny when I told him I would no longer be able to devote myself to our studies. I was thinking of the way I had given up everything for Zen practice many years before.

I continued to study with Lenny and occasionally with X himself the following year, traveling down to Fairlawn and oc-casionally to Williamsburg to my teacher's room in the proj-ects, where he lived alone—without his wife—but now I was outside that strange realm I had entered during the summer. This world receded further and further as the year came on, and soon it became completely closed to me and I gave up my stud-ies altogether. Just before I did, Lenny came to me looking very uncomfortable. "Look," he said, "X has asked me to talk about something with you." Lenny had been one of the most consis-tently generous spirits I had ever known, and having already decided to end my studies with him, I knew I would miss him terribly. But now he seemed deeply embarrassed. "X asked me to tell you," he said, "that once you become his student, you have to support him for the rest of your life and the rest of his life. It's a sacred obligation. You have to contribute to his main-tenance forever."

"I never agreed to any such arrangement," I said.

"I know," Lenny said.

"I'll be happy to pay for my studies thus far, but I'm not going to support X for the rest of my life," I said.

Lenny looked deeply pained. "I'm just telling you what I was asked to tell you," he said.

I gave him a check for what seemed like a fair amount. "I hope this will do," I said.

"I guess it will have to," Lenny said.

I felt some regret at having to leave that vibrant magical world, but not that much regret. I was grateful to have been given this choice, and even more grateful that the choice had been so clear. For the rest of my life, I would know what Kabbalah was and what it was not, and that would turn out to be an important touchstone in a world increasingly crowded with mountebanks and charlatans teaching nonsense in the name of Kabbalah.

## 40  TAKING LEAVE

My synagogue in Monroe was flourishing. In the two years I had been there full time it had doubled in size. I was a success, and we were cozy in our little house by the lake. Beautiful red, gold, and yellow leaves were drifting down out the windows of the sanctuary now. At the top of the meadow there was one magnificent maple whose leaves had turned red overnight. It looked as if it was on fire. I thought of this tree as the Tree of Life of this little congregation named for the Tree of Life. And then one day when I looked out the window, the maple at the top of the hill was gone. One of the members of the congregation had cut it down for firewood.

The days shortened and the color drained from the world. The entire Jewish community of New York suddenly seemed suffocating, narrow, small-minded, smug, and inbred. A heavy darkness settled all around, hemming me in. The trees were now mere sticks.

In January I went to Connecticut to a rabbinical retreat, a new program designed to allow Conservative rabbis to regenerate spiritually. In the afternoons there were sessions on practical issues, and the evenings were devoted to spirituality. I studied with Jonathan Omer-Man, who did outreach in Los Angeles with young Jews seeking spirituality. One evening we all did a spiritual exploration, trying to locate ourselves in the moment. It was very clear to me as well as to everyone else in the group that I was deeply depressed. Jonathan said, "Hanukkah has just passed. Hanukkah is all about spiritual renewal. In the Hanukkah story, there is a *pach shemen*, a jar of oil, hidden in the Temple. Alan, you have to try to locate your pach shemen."

"But I don't know how to find it," I said. Yet even as I said these words, I could feel my depression lifting.

When I got home I found the world had been covered by a pure white snow. It was a wet snow, which made the trees look as if they were wearing lace shawls. Sherril met me at the door and I took her in my arms. I was strangely happy. While I was driving back, it had become clear to me what we had to do. We had to leave Monroe. It was a lovely place, in many ways an ideal place, but I was being called elsewhere. Where, I didn't know. To do what, I had no idea.

I made an appointment with the president of the synagogue and told him that I was leaving, though I would give them plenty of time to find a replacement. We both cried, and he hugged me. I walked out, got into my car, and drove straight up to the rabbinical convention in the Catskills. As soon as I

273

walked in the door, one of my old classmates walked up to me. "Have you heard the news? Beth Sholom, the big congregation in San Francisco, is looking for a rabbi."

As soon as he told me this, I knew for a certainty that I would be going to San Francisco. I knew this despite the fact that there was no rational reason for me to want to go to San Francisco. Northern California was not seen as a desirable place to be a Conservative rabbi. There were no Conservative day schools and there was no kosher food. The area was dominated by the Reform and the unaffiliated, and they had a history of hostility to the State of Israel. Nonetheless, the Bay Area remained a magical place in my imagination.

I knew I was not qualified to apply for this pulpit. I didn't have enough seniority yet for a congregation its size. Moreover, they had always had rabbis who were stars; they wouldn't be looking for some guy who had gone to JTS at age thirty-eight and who had only had one small pulpit. I knew all this, but I also knew that these impediments would somehow work themselves out.

Although I knew this pulpit would be mine, I also knew I couldn't wait passively for it to come to me. To get this job I would have to call up influential people I knew and ask them to recommend me. One of the people I called was a man who moved in the highest circles of San Francisco Jewish society. I had known him when we were kids. He had gone to camp with my friend Howie, and later he had been friends with some of my fraternity brothers at Penn, and I had spent a lot of time with him when he visited them. When I called him, however, he told me he couldn't place my name. Humiliated but steadfast, I asked him to help me to get the job at Beth Sholom.

"That place?" he said. "Why do you want to go there? It's on its last legs."

They called me to come for an interview. I had heard that they had fired their last rabbi and that there was a big schism in the congregation, so I prepared remarks on healing schisms in congregations. I did elaborate preparations for every aspect of the interview, much as I had prepared myself to be called to dokusan in the zendo, and they soon saw in me exactly the person they had been looking for. I found their synagogue dilapidated and their congregation demoralized. But three hundred intelligent people came to Saturday morning services, where they performed a full traditional service, and this thrilled me. "Don't come here. This place is a nightmare. It's about to come apart!" the cantor said to me. "I'm not going to let it come apart," I told him.

"And I won't," I told Norman when he came to pick me up after my interview. Norman was now one of the major teachers at Zen Center. Baker Roshi had been caught engaging in questionable behavior involving sex and money, and they had kicked him out. Instead of having one gurulike leader, Zen Center had decided to have two or three abbots take leadership positions for limited terms.

"For the past ten years," Norman told me, "I've been driving past Beth Sholom on my way between Green Gulch and City Center, and I always had a strange feeling that my destiny was somehow tied up with the place. So when my mother died last year, I went there to say Kaddish. But now that you're going to be the rabbi there, I have this feeling of destiny even stronger. But I don't know what it means."

"It's funny that you should say that, Norman," I said, "because I also have a strong sense of destiny about this job. I feel like I'm being compelled here—for some very specific reason. But what that reason is, I haven't a clue."

We were now driving over the Golden Gate Bridge, and I looked west, through the Golden Gateway. The wind was blowing the fog swiftly toward us, over the Pacific from the east. It billowed around us like pure excitement, and pretty soon it began to envelope us, pouring over us in our little car like God's fresh thoughts.

# PART III

*To Struggle*

*with God*

*Until Your*

*Name Changes*

## 41 THE SHEM'A

Delighted with the success of my visit to San Francisco, I boarded a plane for home. As we rose up through the clouds, the Humash in my lap fell open. I looked to see what story it had opened to; it was the moment when Joseph reveals his identity to his brothers. Their father, Jacob, doesn't know yet that the beloved son he thinks dead is actually alive, and not only alive but the most successful man in the world. Now Joseph tells his brothers, "Go back and tell my father of my glory!" As I read these words, the tears that had been gathering behind my eyes for a very long time began to stream down my face. No one could go back and tell *my* father of *my* glory.

Several months later I arrived back in San Francisco, curious to discover what my work would be and eager to begin it. When I got to my first morning minyan, a man in black Orthodox garb was there waiting for me. He told me a tale of woe. He had been traveling with his mother in Oregon, and she had fallen ill. He had taken her to a hospital there, where they had treated her, but now they refused to release her because he couldn't pay her bill. So he had hightailed it south, to San Francisco, looking for a Jewish community to help them out. He wanted me to appeal to the people at the minyan.

It sounded like a scam to me, but I decided to check it out. When I called the hospital in Oregon, to my surprise, his story turned out to be true. Everyone in the minyan was amazed that I had gone to such lengths to check out the story, and they were a little shocked by my chutzpa when I asked them for money for a stranger on my first day on the job. But they gave generously, and when they did, I felt as if they were giving me authority to be their spiritual leader.

One of the old members of the minyan asked me then if I could give a little impromptu *devar Torah*, a brief sermon. "No," I said. "I'm not prepared." But then I thought to myself, You know a lot of Torah. Surely you can think of something to say. "Okay," I said. "I'll do it."

The parasha was *Balak*. Up until this moment in the story of the Israelites, we have seen them from within the camp, from their own perspective, and from the inside they appear to be a large dysfunctional family—complaining, rebellious, and seething with various discontents. But now suddenly the point of view shifts, and we see them from the outside, as Balak, the King of Moab, sees them approaching his country. In his eyes they are mighty, invincible, an irresistible force. Balak hires the prophet Bilaam to curse them, but, against his will, only blessings come out of Bilaam's mouth. "How lovely are your tents, O Israel!" he finds himself saying. "This is a picture of how we all are," I told the minyan. "On the inside we feel weak, like we can barely function. We think this is reality, but we don't know our own strength. We can't see ourselves as others see us. We're like giants bound by a tiny string."

After minyan, I crossed the hallway from the chapel to my office. The phone was ringing as I opened the door and I ran to answer it. It was a family that lived on Twenty-seventh Avenue and had just had a baby; I told them I would be right over to see them. I stood up to go and the phone rang again. This time it was a man whose father had just died. I took down the address of the family and told them I'd be right over. But as I was going out the door the phone rang again. I turned back to answer it. Another woman had just had a baby. The baby had been born with almost no brain and was not expected to live more than a day. I told them I'd be at the hospital as soon as I could.

After I left this family, I went to the neonatal ward of UCSF Medical Center. The parents of the baby weren't members of my new congregation; in fact, the father wasn't even Jewish. The sadness of the situation was compounded by the fact that the parents had separated, but all four grandparents were there when I arrived, the Jewish grandparents and the Catholic grandparents. The Jewish grandparents wanted a rabbi to be there to say some sort of prayer for the child. They wanted to give him a name because they thought of him as a whole person, and they wanted to mark his death with a prayer as well.

According to Jewish law, you're not supposed to name an infant until the eighth day, until you're sure that it's viable, but this seemed like a poor time to insist on the fine points of halacha. I looked at the baby. He was the most beautiful child I had ever seen, looking completely peaceful, beatific, even. The family hovering around seemed overwhelmed by the odd perfection of this child, of this tiny, brief life. "Why don't you call him 'Shlomo,' I suggested to them. "It means 'wholeness,' 'peace.'" They agreed, and named him Shlomo. Then I said a prayer for him, using part of the prayer for naming a baby and part of the *vidui*, the prayer for someone who is dying, and combined them into one continuum. Often, when I preside at a death, I have the feeling in the end that the life, no matter how long in years, has taken no time at all, and now it was literally true.

As I was leaving the hospital, I looked at the address of the family that had just lost their father. The address, like that of the first baby, was on Twenty-seventh Avenue. But it was on the opposite end. Birth and death were on the opposite ends of the same continuum.

That night the phone woke me. I didn't know where I was. I was sleeping on the floor of our empty flat next to Sherril. Norman had lent us some sleeping bags and futons to use until our beds came. "It's for you," Sherril said. Apparently, a very old and revered woman, a longtime member of the congregation, was dying, and the family needed a rabbi because she wanted to say the *Shem'a*.

When I got to her house, they led me up a winding staircase to her room. She lay sunken into her pillows. It appeared that I was too late; she already seemed to be dead. But then she rose up from death, said the word *shem'a!* and sank back down. The word *shem'a!* (which means "Listen!") is made of the three "mother" sounds, the three fundamental sounds from which all other sounds are derived. The *shin* (shh) is the sound of cacophony, the chaos of all sound at once, "white noise." It shows up on an oscilloscope as a chaos of lines. The *mem* (mmm) is the harmony of all sound, as in "om," and shows up on an oscilloscope as straight balanced lines, equidistant from one another, harmonious. The letter *ayin* is the functional equivalent of the *aleph*, the silence that contains all sound. All the other letters have their origin in these three letters.

The old woman suddenly rose up out of death again to say the second word of the prayer, *Yisrael*, then sank back again, and as I stood by the side of her bed, she continued to do this until the prayer was complete. This prayer, which is called the "watchword of our faith," declares the oneness of all things, the continuum that life and death are on, the final reality, a deeper truth than the dualistic premise of the surrounding culture, the materialist world.

The work I had to do at Beth Sholom was endless, but full of depth and meaning. Beth Sholom had the largest Saturday morning minyan in northern California. I spoke before hundreds of people every week. I was beginning to do important work in the larger community, as well: on behalf of the homeless and the increasingly beleaguered immigrant population of California, and in opposition to capital punishment. Occasionally I spoke about this work from the pulpit on Saturday mornings. These talks were not always received with equanimity. Sometimes people walked out in the middle of them, and sometimes they shouted out their disagreement from their seats, but whenever these talks were over and I turned toward the altar to begin *Musaf*, the concluding service, the room would suddenly be filled with light, I would hear a roaring sound in my ears, and I would feel a great release. God was clapping, I thought.

I had found the synagogue almost dormant when I arrived, and now I instituted many new programs—for young adults, Russian immigrants, women, and other groups—and the place began to feel full of life. I sat on several boards in the community now, I was constantly being asked to give speeches and invocations, and I was invited to host my own TV show on one of the networks. One day toward the end of my first year in San Francisco, I was sitting in my office feeling harried but happy that this work I had been called to was using every ounce of what I had to give, when the phone rang. This time it was a reporter from the *Jewish Bulletin*. "Listen," she said. "We know all about you. We know about your history as a Buddhist. We're going to out you. You can choose to cooperate and give us information, or you can choose not to cooperate. In that case, we will simply write everything we've managed to dig up about you. What do you say? Would you like to cooperate?"

I held my breath until the story came out. I had decided to cooperate so that at last they would get the facts straight, and they did. I expected anger from the community, but anger didn't come. Instead, there was tremendous interest, and Jews who had been practicing Buddhists started lining up outside my office to speak to me. Some of them had been practicing Buddhism for twenty or thirty years, and they were quite happy with it; nevertheless, they felt haunted by their Jewishness, and they had never been able to shake it. They begged me to suggest something for them to do about it. I didn't know what to tell them.

Norman and I decided to hold a colloquium, a panel discussion on Judaism and Buddhism. He and I and several teachers of Jewish meditation would be on the panel. We expected around fifty people, but hundreds of people showed up. What did they all want? Was this why I had been called to San Francisco—to find out?

Norman had asked me to sit on the board of the Zen Center's hospice. When I walked into the room for the first meeting, the chairman began the meeting with a few minutes of silent meditation, which we performed sitting in our chairs. After all those years of sitting in the lotus for hours, I didn't think a few minutes sitting in a chair would have any effect on me, but its effect was profound. Almost immediately, I felt a great cleansing peace coming over my psyche. During the years when I had meditated on a regular basis, I had not come to it, as I did now, from an excruciatingly stressful job. I was working from early in the morning until late at night six, and often seven, days a week. The girls were not adjusting well to San Francisco, and I didn't have the time to give them the attention they needed. I was feeling completely overwhelmed. But in the few moments of silent meditation in that boardroom, I could feel my equilibrium returning. I was stunned by this reminder of the power of meditation.

I decided that we would start a program of meditation before services several times a week at the synagogue. I wasn't sure how I was going to do this, however. My last attempt in Monroe had been a complete failure. I scheduled the program to begin right after I got back from New York, where I was going to another weeklong rabbinic retreat. I had thought of offering to lead meditation at this retreat, and was surprised when I got there to find that morning meditation before davening was already on the daily schedule. The leader was a tall, thin minister from the Alban Institute, a body that studies synagogues and churches. In Monroe, when I had tried to lead the meditation group, I had simply plopped people down, with very little instruction. But the leader of this group led everyone verbally step by step—to check their posture, to notice their breath, to notice when their attention wandered and to gently bring it back. There is no speaking during zazen. Instruction is given *before* sitting. I had never participated in a guided meditation before, and now I saw how effective it was. All the other rabbis attending, who had had no experience meditating and for whom this activity had been, until this point, totally opaque, loved it, too.

The minister began each morning with some light yoga stretching before sitting in order to help people inhabit their bodies and their breath even before sitting down to meditate, and I saw how effective that was, too. The yoga I had always practiced was too strenuous for most people, I realized, but this regimen was just right.

So yoga and directed meditation became part of the practice I offered at my synagogue. The meditation group changed the whole tenor of the Friday night minyan. Suddenly the service had great density and feeling.

A group of people had already started a center for Jewish meditation in Berkeley, and I interviewed one of them on my TV show. Afterward, we discussed the idea that I might like to work with them. Norman, who was a guest on my show the same week, suggested that he and I do a workshop together instead, in a *yurt* (the Mongolian-style structure used for such things) at Zen Center's Green Gulch Farm. My goal was to help Jews deepen their Jewish practice with Buddhist-style meditation techniques, and Norman's interest was in reaching out to Jewish Buddhists who wanted to have some way to express their Jewishness. We put up some flyers, and within days the workshop was sold out.

Our idea was not to have an exercise in comparative religion, but simply to practice the two disciplines side by side. Norman and I would alternate as the leader throughout the day. We would begin with light yoga stretching, followed by meditation, which would be followed by a Jewish prayer service. Then we would meditate again, study a Jewish text, and have lunch. After lunch we would do yoga again, meditate again, and then study a Buddhist text, which would be followed by a Jewish prayer service, more meditation, and a closing circle. The point of alternating practices was to see what effect they had on each other.

Everything went very well until we got to the Jewish prayer service, and then all hell broke loose. My assumption was that the meditation would open people to the deep spirituality and beauty of the Jewish prayer service as it had in my meditation group at Beth Sholom, but what happened was almost exactly the opposite. The meditation had served, instead, to open them to their deep anger with Judaism, and with the Jewish prayer service in particular. They felt excluded by it. They felt shut out by the fact that it was in Hebrew, a language they didn't understand. The English translations only made things worse; the language was archaic and sexist. Why pray to a God of our fathers, they wanted to know. What was God anyway? What was this reward and punishment business? The God of the prayerbook seemed like an abusive father. The service made them feel impotent. They didn't know what to do with it. They couldn't get inside it. They were furious, and I, of course, as the representative of the Jewish tradition, became the object of their anger.

"What happened?" Sherril asked, when I came home, ashen and shaken.

"Buddhists nine, Jews three," I told her.

It might have all ended there, except that Norman and I had already scheduled a weeklong retreat at Tassajara that summer. It, too, had sold out almost immediately, and there was a long waiting list. Now it was with terror in my heart that I drove over the precipitous one-lane mountain road to the monastery.

Part of the reason for the popularity of this workshop, of course, was simply that it was being given at Tassajara, now one of the most beautiful mountain resorts in the west, with beautiful new Japanese-style bathhouse, breathtaking views, and a world-class gourmet vegetarian kitchen. This probably accounted for the fact that about half a dozen innocent Christians signed up for the workshop, including two housewives from San Diego and a patrician farmer from New England whose family regarded the people who came over on the Mayflower as latecomers. How surprised these innocents were to suddenly find themselves in the middle of a weeklong psychodrama on Jewish angst, alienation, and reconciliation, because it didn't take long for the anger that had surfaced at Green Gulch to surface here as well.

After the experience at Green Gulch, I had made a considerable effort to abbreviate the Jewish prayer service and to make it more meaningful, but I wasn't willing to compromise on the Hebrew, and obviously I hadn't abbreviated enough. One prayer service was all it took to provoke a rage among many of the participants, making what happened at Green Gulch seem tame. It came spilling out of the dining room and the bathhouse, the same complaints: "The Hebrew shut us out . . . the language was archaic and not what we felt in our hearts . . . the service excludes us . . . the language affronts us. In short, we feel repelled by the religion and the people we're supposed to belong to. It's supposed to offer us spiritual nourishment and it doesn't. It turns us away."

And again, I was the lightning rod for all this anger. I found my own anger building, and I felt myself becoming more and more defensive. There were now actual shouting matches out in the courtyard and on the paths where other people walked silently, bowing mutely to each other in greeting. "Don't you people take any responsibility at all for your own alienation?" I shouted. "How is it possible that you've made it to your fiftieth year without learning any Hebrew? When *I* began to realize the spiritual potential of Judaism, I stopped everything and sat down for two or three years and I *learned* Hebrew. If Judaism were important to you, if you weren't trying to run away from it so hard, you would have done the same," I shouted stupidly.

But after my initial anger and defensiveness were spent, I began to hear something I hadn't noticed before. There was real hurt in their anger. Clearly, if they didn't want a connection with Judaism, they wouldn't have come to this workshop. If they didn't feel a deep sense of frustration about their Judaism, they wouldn't feel so angry, they'd merely feel indifferent. But what I was getting from them was anything but indifference.

So that night, Norman and I sat down and redesigned the whole workshop, especially the Jewish prayer service. The first thing we did was to simplify. I had previously abbreviated the service by about a third; now it was obvious that the cuts had to be much more drastic. In the end, we reduced the daily service to half a dozen tiny sections, a few dozen lines.

But before we started cutting, we made a few crucial additions as well. Norman had a vague memory of singing a song in

Hebrew that had affected him very deeply once. He reconstructed part of the melody for me and I recognized it immediately—Shlomo Carlbach's version of *Pitchu Li Sharey Tzedek*, "Open the gates of righteousness for me and I will go through them and praise God." For the rest of the week we sang this song every morning as we were coming out of meditation. It had a riveting effect on the group.

A colleague of mine, Eddie Feld, once told me that when he was a teenager, he had a job working as a waiter in a bungalow colony in the Catskills for Bobover Chasidim, a Jewish sect. The Bobovers are famous for their wildly ecstatic and deeply spiritual dancing, and, in fact, he saw the Bobovers dancing this way all summer. So one night, the waiters thought it would be amusing if they came out to serve the meal, trays raised and dancing wildly. It was their way of expressing appreciation for the Bobover dancing, but it wasn't received that way. The Bobovers were horrified, and made them stop immediately.

"This is not the way we do things," the Bobover Rebbe told them. "We don't just start dancing right away. First we sing a song with words, and when we are completely full of the words, we sing a *nigun*, a song without words. And when that song has filled every cell of our body and soul and we are so full of it that we just can't stand it anymore, then we get up and dance."

So, I decided, we would start the next prayer service at Tassajara with a song without words. But which one? All the nigunim I knew were hopelessly complicated, and that was the very problem we were trying to remedy.

The next morning, when I stepped out of my cabin and looked up at the mountains, I heard them singing a nigun, a tune of such perfect simplicity and intense emotion—a song without words—I felt it deep in my heart. We began our service every day for the rest of the week chanting this nigun, and I began to feel the anger dissipating between the notes.

Next we said the *Birchot Hashachar*, the repetitive, incantational lines with which we start every morning service, lines that celebrate the ordinary miracle of waking up to life and to this world, and I invited people to add lines expressing their gratitude for the ordinary miracles of their own lives, in a mixture of Hebrew and English: *Baruch Ata Adonai, Eloheinu Melech Haolam,* "Blessed be God, master of the universe . . . who brought me to this beautiful mountain valley . . . or, who gave me time to be with my daughter . . . or, who enabled us to learn from suffering and anger," people sang.

Then we sang one line from one of the dozens of psalms ordinarily said, but we sang it in a three-part round, and it was very beautiful: *Col Hanshema Tehalel Ya Haleluyah,* "Every living being thanks God . . . or, Every breathing thing thanks God . . . or, Every breath expresses thanks to God."

After that we went straight to the *Barhu,* which we performed standing in a circle. Each person in turn made the call and had the exhilarating experience of provoking a response from the group. The rhythm of the simple Hebrew built as we made our way around the circle (even the gentiles chimed in), and we all heard the hermetic essence, the heavenly host of angels echoing God's praises to each other.

From there we went to the *Shem'a,* but only the first six words, which we said over and over until we were infused with them. The words spoke to us of the miracle of awareness and the mind-boggling idea that there is a oneness in all things, that despite appearances, we do live in a coherent world, and that God is precisely the ground of that oneness and that co-herence.

We concluded with the *Amidah*—perhaps the deepest and most important of all our prayers—the prayer that begins by ac-knowledging that we are part of a great stream of spiritual consciousness from which we and our ancestors have been addressing God for the past several thousand years, and this we said lovingly, slowly, and responsively, beautiful Hebrew phrase by beautiful Hebrew phrase. *Baruch Ata Adonai*, I would chant, *Baruch Ata Adonai* they would repeat, and we would go through the first few paragraphs like this and then continue the rest of the *Amidah* in silence. The rhythm and force of the Hebrew, slowed down and simplified, was becoming irresistible, and I felt a great gateway of space and silence opening up between the words, and the people's souls began to pour through these gates.

They were hooked. Even the gentiles were hooked. They said the prayers with us and were deeply moved by them, and as we went on, I realized that this was having a transforming effect on the Jewish Buddhists among us. The Christians were not only being tolerant of their Jewishness, they were actively sup-porting it and participating in it. It was like when you're a teenager and your father makes a terrible joke, and you're dying with embarrassment, but then someone from outside the family who you really respect (one of your friends, maybe) laughs at the joke and tells you how great your father is. What a relief! Suddenly you see your father in a new light. He is terrific and you can stop being so angry at him for being dumb and embar-rassing you. And the relief comes because secretly you have loved him very deeply all along.

The truth is, I had already begun to suspect that there was a connection between these people's anger at Judaism and their anger at their fathers and mothers. One of the most poignant moments of the week occurred on the last day, when the woman who had been the angriest of the angry—the ringleader of the insurrection of rage on the first day—asked me to say Kaddish for her father. She had never done it before. She had had a terrible relationship with him, and then he had abandoned her by dying when she was a teenager. Suddenly I remembered how at the first workshop at Green Gulch a young man had said something shocking—all the more so, because it obviously came from the bottom of his heart and because so many others there identified with it. He said, "Judaism is my family, and I just don't know if I want to be part of my family anymore. And I don't know if I want to be part of Judaism anymore, either."

But, of course, there is nothing he can do about it. He is and always will be part of his family, whether he chooses to be or not. They are inside him, whether they are alive or dead, here or in Boston, in monasteries or in synagogues. There is nothing on earth he can do to get away from them, or they from him.

I thought about how I had fought with my own father when I was young, and when I was not so young, even when he was dying in the hospital. It was now twelve years since my father had died, since he had been buried in the family plot in New Jersey. In the spring of 1995 I had led a congregational trip to Israel. On our way we were to change planes in New Jersey, and as the plane came in for a landing at Newark, I suddenly realized what day it was—the anniversary of my father's death, the day of my father's *yahrtzeit*, the day when it is traditional to visit his grave. And, miraculously, there I was in New Jersey, with a few hours to spare before boarding the plane for Israel.

It was late, but the gates to the cemetery were still open when I pulled up in a cab. Standing there by my father's grave, in the grass that grew there perpetually, I experienced what I always felt there—that my father's soul is intimately bound up in my own soul, that he is inextricably a part of me, that at the deepest recesses of my soul he and I dissolve into a single light and that light is the core of my life. There is nothing I could ever do that would change that, nor, it was now clear, would I ever want to.

I stood there for a few moments in silence. Then little by little, all my deepest anxieties and regrets—my worries about the girls, my stress about the synagogue, my guilt for having abandoned my mother—began to well up in my heart. The next instant I felt it all dissolve in the light of my father's being. I could feel his love for me rising up and covering me like a cloak. Out of the corner of my eye I could see the cabbie motioning for me to come back. He was worried I would miss my plane. "One more minute," I said. I still had to say the "El Mole Rachamim" for my father. As I began to say it, the minor strains of the ancient Hebrew chant spread down through the leaves of grass and then rose up into the shimmering trees. "God, full of compassion, who lives in the heights, may the soul of Isaiah ben haRav Yitzhak, Isaiah son of Rabbi Isaac, find proper rest under the wings of the divine presence . . . may his soul be bound up in the bond of eternal life . . ." When I was done, I bent down, picked up a pebble, and placed it on my father's headstone. Then I turned and strode swiftly back to the waiting cab.

## 43 OUR DIVINE NAME

Meditation and Jewish practice lead us to experience the oneness of all beings. We are all connected; each of us is created in the divine image, and other people's suffering is our own. Therefore, we have no choice but to try to heal it. But our instinct is to always run away from suffering, to deny it. We demonize the homeless and the needy because we see our own darkness in them, our own predilection for death and failure, and we try to get them out of sight. "It's their own fault," we say, and, increasingly, our response to homelessness and poverty has turned on various strategies for keeping the homeless and the poor at bay. But the first noble truth is that everything is suffering, and both Judaism and Buddhism insist that the only appropriate response to this suffering is to turn toward it, to attend to it. Avalokiteshvara, the Bodhisattva of Compassion, is "The Hearer of the Cries of the World," and in the Torah God is repeatedly described as hearing the cries of the oppressed. Serious engagement in meditation and Jewish practice lead inevitably to social action, to the attempt to heal suffering in the public as well as in the private domain. For me, in San Francisco, this has meant becoming an advocate for the homeless.

With Sister Bernie Galvin and a small group of San Francisco clergy, I began to fight the oppressive measures the city of San Francisco had adopted in a futile effort to rid the streets of the homeless. We were arrested several times, and the homeless population of San Francisco tripled in size before we turned our attention to trying to save low-income housing from being destroyed in San Francisco (close to 15,000 people were sleeping on the streets every night, and hundreds were dying there every year). In 1998 we got a ballot initiative passed to save this housing. We had no money for our campaign, no power, and no media, but we appealed to the inner light, the image of God in people, instead of their darkness, and this is why, I believe, we won the initiative. People desperately want to be touched in this place, but politicians are more likely to manipulate them with fear and anger. Huge majorities of Californians have voted to close our borders to the poor, to do away with affirmative action and bilingual education, and to support capital punishment. Appeals to darkness have been setting the political agenda.

Whenever I have been called upon to give a speech on behalf of the homeless or other victims of injustice, the speeches have surprised me by coming to me fully formed, and these have all been my best, my deepest and most eloquent speeches. In all these situations I have felt quite literally inspired, as if the words were coming to me from outside myself, and I have come to understand that my ability to speak is a divine instrument.

And yet each time I speak, if there is applause or if I receive any kind of recognition, a wave of nausea washes over me. I feel disgust at myself for trying to draw attention to myself.

When I was an infant, I got more attention than a Persian prince. My mother had three sisters, all living in the same building in Coney Island. I was my parents' first child, my aunts' first nephew, and my grandparents' first grandchild. I was the only baby in the family, and everyone doted on me. But after a few years, all that changed. My aunts had children of their own, and then my father became quite ill and my sister had to undergo a series of operations on her leg. My mother now spent most of her time running back and forth between hospitals in Manhattan. In a few short years, I had gone from feast to famine, and, as a consequence, I grew up with an insatiable thirst for attention.

Now I often find myself in front of large groups of people, all focused on me and what I'm saying, and I've begun to realize that I have manipulated unconsciously to make this happen. I'm not completely comfortable with this; in fact, I'm quite uncomfortable with it and always have been. Back when all the attention was focused on my father and my sister, I knew that they really needed it and I didn't, so any desire for attention was clearly selfish, and when the desire welled up, as it always did, I felt horribly guilty. As I grew up, I hid out for many years, first in a cabin in faraway Mendocino County, then in a tiny room over a deli in Berkeley, and then in a monastery high in the Los Padres Mountains. Even when I first became a rabbi, I hid out in a small congregation, off in the woods, still trying to resist the temptation to draw attention to myself.

But now this need for attention, it seemed to me, had finally prevailed. I was the rabbi of a major congregation; hundreds of people came to hear me speak every week. I was president of the Board of Rabbis and was frequently called upon to speak on ceremonial occasions and at times of public crisis. I had finally given in to my secret desire.

Rabbi Yitzak of Akko, who lived in Israel at the time just before the flowering of Safetian Kabbalah, told the story of a vagrant who saw a beautiful princess coming out of the bathhouse one day. He sighed a deep sigh and said, "Would that I could do with her as I liked." "That will come to pass in the graveyard, but not here," the princess said. She meant to brush him off, of course, but he rejoiced, because he thought she was telling him to meet her at the graveyard for an assignation. So he went right to the graveyard to wait for her, and there he devoted all of his thoughts to her, thinking of her beauty. And he waited there many days. After a while, because of his intense longing and his intense concentration, his soul separated from all things sensual, including the woman herself, and he communed with God. Afterward, he became a perfect servant and holy man of God, and his blessings were beneficial to all passersby. Our impulses, even what seem to be our basest impulses, are divine in origin.

All my life I had regarded my need for attention as a terrible defect, an ugly lust. And yet, if I hadn't finally managed to get attention focused on me, would I have been able to rally people to protect the homeless or bring meditation to the synagogue or do any of the things I was proudest of? It was this thing I hated most about myself that was enabling me to do good in the world, all the work I thought of as God's work. Could it be that what I had always thought of as a neurotic need, a need I had struggled against all my life, was really my divine name? What if, instead of trying to suppress what I thought of as my greatest weakness, I turned a soft eye on the way I was made? Would I, like Jacob, see that it was actually my greatest strength?

This is the most important transformation of all, the transformation Jacob undergoes when he wrestles with the angel of God and discovers that his inclination for grasping and dissatisfaction is really his divine name: *Yisrael,* He struggled with God. This is the transformation we undergo when we realize that our inner darkness, the quality that we see as our ugliness, our evil, is precisely what is most meaningful about us, what is important, what is holy about us. It's just that in our unconsciousness we have come to act on it inappropriately, to cover it over with a base human inclination, and that's what we really hate.

Each of us has a divine name. Mindfulness is the key to unlocking its secret. The term in the Talmud for mindfulness is *kavanat lev,* "the directing of the heart." Real mindfulness comes about not by an act of violence against our consciousness, not by force, not by trying to control our consciousness, but rather, by a kind of directed compassion, a softening of our awareness, a loving embrace of our lives, a soft letting be.

What would happen if we were willing to look more deeply at the things we don't like about ourselves instead of beating ourselves up about them? Maybe, just maybe, they would turn out to be strengths and not weaknesses after all.

Our impulses, even what seem to be our basest impulses, are divine in origin. The impulse itself is almost never a problem. The problem is that we just don't see it in the proper light, we have not become mindful of its true nature, and we act on it unconsciously and inappropriately. But the impulse itself is from God.

What is it about ourselves that we really hate? What is it we would do anything to change? And how is the very thing we hate our divine name? How might it express our purpose in life, the reason God brought us here? This is the kind of question we might spend our whole lives wrestling with. But if we turn a soft, loving eye on the thing we can't stand about ourselves and keep it there until the thing we can't stand falls away, this wrestling will become a loving embrace and our divine name will emerge in its stead.

# WHAT I LEARNED FROM BUDDHISM ABOUT HOW TO SAVE JUDAISM

In his recent book, *After Heaven,* the sociologist Richard Wutnow describes three stages in the development of American spirituality. I can see these same stages in my own spiritual path. I was born into Judaism. Judaism was the place where I lived, the religion and culture that permeated the streets of my native Brooklyn, the family and the larger sense of peoplehood from which I drew my identity, and it was the synagogue that I came to identify as sacred space, the place where I could speak to God. Although I felt God's presence in the forest, the synagogue, the sacred space, was God's address, the place where God could be reached most dependably. To the degree that I thought about it then, I defined my spirituality in terms of my place in this sacred space and the larger spiritual family I had been born to. And this situation prevailed until I went to college.

Then I embarked on the second great division of my spiritual life: a period of seeking. I had no unfriendly feelings toward Judaism; I simply didn't see Judaism as a serious spiritual path, so I set out. It was a kind of undisciplined journey, and I'm not even sure I knew I was on it at first, but by the time I came of age, the search for a spiritual path had become the center of my life. And then, finally, I found Zen Buddhism and began the third of the major divisions of my spiritual life: the period characterized by spiritual practice. I am in that phase still, and I fully expect to be in it for the rest of my life.

Zen, or at least the Zen that I followed, wasn't a theology, and it wasn't a home, and it certainly wasn't spiritual consumerism. It didn't promise great visions or spiritual epiphanies. It was a practice characterized by rigorous discipline, by what we did and how thoroughly and regularly we did it. So perhaps it's not surprising that when I returned to Judaism, some ten years later, I saw it primarily as practice, a spiritual practice of great depth and integrity—daily prayer, Shabbat, kashrut, the yearly cycle of holidays—the lineaments of an ancient and disciplined practice. These were the elements that had informed Jewish spirituality since the beginning of Judaism. But by and large they had been discarded by American Jews in this century, who, ironically, now find themselves dissatisfied with Judaism and looking elsewhere for spiritual gratification.

Little by little we are recovering a sense of Jewish practice. For some, particularly the young and the highly romantic, this means a return to Orthodoxy, the branch of Judaism that retained this sense most successfully over the past century. But time only flows one way. I discovered this in my own flirtation with Orthodoxy, which I admired for the intensity of its practice but which I felt required me to make a painful squint that shut out more of reality than I was comfortable doing.

Orthodoxy requires one to believe things about the sacred texts of our religion that we know not to be true and forbids open, intellectual questioning about the origin of these texts. It has frozen the classical evolutionary thrust of Judaism and left it completely unable to deal with new historical circumstances, such as the changing status of women and homosexuals. I don't believe we can go back without giving up more than we ought to be willing to give up. Judaism owes Orthodoxy a substantial and largely unacknowledged debt, and given the current acrimony among the various Jewish denominations, it is not likely to be acknowledged any time soon. The simple truth, however, is that Orthodoxy sustained serious Jewish spirituality, albeit a particular version of it, when no one else on this planet showed the slightest interest in doing so. I feel enormous gratitude to the Orthodox movement for this and I wish them well. But their version cannot be my own. The spiritual constriction required to keep modernity at bay is just too painful for me, and I rather suspect that when the romance wears off, most of Orthodoxy's new adherents will come to feel the same way.

Eighty percent of the Jewish people never set foot in any synagogue, even on the High Holidays, and those who do, use synagogues far too often as places where one can comfortably fall asleep—as safe refuge from any experience of the transcendent. Those who realize that their spiritual needs are real are out seeking. A whole Jewish movement—the Renewal Movement—has arisen in response to this need. We owe the Renewal Movement a substantial debt as well. It has named what is presently the most compelling item on the American Jewish agenda—the renewal of Jewish spirituality. But so far, it has shown far too little in the way of serious spiritual discipline. Pointing to the spiritual emptiness of mainstream Judaism, its adherents go from peak experience to peak experience, from retreat to workshop to concert.

But so far there has been too little in between; too few enduring disciplines, too little in the way of a daily, intentional invoking of the sacred, and no consistent methodology for invoking this sense. Rabbi Zalman Schachter, a seminal force in American Jewish spirituality and the spiritual father of the Renewal Movement, has acknowledged this weakness himself. "We have succeeded in creating a Holiday Inn," Schachter said in his farewell address to the movement a few years ago, "but what we really need is a home."

The Jewish Renewal Movement is still a very young movement, and all this may well come with time. Institutions like Jonathan Omer-Man's Metivta in Los Angeles and Chachmat HaLev in Berkeley are striving mightily toward the committed practice of Jewish meditation, but they are still a ways off and exist pretty much on the periphery of Jewish life. I wish them well, too. I feel a kinship with these institutions. I share their vision. But if Judaism is to survive in this country, it will be because it has succeeded in retrieving this sense of practice and bringing it into the mainstream. It will be because it sees itself again not primarily as an ethnicity or an occasional church or a dwelling place, but a practice—a set of intentional gestures capable of transforming us, of deepening our relationship to the sacred.

It may very well be left to institutions like my own synagogue—mainstream institutions that have inherited a serious subculture of spiritual discipline—to develop this practice model, not just because it will enhance our chances of surviving, but because it will enliven us again; it will help us move from a need for security to a practice that could bring us closer to the only sure sense of security there is: a sense of the sacred. And the key to this renewed sense of practice may be meditation and the implementation of a contemplative service, ideas borrowed from Buddhism.

Some see this borrowing as a betrayal and a threat to religious identity. In some quarters, the old exclusive doctrines are reasserted more stridently than ever as their adherents retreat into denominational ghettos. But it takes enormous energy to hold the rest of the world at bay, energy we can gain access to when we open ourselves to others, energy we can use for healing. Interdenominational and interreligious angst waste our energy, sap our evolutionary power. Why not just let go of it?

We don't really have to give up a thing. In fact, in order for this to work, we have to reclaim our particular identities more forcefully than we have been willing to do so far in this century. The wrong turn Judaism began to take in the nineteenth century was giving up its particularity—the sense of observance that had kept it alive for so long—in the mistaken belief that these practices were alienating Jews from their fellow human beings. The fact is, exactly the opposite is true. People who are observant and committed are not threatened by opening to others. They are rooted in the way they live, not in some flimsy idea of ethnicity.

Practice, or the idea of spiritual discipline, is a Jewish idea I learned from Buddhism. It was in a Buddhist monastery, meditating, that I realized who I really am. I am a Jew. A Jew can use the practice of meditation to illuminate his or her Jewish soul. And meditation can help us to slow down enough so that we

306

can once again experience the beauty of the Jewish path. I have seen this happen at my own synagogue. We have had four weekly meditation groups there for the past five years. They have enriched our prayer services and our study of Torah.

McLuhan is out of date. We no longer live in a global village, we live in a global apartment house, and the walls are very thin. It is no longer possible to close ourselves off from each other the way we used to. Why can't we nurture each other, use what the other has to offer while maintaining our fundamental integrity? Why can't religious men and women across the globe pool the special insights of their faiths for the benefit of all?

I performed a wedding downtown the week before Pesach. The parents of the groom, a nice couple from San Antonio, Texas, told me that their son and his new wife were going to take them to Israel in a few weeks to celebrate their golden wedding anniversary. They had been married fifty years ago, a few weeks before the signing of the Israeli Declaration of Independence. Both had immigrated to Israel from the death camps of Poland. He was a soldier in the Israeli Army, and she fought in the Haganah. The War of Independence was already in full swing. There were no guests at the wedding; it was far too dangerous for that. The rabbi and his assistant were the only witnesses. Yellow tracers from the phosphorous bullets used to light up the frontier filled the air overhead as the *Sheva Brachot*, the Seven Blessings, were pronounced.

Now, exactly fifty years later, I was pronouncing the Sheva

Brachot for their American son and his bride. She was a beautiful and brilliant Korean woman. Her parents stood just outside the chuppah, her mother a figure of impeccable dignity in
full Korean ceremonial dress: a green silk robe with an immense green bow in the back. I had come to know the bride
and groom quite well over the past year, having presided over
her conversion to Judaism. They had a wonderful relationship
and seldom fought. In fact, the only point of tension between
them was that she seemed much more passionate about Judaism
and Jewish observance than he was. As Jewish custom required,
she had gone to the mikvah the previous week and fasted this
entire day, and now this lovely Korean woman was deeply immersed in the profound and particular spiritual experience of a
Jewish wedding. Her eyes filled with tears of joy as I intoned the
Sheva Brachot. Her new in-laws caught her glance for a moment, and their eyes filled with tears as well. They loved her
very much, had loved her from the first time they'd met her. I
could see this couple standing under the yellow streamers fifty
years ago in Israel. This moment was an unanticipated consequence of that one.

It was springtime and I felt good about the way things had
been going at the synagogue. Things at home were going well,
too. Hannah was almost eighteen and had been accepted to the
School of Visual Art in New York for next year. Malka would
be a junior in high school, and although she hadn't found her
particular passion yet, I was confident that she would. I believed this because Steve, at the age of thirty, had recently
found his. After years as a starving musician, he decided to go
back to school to become an entomologist. He has found his
"divine name."

In early summer he came with us to Martha's Vineyard,

where the whole family gathered for Jason's oldest daughter's bat mitzvah. One day Steve invited me to go with him to the Martha's Vineyard Nature Preserve. Midway through the hike a rainstorm came up, and we had to take refuge in a little shack on the banks of a lake. The shack was an observatory for the birds of the preserve. Next to a big picture window was a large chart showing all the birds in that region. The idea was that you were supposed to look out the window and identify the birds depicted on the chart. I was quite happy to sit there in the rain and do just that, but Steve had other ideas. He wanted to look not *through* the window at what was outside, but rather, at the window itself. The window, he soon pointed out, was a very active world in and of itself, a nature preserve, as it were, for insect life. There was a circle on the window, which I had taken for a spot of annoying *shmutz*, something obscuring my view of the lake, but when Steve drew my full attention to this spot, it became clear that the circle was a beautiful and delicate membrane holding half a dozen perfectly formed spherical silver eggs. Then Steve drew my attention to an incredible fly sitting in the middle of the window. This fly was a metallic silver and looked like some sort of Art Deco flying machine, a silvery batmobile with silky silver wings. So soon it became clear: this window wasn't just something through which the world was viewed; it was a world in itself, a place with a life of its own.

Suddenly I knew what I would tell my congregation the first night of Rosh Hashana. I would tell them that the essential act of the High Holidays is *teshuvah*, a turning toward mindfulness, and the first step in this process is a kind of turning in to examine our perceptive mechanisms, the way we see the world. It is a shifting of our gaze from the world itself to the window through which we see it, because that window, the screen of our consciousness, is not just a blank transparent medium. Rather, it is a world unto itself, a world teeming with life, and that life affects what we see. And because that life makes us see the world differently, the first step in teshuvah is to look at the window itself. When the shofar blows, it reminds us to turn our gaze inward, to shift our focus from the outside world to the window through which we view this world, and the considerable activity taking place there. It is precisely this activity that we need to make teshuvah about.

We always read the Torah portion *Netzavim* the week before Rosh Hashana, and in the beautiful and mystical sense of efficiency that informs the yearly cycle of Torah readings, Parshat Netzavim contains some straightforward and useful advice on how we make teshuvah, and, particularly, how we begin the process. Teshuvah, Parshat Netzavim informs us, is not up in heaven, nor is it far across the sea. No, the Torah insists, this business of teshuvah is extremely close to us, in fact it is the closest thing to us there is. It is in our hearts and mouths. And so the beginning of the process of teshuvah is to shift our consciousness—our awareness—from things that are distant from us to things that are very close, from things that are external— outside us—to things that are inside, from the stars and the sea to our mouths and our hearts, from the birds outside the window to the window itself.

What do you need to make teshuvah about? That pain that is pressing on your heart right now, those words just on the edge of articulation, lying between your heart and your mouth. So how do you begin the process of teshuvah? First, you turn in and try to see what's on your heart; try to feel the pain pressing on it at this very moment.

But how do you do this? How do you look at your heart? Did

you ever try to see your heart? It's a very tricky thing. Your heart tends to be invisible, inscrutable, especially to you. Every once in a while you might actually sneak up on it; you might suddenly turn your attention to your heart and catch it unawares; you might even catch a glimpse of what's going on there. But usually indirection works better; usually the problem is that we are unconscious of what we really need to work on, and when we try to peer directly into our heart, we don't see anything; it's illusive, it's murky; the harder we look, the less we see. So how do we see this thing that is so close to us that we can't see the forest for the trees?

The physiologist Herbert Benson, who did pioneering work on meditation, discovered that there was something common to all meditation practices, which he called the relaxation response. According to Benson, it was the relaxation response that seemed to produce the brain wave and the psychospiritual changes we usually associate with meditation. The active ingredient in this process was that the meditation technique had a point of focus at its center. If it was Zen meditation, the point of focus was the breath and the posture. If it was Jewish prayer, the point of focus was the siddur, the words of the prayerbook. What all these activities had in common was that one would try to center one's attention on the point of focus. Inevitably a thought or a noise or a bodily sensation would intrude, and when this happened, one simply took note of the thought or the noise or the sensation that had done so, let it rise up as it wanted to, and fall away of its own accord, as it always did when left alone. Then one simply brought one's attention gently back to the point of focus, to the breath or the words of the siddur, and it was this bringing back, this teshuvah, this returning to the point of focus, to the actual experience of one's life, that was the active ingredient in meditation, the gesture Benson isolated as being responsible for the changes in consciousness we call meditation.

During the High Holidays we spend an inordinate amount of time sitting in the synagogue with a prayerbook in our laps, and certainly our minds will wander, whether we wish them to or not. But if we just sit and try to focus on the *machzor*, the High Holiday prayerbook, and continually try to bring our awareness back to it every time we realize it has been carried away—every time we find ourselves daydreaming or having fantasies about the good-looking person four aisles away or gossiping to ourselves about that person behind us we don't like—we will be participating in an important spiritual process; we will be beginning a spiritual transformation.

And here is something else Dr. Benson noticed, and he was neither the first nor the only one to notice it; the Rambam had noticed it a thousand years before him. The particular thought that carries your thought away from the machzor does not arise at random or by accident. It is extremely significant. It is precisely what you need to make teshuvah about, precisely what Parshat Netzavim was talking about when it told us teshuvah was extremely close to us, in our hearts. If you really try this for the ten days between Rosh Hashana and Yom Kippur, you'll find that the same thoughts or patterns of thoughts, the same fantasies, the same regrets, the same anxieties keep carrying your attention away. And if you continue in your efforts to make teshuvah, to bring your awareness back to your actual circumstances, in this case, the words of the machzor, these recurring concerns will become clearer and clearer to you. The unresolved elements of our life keep repeating themselves until we get them right, the Rambam assures us in his treatise on teshuvah. The thoughts that keep arising in our mind, particularly those thoughts with enough force to carry our awareness away, keep arising out of some unresolved point of tension. So it is an extremely useful thing to be aware of them, and we become aware of them not by trying to focus on them directly, but rather, by trying to focus on something else, like our breath, or our body, or the words of the machzor, and letting these thoughts rise up of their own accord. They always will. If they didn't, they wouldn't be important.

And I don't just know this from Benson or from the Rambam; I know this from my own experience, from my own teshuvah, my own return to Judaism. Ten years of doing intense meditation, ten years of developing focus on my breath and my posture, finally illuminated my own unconscious material for me. I was very familiar with precisely what it was that kept rising up and carrying my consciousness away from the present moment of my life. I had been watching this happen for ten years, and what amazed me in the end was how Jewish so much of this unconscious material was—how much of my unconscious was absorbed with the Jewishness I had held at such a distance for so long. And the more I became aware of this unconscious material, the more it became apparent to me that I had to turn toward it, that it was significant, that it was neither random nor incidental, but rather, the key to my soul, the map to the path I had to travel next.

We all have such a map. We all have such a key. And it waits to be discovered, not outside of us, but right there on the tip of our tongue, right there on top of our heart, not outside the window but in the window itself. The bad news is, we can't find it if we look at it directly; the good news is, it will come and find us if we let it. It will come and find us while we're praying, while we're trying to focus on these prayers, on this ancient communal call to God. God will answer us, if we're listening.

# About JEWISH LIGHTS Publishing

People of all faiths and backgrounds yearn for books that attract, engage, educate and spiritually inspire.

Our principal goal is to stimulate thought and help all people learn about who the Jewish People are, where they come from, and what the future can be made to hold. While people of our diverse Jewish heritage are the primary audience, our books speak to people in the Christian world as well and will broaden their understanding of Judaism and the roots of their own faith.

We bring to you authors who are at the forefront of spiritual thought and experience. While each has something different to say, they all say it in a voice that you can hear.

Our books are designed to welcome you and then to engage, stimulate and inspire. We judge our success not only by whether or not our books are beautiful and commercially successful, but by whether or not they make a difference in your life.

We at Jewish Lights take great care to produce beautiful books that present meaningful spiritual content in a form that reflects the art of making high quality books. Therefore, we want to acknowledge those who contributed to the production of this book.

Stuart M. Matlins, Publisher

### PRODUCTION
Marian B. Wallace & Bridgett Taylor

### EDITORIAL
Sandra Korinchak, Emily Wichland,
Martha McKinney & Amanda Dupuis

### COVER / TEXT PRINTING & BINDING
Versa Press, East Peoria, Illinois

# The Way Into... Series

A major 14-volume series to be completed over the next several years, *The Way Into...* provides an accessible and usable "guided tour" of the Jewish faith, its people, its history and beliefs—in total, an introduction to Judaism for adults that will enable them to understand and interact with sacred texts. Each volume is written by a major modern scholar and teacher, and is organized around an important concept of Judaism. *The Way Into...* will enable all readers to achieve a real sense of Jewish cultural literacy through guided study. Forthcoming volumes include:

### The Way Into Torah
by *Dr. Norman J. Cohen*
What is "Torah"? What are the different approaches to studying Torah? What are the different levels of understanding Torah? For whom is the study intended? Explores the origins and development of Torah, why it should be studied and how to do it.
6 x 9, 176 pp, HC, ISBN 1-58023-028-8 **$21.95**

### The Way Into Jewish Prayer
by *Dr. Lawrence A. Hoffman*
Opens the door to 3,000 years of the Jewish way to God by making available all you need to feel at home in Jewish worship. Provides basic definitions of the terms you need to know as well as thoughtful analysis of the depth that lies beneath Jewish prayer.
6 x 9, 224 pp, HC, ISBN 1-58023-027-X **$21.95**

### The Way Into Jewish Mystical Tradition
by *Rabbi Lawrence Kushner*
Explains the principles of Jewish mystical thinking, their religious and spiritual significance, and how they relate to our lives. A book that allows us to experience and understand the Jewish mystical approach to our place in the world.
6 x 9, 224 pp, HC, ISBN 1-58023-029-6 **$21.95**

### The Way Into Encountering God in Judaism
by *Dr. Neil Gillman*
Explains how Jews have encountered God throughout history—and today—by exploring the many metaphors for God in Jewish tradition. Explores the Jewish tradition's passionate but also conflicting ways of relating to God as Creator, relational partner, and a force in history and nature.
6 x 9, 240 pp, HC, ISBN 1-58023-025-3 **$21.95**

# Theology/Philosophy

## A Heart of Many Rooms: *Celebrating the Many Voices within Judaism*
by *Dr. David Hartman*  AWARD WINNER!

Addresses the spiritual and theological questions that face all Jews and all people today. From the perspective of traditional Judaism, Hartman shows that commitment to both Jewish tradition and to pluralism can create understanding between people of different religious convictions. 6 x 9, 352 pp, HC, ISBN 1-58023-048-2 **$24.95**

## A Living Covenant: *The Innovative Spirit in Traditional Judaism*
by *Dr. David Hartman*  AWARD WINNER!

Winner, National Jewish Book Award. Hartman reveals a Judaism grounded in covenant—a relational framework—informed by the metaphor of marital love rather than that of parent-child dependency. 6 x 9, 368 pp, Quality PB, ISBN 1-58023-011-3 **$18.95**

 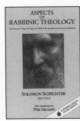   

**These Are the Words:** *A Vocabulary of Jewish Spiritual Life*
by Arthur Green  6 x 9, 304 pp, Quality PB, ISBN 1-58023-107-1 **$18.95**

**Evolving Halakhah:** *A Progressive Approach to Traditional Jewish Law*
by Rabbi Dr. Moshe Zemer  6 x 9, 480 pp, HC, ISBN 1-58023-002-4 **$40.00**

**The Death of Death:** *Resurrection and Immortality in Jewish Thought*  AWARD WINNER!
by Dr. Neil Gillman  6 x 9, 336 pp, Quality PB, ISBN 1-58023-081-4 **$18.95**;
HC, ISBN 1-879045-61-3 **$23.95**

**Aspects of Rabbinic Theology** by Solomon Schechter; New Intro. by Dr. Neil Gillman
6 x 9, 448 pp, Quality PB, ISBN 1-879045-24-9 **$19.95**

**The Last Trial:** *On the Legends and Lore of the Command to Abraham to Offer Isaac as a Sacrifice* by Shalom Spiegel; New Intro. by Judah Goldin
6 x 9, 208 pp, Quality PB, ISBN 1-879045-29-X **$17.95**

**Judaism and Modern Man:** *An Interpretation of Jewish Religion* by Will Herberg;
New Intro. by Dr. Neil Gillman  5½ x 8½, 336 pp, Quality PB, ISBN 1-879045-87-7 **$18.95**

**Seeking the Path to Life**  AWARD WINNER!
*Theological Meditations on God and the Nature of People, Love, Life and Death*
by Rabbi Ira F. Stone
6 x 9, 160 pp, Quality PB, ISBN 1-879045-47-8 **$14.95**; HC, ISBN 1-879045-17-6 **$19.95**

**The Spirit of Renewal:** *Finding Faith after the Holocaust*  AWARD WINNER!
by Rabbi Edward Feld
6 x 9, 224 pp, Quality PB, ISBN 1-879045-40-0 **$16.95**

**Tormented Master:** *The Life and Spiritual Quest of Rabbi Nahman of Bratslav*
by Dr. Arthur Green
6 x 9, 416 pp, Quality PB, ISBN 1-879045-11-7 **$18.95**

# Healing/Wellness/Recovery

## Jewish Pastoral Care
### *A Practical Handbook from Traditional and Contemporary Sources*
Ed. by *Rabbi Dayle A. Friedman*
Gives today's Jewish pastoral counselors practical guidelines based in the Jewish tradition.
6 x 9, 464 pp, HC, ISBN 1-58023-078-4 **$35.00**

## Healing of Soul, Healing of Body
### *Spiritual Leaders Unfold the Strength & Solace in Psalms*
Ed. by *Rabbi Simkha Y. Weintraub, CSW,* for The National Center for Jewish Healing
A source of solace for those who are facing illness, as well as those who care for them.
Provides a wellspring of strength with inspiring introductions and commentaries by eminent
spiritual leaders reflecting all Jewish movements.
6 x 9, 128 pp, Quality PB, Illus., 2-color text, ISBN 1-879045-31-1 **$14.95**

## Jewish Paths toward Healing and Wholeness
### *A Personal Guide to Dealing with Suffering*
by *Rabbi Kerry M. Olitzky*; Foreword by *Debbie Friedman*
Why me? Why do we suffer? How can we heal? Grounded in personal experience with
illness and Jewish spiritual traditions, this book provides healing rituals, psalms and
prayers that help readers initiate a dialogue with God, to guide them along the complicated path of healing and wholeness.
6 x 9, 192 pp, Quality PB, ISBN 1-58023-068-7 **$15.95**

 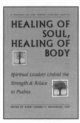   

Twelve Jewish Steps to Recovery: *A Personal Guide to Turning from Alcoholism &*
*Other Addictions . . . Drugs, Food, Gambling, Sex . . .* by Rabbi Kerry M. Olitzky &
Stuart A. Copans, M.D. Preface by Abraham J. Twerski, M.D.; Intro. by Rabbi Sheldon Zimmerman;
"Getting Help" by JACS Foundation 6 x 9, 144 pp, Quality PB, ISBN 1-879045-09-5 **$13.95**

One Hundred Blessings Every Day: *Daily Twelve Step Recovery Affirmations,*
*Exercises for Personal Growth & Renewal Reflecting Seasons of the Jewish Year*
by Rabbi Kerry M. Olitzky  4½ x 6½, 432 pp, Quality PB, ISBN 1-879045-30-3 **$14.95**

Recovery from Codependence: *A Jewish Twelve Steps Guide to Healing Your Soul*
by Rabbi Kerry M. Olitzky   6 x 9, 160 pp, Quality PB, ISBN 1-879045-32-X **$13.95**;
HC, ISBN 1-879045-27-3 **$21.95**

Renewed Each Day: *Daily Twelve Step Recovery Meditations Based on the Bible*
by Rabbi Kerry M. Olitzky & Aaron Z. *Vol. I: Genesis & Exodus; Vol. II: Leviticus,*
*Numbers and Deuteronomy*
*Vol. I:* 6 x 9, 224 pp, Quality PB, ISBN 1-879045-12-5 **$14.95**
*Vol. II:* 6 x 9, 280 pp, Quality PB, ISBN 1-879045-13-3 **$14.95**

# Life Cycle/Grief

## Moonbeams
### A Hadassah Rosh Hodesh Guide
Ed. by *Carol Diament, Ph.D.*

This hands-on "idea book" focuses on *Rosh Hodesh*, the festival of the new moon, as a source of spiritual growth for Jewish women. A complete sourcebook that will initiate or rejuvenate women's study groups, it is also perfect for women preparing for *bat mitzvah*, or for anyone interested in learning more about *Rosh Hodesh* observance and what it has to offer. 8½ x 11, 240 pp, Quality PB, ISBN 1-58023-099-7 **$20.00**

## Mourning & Mitzvah: *A Guided Journal for Walking the Mourner's Path through Grief to Healing, 2nd Ed.* with *Over 60 Guided Exercises*
by *Anne Brener, L.C.S.W.*; Foreword by *Rabbi Jack Riemer*; Intro. by *Rabbi William Cutter*

For those who mourn a death, for those who would help them, for those who face a loss of any kind, Brener teaches us the power and strength available to us in the fully experienced mourning process. 7½ x 9, 304 pp, Quality PB, ISBN 1-58023-113-6 **$19.95**

 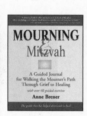   

Tears of Sorrow, Seeds of Hope
*A Jewish Spiritual Companion for Infertility and Pregnancy Loss*
by Rabbi Nina Beth Cardin   6 x 9, 192 pp, HC, ISBN 1-58023-017-2 **$19.95**

Lifecycles
**V. 1:** *Jewish Women on Life Passages & Personal Milestones* AWARD WINNER!
Ed. and with Intros. by Rabbi Debra Orenstein
**V. 2:** *Jewish Women on Biblical Themes in Contemporary Life* AWARD WINNER!
Ed. and with Intros. by Rabbi Debra Orenstein and Rabbi Jane Rachel Litman
*V. 1:* 6 x 9, 480 pp, Quality PB, ISBN 1-58023-018-0 **$19.95**; HC, ISBN 1-879045-14-1 **$24.95**
*V. 2:* 6 x 9, 464 pp, Quality PB, ISBN 1-58023-019-9 **$19.95**; HC, ISBN 1-879045-15-X **$24.95**

A Heart of Wisdom: *Making the Jewish Journey from Midlife through the Elder Years*
Ed. by Susan Berrin; Foreword by Harold Kushner
6 x 9, 384 pp, Quality PB, ISBN 1-58023-051-2 **$18.95**; HC, ISBN 1-879045-73-7 **$24.95**

Grief in Our Seasons: *A Mourner's Kaddish Companion*
by Rabbi Kerry M. Olitzky 4½ x 6½, 448 pp, Quality PB, ISBN 1-879045-55-9 **$15.95**

Parenting As a Spiritual Journey
*Deepening Ordinary & Extraordinary Events into Sacred Occasions*
by Rabbi Nancy Fuchs-Kreimer 6 x 9, 224 pp, Quality PB, ISBN 1-58023-016-4 **$16.95**

A Time to Mourn, A Time to Comfort: *A Guide to Jewish Bereavement and Comfort*
by Dr. Ron Wolfson 7 x 9, 336 pp, Quality PB, ISBN 1-879045-96-6 **$18.95**

When a Grandparent Dies
*A Kid's Own Remembering Workbook for Dealing with Shiva and the Year Beyond*
by Nechama Liss-Levinson, Ph.D.
8 x 10, 48 pp, HC, Illus., 2-color text, ISBN 1-879045-44-3 **$15.95**

So That Your Values Live On: *Ethical Wills & How to Prepare Them*
Ed. by Rabbi Jack Riemer & Professor Nathaniel Stampfer
6 x 9, 272 pp, Quality PB, ISBN 1-879045-34-6 **$17.95**

# Life Cycle & Holidays

## How to Be a Perfect Stranger, In 2 Volumes
### A Guide to Etiquette in Other People's Religious Ceremonies
Ed. by *Stuart M. Matlins* & *Arthur J. Magida* **AWARD WINNER!**

*What will happen? What do I do? What do I wear? What do I say? What are their basic beliefs? Should I bring a gift?* In question-and-answer format, explains the rituals and celebrations of America's major religions/denominations, helping an interested guest to feel comfortable, participate to the fullest extent possible, and avoid violating anyone's religious principles. Not presented from the perspective of any particular faith.

Vol. 1: *America's Largest Faiths*, 6 x 9, 432 pp, HC, ISBN 1-879045-39-7 **$24.95**

Vol. 2: *Other Faiths in America*, 6 x 9, 416 pp, HC, ISBN 1-879045-63-X **$24.95**

## Putting God on the Guest List, 2nd Ed.
### How to Reclaim the Spiritual Meaning of Your Child's Bar or Bat Mitzvah
by *Rabbi Jeffrey K. Salkin* **AWARD WINNER!**

The most influential book about finding core spiritual values in American Jewry's most misunderstood ceremony. 6 x 9, 224 pp, Quality PB, ISBN 1-879045-59-1 **$16.95**

For Kids—Putting God on Your Guest List
*How to Claim the Spiritual Meaning of Your Bar or Bat Mitzvah*
by Rabbi Jeffrey K. Salkin  6 x 9, 144 pp, Quality PB, ISBN 1-58023-015-6 **$14.95**

Bar/Bat Mitzvah Basics: *A Practical Family Guide to Coming of Age Together*
Ed. by Cantor Helen Leneman  6 x 9, 240 pp, Quality PB, ISBN 1-879045-54-0 **$16.95**; HC, ISBN 1-879045-51-6 **$24.95**

The New Jewish Baby Book  **AWARD WINNER!**
*Names, Ceremonies, & Customs—A Guide for Today's Families*
by Anita Diamant  6 x 9, 336 pp, Quality PB, ISBN 1-879045-28-1 **$16.95**

Hanukkah: The Art of Jewish Living
by Dr. Ron Wolfson  7 x 9, 192 pp, Quality PB, Illus., ISBN 1-879045-97-4 **$16.95**

The Shabbat Seder: The Art of Jewish Living
by Dr. Ron Wolfson  7 x 9, 272 pp, Quality PB, Illus., ISBN 1-879045-90-7 **$16.95**
Also available are these helpful companions to *The Shabbat Seder:* Booklet of the Blessings and Songs, ISBN 1-879045-91-5 **$5.00**; Audiocassette of the Blessings, DN03 **$6.00**; Teacher's Guide, ISBN 1-879045-92-3 **$4.95**

The Passover Seder: The Art of Jewish Living
by Dr. Ron Wolfson  7 x 9, 352 pp, Quality PB, Illus., ISBN 1-879045-93-1 **$16.95**
Also available are these helpful companions to *The Passover Seder:* Passover Workbook, ISBN 1-879045-94-X **$6.95**; Audiocassette of the Blessings, DN04 **$6.00**; Teacher's Guide, ISBN 1-879045-95-8 **$6.95**

The Jewish Gardening Cookbook: *Growing Plants & Cooking for Holidays & Festivals*
by Michael Brown  6 x 9, 224 pp, Illus., Quality PB, ISBN 1-58023-116-0 **$16.95**; HC, ISBN 1-58023-004-0 **$21.95**

# Children's Spirituality

## God Said Amen
by *Sandy Eisenberg Sasso*
Full-color illus. by *Avi Katz*

For ages
4 & up

A warm and inspiring tale of two kingdoms: one overflowing with water but without oil to light its lamps; the other blessed with oil but no water to grow its gardens. The kingdoms' rulers ask God for help but are too stubborn to ask each other. It takes a minstrel, a pair of royal riding-birds and their young keepers, and a simple act of kindness to show that they need only reach out to each other to find God's answer to their prayers.

9 x 12, 32 pp, HC, Full-color illus., ISBN 1-58023-080-6 **$16.95**

## For Heaven's Sake

For ages
4 & up

by *Sandy Eisenberg Sasso*; Full-color illus. by *Kathryn Kunz Finney*

Everyone talked about heaven: "Thank heavens." "Heaven forbid." "For heaven's sake, Isaiah." But no one would say what heaven was or how to find it. So Isaiah decides to find out, by seeking answers from many different people.
9 x 12, 32 pp, HC, Full-color illus., ISBN 1-58023-054-7 **$16.95**

## But God Remembered
Stories of Women from Creation to the Promised Land

For ages
8 & up

by *Sandy Eisenberg Sasso*; Full-color illus. by *Bethanne Andersen*

A fascinating collection of four different stories of women only briefly mentioned in biblical tradition and religious texts. Vibrantly brings to life courageous and strong women from ancient tradition; all teach important values through their actions and faith.
9 x 12, 32 pp, HC, Full-color illus., ISBN 1-879045-43-5 **$16.95**

## God in Between

For ages
4 & up

by *Sandy Eisenberg Sasso*; Full-color illus. by *Sally Sweetland*

If you wanted to find God, where would you look? A magical, mythical tale that teaches that God can be found where we are: within all of us and the relationships between us.
9 x 12, 32 pp, HC, Full-color illus., ISBN 1-879045-86-9 **$16.95**

## A Prayer for the Earth: The Story of Naamah, Noah's Wife **AWARD WINNER!**
by *Sandy Eisenberg Sasso*; Full-color illus. by *Bethanne Andersen*

This new story, based on an ancient text, opens readers' religious imaginations to new ideas about the well-known story of the Flood. When God tells Noah to bring the animals of the world onto the ark, God also calls on Naamah, Noah's wife, to save each plant on Earth.
9 x 12, 32 pp, HC, Full-color illus., ISBN 1-879045-60-5 **$16.95**

# Children's Spirituality

## In Our Image
### *God's First Creatures*
by *Nancy Sohn Swartz*
Full-color illus. by *Melanie Hall*

*For ages 4 & up*

A playful new twist on the Creation story—from the perspective of the animals. Celebrates the interconnectedness of nature and the harmony of all living things. "The vibrantly colored illustrations nearly leap off the page in this delightful interpretation." —*School Library Journal*

9 x 12, 32 pp, HC, Full-color illus., ISBN 1-879045-99-0 **$16.95**

## God's Paintbrush
by *Sandy Eisenberg Sasso*; Full-color illus. by *Annette Compton*

*For ages 4 & up*

Invites children of all faiths and backgrounds to encounter God openly in their own lives. Wonderfully interactive; provides questions adult and child can explore together at the end of each episode.
11 x 8½, 32 pp, HC, Full-color illus., ISBN 1-879045-22-2 **$16.95**

*Also available: A Teacher's Guide:* **A Guide for Jewish & Christian Educators and Parents**
8½ x 11, 32 pp, PB, ISBN 1-879045-57-5 **$6.95**

**God's Paintbrush Celebration Kit** 9½ x 12, HC, Includes 5 sessions/40 full-color Activity Sheets and Teacher Folder with complete instructions, ISBN 1-58023-050-4 **$21.95**

## In God's Name
by *Sandy Eisenberg Sasso*; Full-color illus. by *Phoebe Stone*

*For ages 4 & up*

Like an ancient myth in its poetic text and vibrant illustrations, this award-winning modern fable about the search for God's name celebrates the diversity and, at the same time, the unity of all the people of the world.
9 x 12, 32 pp, HC, Full-color illus., ISBN 1-879045-26-5 **$16.95**

## What Is God's Name? (A Board Book)

*For ages 0–4*

An abridged board book version of the award-winning *In God's Name.*
5 x 5, 24 pp, Board, Full-color illus., ISBN 1-893361-10-1 **$7.95**

## The 11th Commandment: Wisdom from Our Children
by *The Children of America*

*For all ages*

"If there were an Eleventh Commandment, what would it be?" Children of many religious denominations across America answer this question—in their own drawings and words. "A rare book of spiritual celebration for all people, of all ages, for all time."—*Bookviews*
8 x 10, 48 pp, HC, Full-color illus., ISBN 1-879045-46-X **$16.95**

# *Children's Spirituality*

## Because Nothing Looks Like God

by *Lawrence and Karen Kushner*
Full-color illus. by *Dawn W. Majewski*

**For ages 4 & up**

MULTICULTURAL, NONDENOMINATIONAL, NONSECTARIAN

What is God like? The first collaborative work by husband-and-wife team Lawrence and Karen Kushner introduces children to the possibilities of spiritual life. Real-life examples of happiness and sadness—from goodnight stories, to the hope and fear felt the first time at bat, to the closing moments of life—invite us to explore, together with our children, the questions we all have about God, no matter what our age.

11 x 8½, 32 pp, HC, Full-color illus., ISBN 1-58023-092-X **$16.95**

## Where Is God? (A Board Book)

**For ages 0–4**

by *Lawrence and Karen Kushner;* Full-color illus. by *Dawn W. Majewski*

Gently invites children to become aware of God's presence all around them. Abridged from *Because Nothing Looks Like God* by Lawrence and Karen Kushner.
5 x 5, 24 pp, Board, Full-color illus., ISBN 1-893361-17-9 **$7.95**

## Sharing Blessings

**For ages 6 & up**

Children's Stories for Exploring the Spirit of the Jewish Holidays
by *Rahel Musleah* and *Rabbi Michael Klayman*
Full-color illus. by *Mary O'Keefe Young*

What is the spiritual message of each of the Jewish holidays? How do we teach it to our children? Many books tell children about the historical significance and customs of the holidays. Now, through engaging, creative stories about one family's preparation, *Sharing Blessings* explores ways to get into the *spirit* of 13 different holidays.
8½ x 11, 64 pp, HC, Full-color illus., ISBN 1-879045-71-0 **$18.95**

## The Book of Miracles

**For ages 9 & up**

A Young Person's Guide to Jewish Spiritual Awareness
by *Lawrence Kushner*

Introduces kids to a way of everyday spiritual thinking to last a lifetime. Kushner, whose award-winning books have brought spirituality to life for countless adults, now shows young people how to use Judaism as a foundation on which to build their lives.
6 x 9, 96 pp, HC, 2-color illus., ISBN 1-879045-78-8 **$16.95**

# Spirituality

## My People's Prayer Book: *Traditional Prayers, Modern Commentaries*
Ed. by *Dr. Lawrence A. Hoffman*
Provides a diverse and exciting commentary to the traditional liturgy, helping modern men and women find new wisdom in Jewish prayer, and bring liturgy into their lives. Each book includes Hebrew text, modern translation, and commentaries *from all perspectives* of the Jewish world.
Vol. 1—*The Sh'ma and Its Blessings,* 7 x 10, 168 pp, HC, ISBN 1-879045-79-6 **$23.95**
Vol. 2—*The Amidah,* 7 x 10, 240 pp, HC, ISBN 1-879045-80-X **$23.95**
Vol. 3—*P'sukei D'zimrah* (Morning Psalms), 7 x 10, 240 pp, HC, ISBN 1-879045-81-8 **$23.95**
Vol. 4—*Seder K'riat Hatorah* (The Torah Service), 7 x 10, 264 pp, ISBN 1-879045-82-6 **$23.95**

   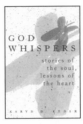 

### Becoming a Congregation of Learners
*Learning as a Key to Revitalizing Congregational Life*   by Isa Aron, Ph.D.;
Foreword by Rabbi Lawrence A. Hoffman, Co-Developer, Synagogue 2000
6 x 9, 304 pp, Quality PB, ISBN 1-58023-089-X **$19.95**

### Self, Struggle & Change
*Family Conflict Stories in Genesis and Their Healing Insights for Our Lives*
by Dr. Norman J. Cohen  6 x 9, 224 pp, Quality PB, ISBN 1-879045-66-4 **$16.95;**
HC, ISBN 1-879045-19-2 **$21.95**

### Voices from Genesis: *Guiding Us through the Stages of Life*
by Dr. Norman J. Cohen   6 x 9, 192 pp, Quality PB, ISBN 1-58023-118-7 **$16.95;**
HC, ISBN 1-879045-75-3 **$21.95**

### God Whispers: *Stories of the Soul, Lessons of the Heart*
by Rabbi Karyn D. Kedar  6 x 9, 176 pp, Quality PB, ISBN 1-58023-088-1 **$15.95**

### Being God's Partner: *How to Find the Hidden Link Between Spirituality and Your Work*
by Rabbi Jeffrey K. Salkin; Intro. by Norman Lear  **AWARD WINNER!**
6 x 9, 192 pp, Quality PB, ISBN 1-879045-65-6 **$16.95**; HC, ISBN 1-879045-37-0 **$19.95**

### ReVisions: *Seeing Torah through a Feminist Lens*  **AWARD WINNER!**
by Rabbi Elyse Goldstein 5½ x 8½, 224 pp. Quality PB, ISBN 1-58023-117-9 **$16.95;**
208 pp, HC, ISBN 1-58023-047-4 **$19.95**

### Soul Judaism: *Dancing with God into a New Era*
by Rabbi Wayne Dosick 5½ x 8½, 304 pp, Quality PB, ISBN 1-58023-053-9 **$16.95**

### Finding Joy: *A Practical Spiritual Guide to Happiness*  **AWARD WINNER!**
by Rabbi Dannel I. Schwartz with Mark Hass
6 x 9, 192 pp, Quality PB, ISBN 1-58023-009-1 **$14.95**; HC, ISBN 1-879045-53-2 **$19.95**

### "Who Is a Jew?" *Conversations, Not Conclusions*  by Meryl Hyman
6 x 9, 272 pp, Quality PB, ISBN 1-58023-052-0 **$16.95**; HC, ISBN 1-879045-76-1 **$23.95**

# Ecology/Spirituality

**Torah of the Earth:** *Exploring 4,000 Years of Ecology in Jewish Thought*
In 2 Volumes Ed. by *Rabbi Arthur Waskow*

Major new resource offering us an invaluable key to understanding the intersection of ecology and Judaism. Leading scholars provide us with a guided tour of ecological thought from four major Jewish viewpoints.
Vol. 1: *Biblical Israel & Rabbinic Judaism,* 6 x 9, 272 pp, Quality PB, ISBN 1-58023-086-5 **$19.95**
Vol. 2: *Zionism & Eco-Judaism,* 6 x 9, 336 pp, Quality PB, ISBN 1-58023-087-3 **$19.95**

**Broken Tablets:** *Restoring the Ten Commandments and Ourselves*
Ed. by *Rabbi Rachel S. Mikva*; Intro. by *Rabbi Lawrence Kushner*;
Afterword by *Rabbi Arnold Jacob Wolf* **AWARD WINNER!**

Twelve outstanding spiritual leaders each share profound and personal thoughts about these biblical commands and why they have such a special hold on us.
6 x 9, 192 pp, HC, ISBN 1-58023-066-0 **$21.95**

**Ecology & the Jewish Spirit:** *Where Nature & the Sacred Meet* Ed. and with Intros. by
Ellen Bernstein 6 x 9, 288 pp, Quality PB, ISBN 1-58023-082-2 **$16.95**;
HC, ISBN 1-879045-88-5 **$23.95**

**God & the Big Bang**
*Discovering Harmony Between Science & Spirituality* **AWARD WINNER!**
by Daniel C. Matt
6 x 9, 216 pp, Quality PB, ISBN 1-879045-89-3 **$16.95**

**Israel—A Spiritual Travel Guide** **AWARD WINNER!**
*A Companion for the Modern Jewish Pilgrim*
by Rabbi Lawrence A. Hoffman 4¾ x 10, 256 pp, Quality PB, ISBN 1-879045-56-7 **$18.95**

**Godwrestling—Round 2:** *Ancient Wisdom, Future Paths* **AWARD WINNER!**
by Rabbi Arthur Waskow
6 x 9, 352 pp, Quality PB, ISBN 1-879045-72-9 **$18.95**; HC, ISBN 1-879045-45-1 **$23.95**

**The Year Mom Got Religion:** *One Woman's Midlife Journey into Judaism*
by Lee Meyerhoff Hendler 6 x 9, 208 pp, Quality PB, ISBN 1-58023-070-9 **$15.95**

**Israel:** *An Echo of Eternity* by Abraham Joshua Heschel; New Intro. by
Dr. Susannah Heschel 5½ x 8, 272 pp, Quality PB, ISBN 1-879045-70-2 **$18.95**

**The Earth Is the Lord's:** *The Inner World of the Jew in Eastern Europe*
by Abraham Joshua Heschel 5½ x 8, 112 pp, Quality PB, ISBN 1-879045-42-7 **$13.95**

**A Passion for Truth:** *Despair and Hope in Hasidism* by Abraham Joshua Heschel
5½ x 8, 352 pp, Quality PB, ISBN 1-879045-41-9 **$18.95**

**Your Word Is Fire:** *The Hasidic Masters on Contemplative Prayer*
Ed. and Trans. with a New Introduction by Dr. Arthur Green and Dr. Barry W. Holtz
6 x 9, 160 pp, Quality PB, ISBN 1-879045-25-7 **$14.95**

# Spirituality & More

## The Jewish Lights Spirituality Handbook
### *A Guide to Understanding, Exploring & Living a Spiritual Life*
Ed. by *Stuart M. Matlins, Editor-in-Chief, Jewish Lights Publishing*
Rich, creative material from over 50 spiritual leaders on every aspect of Jewish spirituality today: prayer, meditation, mysticism, study, rituals, special days, the everyday, and more.
6 x 9, 304 pp, Quality PB, ISBN 1-58023-093-8 **$16.95**; HC, ISBN 1-58023-100-4 **$24.95**

## Six Jewish Spiritual Paths: *A Rationalist Looks at Spirituality*
by *Rabbi Rifat Sonsino*
The quest for spirituality is universal, but which path to spirituality is right *for you?* A straight-forward, objective discussion of the many ways—each valid and authentic—for seekers to gain a richer spiritual life within Judaism. 6 x 9, 208 pp, HC, ISBN 1-58023-095-4 **$21.95**

## Restful Reflections: *Nighttime Inspiration to Calm the Soul, Based on Jewish Wisdom* by *Rabbi Kerry M. Olitzky* and *Rabbi Lori Forman*
Wisdom to "sleep on." For each night of the year, an inspiring quote from a Jewish source and a personal reflection on it from an insightful spiritual leader helps you to focus on your spiritual life and the lessons your day has offered. The companion to *Sacred Intentions: Daily Inspiration to Strengthen the Spirit, Based on Jewish Wisdom* (see below).
4½ x 6½, 448 pp, Quality PB, ISBN 1-58023-091-1 **$15.95**

 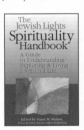   

Sacred Intentions: *Daily Inspiration to Strengthen the Spirit, Based on Jewish Wisdom*
by Rabbi Kerry M. Olitzky and Rabbi Lori Forman
4½ x 6½, 448 pp, Quality PB, ISBN 1-58023-061-X **$15.95**

The Enneagram and Kabbalah: *Reading Your Soul*
by Rabbi Howard A. Addison 6 x 9, 176 pp, Quality PB, ISBN 1-58023-001-6 **$15.95**

Embracing the Covenant: *Converts to Judaism Talk About Why & How*
Ed. and with Intros. by Rabbi Allan L. Berkowitz and Patti Moskovitz
6 x 9, 192 pp, Quality PB, ISBN 1-879045-50-8 **$15.95**

Shared Dreams: *Martin Luther King, Jr. and the Jewish Community*
by Rabbi Marc Schneier; Preface by Martin Luther King III
6 x 9, 240 pp, HC, ISBN 1-58023-062-8 **$24.95**

Mystery Midrash: *An Anthology of Jewish Mystery & Detective Fiction*
Ed. by Lawrence W. Raphael; Preface by Joel Siegel, ABC's *Good Morning America*
6 x 9, 304 pp, Quality PB, ISBN 1-58023-055-5 **$16.95**

Wandering Stars: *An Anthology of Jewish Fantasy & Science Fiction* Ed. by Jack Dann; Intro. by Isaac Asimov 6 x 9, 272 pp, Quality PB, ISBN 1-58023-005-9 **$16.95**

More Wandering Stars
*An Anthology of Outstanding Stories of Jewish Fantasy and Science Fiction*
Ed. by Jack Dann; Intro. by Isaac Asimov 6 x 9, 192 pp, Quality PB, ISBN 1-58023-063-6 **$16.95**

# Spirituality/Jewish Meditation

## Discovering Jewish Meditation
### Instruction & Guidance for Learning an Ancient Spiritual Practice
by *Nan Fink Gefen*

Gives readers of any level of understanding the tools to learn the practice of Jewish meditation on your own, starting you on the path to a deep spiritual and personal connection to God and to greater insight about your life. 6 x 9, 208 pp, Quality PB, ISBN 1-58023-067-9 **$16.95**

## Entering the Temple of Dreams: *Jewish Prayers, Movements, and Meditations for the End of the Day* by *Tamar Frankiel* and *Judy Greenfeld*

Nighttime spirituality is much more than bedtime prayers! Here, you'll uncover deeper meaning to familiar nighttime prayers—and learn to combine the prayers with movements and meditations to enhance your physical and psychological well-being.
7 x 10, 192 pp, Illus., Quality PB, ISBN 1-58023-079-2 **$16.95**

## The Handbook of Jewish Meditation Practices
### A Guide for Enriching the Sabbath and Other Days of Your Life
by *Rabbi David A. Cooper*

Gives us ancient and modern Jewish tools—Jewish practices and traditions, easy-to-use meditation exercises, and contemplative study of Jewish sacred texts—to help us quiet our minds and refresh our souls. 6 x 9, 208 pp, Quality PB, ISBN 1-58023-102-0 **$16.95**

 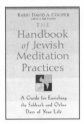 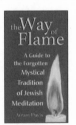 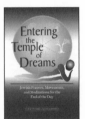 

## Meditation from the Heart of Judaism
### Today's Teachers Share Their Practices, Techniques, and Faith
Ed. by Avram Davis 6 x 9, 256 pp, Quality PB, ISBN 1-58023-049-0 **$16.95**;
HC, ISBN 1-879045-77-X **$21.95**

## The Way of Flame: *A Guide to the Forgotten Mystical Tradition of Jewish Meditation*
by Avram Davis 4½ x 8, 176 pp, Quality PB, ISBN 1-58023-060-1 **$15.95**

## Minding the Temple of the Soul: *Balancing Body, Mind, and Spirit through Traditional Jewish Prayer, Movement, and Meditation*
by Tamar Frankiel and Judy Greenfeld 7 x 10, 184 pp, Quality PB, Illus.,
ISBN 1-879045-64-8 **$16.95**; Audiotape of the Blessings and Meditations (60-min. cassette),
JN01 **$9.95**; Videotape of the Movements and Meditations (46-min.), S507 **$20.00**

## The Empty Chair: *Finding Hope and Joy—*
*Timeless Wisdom from a Hasidic Master, Rebbe Nachman of Breslov* AWARD WINNER!
4 x 6, 128 pp, Deluxe PB, 2-color text, ISBN 1-879045-67-2 **$9.95**

## The Gentle Weapon: *Prayers for Everyday and Not-So-Everyday Moments*
Adapted from the Wisdom of Rebbe Nachman of Breslov
4 x 6, 144 pp, Deluxe PB, 2-color text, ISBN 1-58023-022-9 **$9.95**

# *Spirituality*

### Does the Soul Survive?
*A Jewish Journey to Belief in Afterlife, Past Lives & Living with Purpose*
by *Rabbi Elie Kaplan Spitz;* Foreword by *Brian L. Weiss, M.D.*

Do we have a soul that survives our earthly existence? To know the answer is to find greater understanding, comfort and purpose in our lives. Here, Spitz relates his own experiences and those shared with him by people he has worked with as a rabbi, and shows us that belief in afterlife and past lives, so often approached with reluctance, is in fact true to Jewish tradition.
6 x 9, 288 pp, HC, ISBN 1-58023-094-6 **$21.95**

### The Women's Torah Commentary: *New Insights from Women Rabbis on the 54 Weekly Torah Portions* Ed. by *Rabbi Elyse Goldstein*

For the first time, women rabbis provide a commentary on the entire Torah. More than 25 years after the first woman was ordained a rabbi in America, these inspiring teachers bring their rich perspectives to bear on the biblical text. In a week-by-week format; a perfect gift for others, or for yourself. 6 x 9, 496 pp, HC, ISBN 1-58023-076-8 **$34.95**

### Bringing the Psalms to Life
*How to Understand and Use the Book of Psalms* by *Rabbi Daniel F. Polish*

Here, the most beloved—and least understood—of the books in the Bible comes alive. This simultaneously insightful and practical guide shows how the psalms address a myriad of spiritual issues in our lives: feeling abandoned, overcoming illness, dealing with anger, and more.
6 x 9, 208 pp, HC, ISBN 1-58023-077-6 **$21.95**

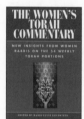    

**Stepping Stones to Jewish Spiritual Living:** *Walking the Path Morning, Noon, and Night*
by Rabbi James L. Mirel & Karen Bonnell Werth
6 x 9, 240 pp, Quality PB, ISBN 1-58023-074-1 **$16.95**

**The Business Bible**
*10 New Commandments for Bringing Spirituality & Ethical Values into the Workplace*
by Rabbi Wayne Dosick 5½ x 8½, 208 pp, Quality PB, ISBN 1-58023-101-2 **$14.95**

**Moses—The Prince, the Prophet:** *His Life, Legend & Message for Our Lives*
by Rabbi Levi Meier, Ph.D. 6 x 9, 224 pp, Quality PB, ISBN 1-58023-069-5 **$16.95**

**Ancient Secrets:** *Using the Stories of the Bible to Improve Our Everyday Lives*
by Rabbi Levi Meier, Ph.D. 5½ x 8½, 288 pp, Quality PB, ISBN 1-58023-064-4 **$16.95**

*Or phone, fax, mail or e-mail to:* **JEWISH LIGHTS** Publishing
Sunset Farm Offices, Route 4 • P.O. Box 237 • Woodstock, Vermont 05091
Tel: (802) 457-4000 • Fax: (802) 457-4004 • www.jewishlights.com
*Credit card orders:* **(800) 962-4544** (9AM–5PM ET Monday–Friday)
*Generous discounts on quantity orders. SATISFACTION GUARANTEED. Prices subject to change.*